SOCIAL WORK PRACTICE
WITH IMMIGRANTS AND REFUGEES

FOUNDATIONS OF SOCIAL WORK KNOWLEDGE,
FREDERIC G. REAMER, SERIES EDITOR

Foundations of Social Work Knowledge
Frederic G. Reamer, Series Editor

Social work has a unique history, purpose, perspective, and method. The primary purpose of this series is to articulate these distinct qualities and to define and explore the ideas, concepts, and skills that together constitute social work's intellectual foundations and boundaries and its emerging issues and concerns.

To accomplish this goal, the series will publish a cohesive collection of books that address both the core knowledge of the profession and its newly emerging topics. The core is defined by the evolving consensus, as primarily reflected in the Council of Social Work Education's Curriculum Policy Statement, concerning what courses accredited social work education programs must include in their curricula. The series will be characterized by an emphasis on the widely embraced ecological perspective; attention to issues concerning direct and indirect practice; and emphasis on cultural diversity and multiculturalism, social justice, oppression, populations at risk, and social work values and ethics. The series will have a dual focus on practice traditions and emerging issues and concepts.

David G. Gil, *Confronting Injustice and Oppression: Concepts and Strategies for Social Workers*

George Alan Appleby and Jeane W. Anastas, *Not Just a Passing Phase: Social Work with Gay, Lesbian, and Bisexual People*

Frederic G. Reamer, *Social Work Research and Evaluation Skills*

SOCIAL WORK PRACTICE
WITH IMMIGRANTS AND REFUGEES

Edited by

Pallassana R. Balgopal

COLUMBIA UNIVERSITY PRESS   NEW YORK

Columbia University Press
Publishers Since 1893
New York   Chichester, West Sussex

Copyright © 2000 Columbia University Press

All rights reserved

Library of Congress Cataloging-in-Publication Data
Social work practice with immigrants and refugees / [edited by] Pallassana R. Balgopal.
    p. cm. — (Foundations of social work knowledge)
    Includes bibliographical references and index.
    ISBN 0–231–10856–7 (alk. paper) — ISBN 0–231–10857–5 (pbk. : alk. paper)
    1. Social work with immigrants—United States 2. Immigrants—United States
    3. Refugees—United States. 4. Emigration and immigration law—United States.
    5. United States—Emigration and immigration—Social aspects.
    I. Balgopal, Pallassana R. II. Series.
    HV4010.S629 2000
    362.87′0973—dc21   00–020725

Casebound editions of Columbia University Press books
are printed on permanent and durable acid-free paper.
Printed in the United States of America
c 10 9 8 7 6 5 4 3 2 1
p 10 9 8 7 6 5 4 3 2 1

To my wife Shyamala Balgopal
for teaching our children to be true Americans
while retaining the Hindu dharma

CONTENTS

PREFACE

From its inception, the United States has been a land of immigrants. Likewise, the field of social work has a long history of working with immigrants and refugees. In the nineteenth century, charity organizations and missions assisted with social welfare services to immigrants and their families, and at the beginning of the social work profession, the "friendly visitor" helped families in need. The settlement house movement in the late nineteenth century focused on improving the environment and quality of life by teaching English and American values to the immigrant communities. Neighborhood centers were opened all over the United States, providing a variety of services.

During its first years, the majority of immigrants to the United States were from Europe, plus those individuals who were brought from Africa by force as slaves. The long-standing quota system regulating the number of immigrants from each country was finally abolished with the passage of the Immigration Act of 1965, resulting in increased numbers of immigrants from Asia and Latin America. Then the Immigration Reform and Control Act of 1986 enabled illegal immigrants who had been in the United States for more than five years to claim legal residence.

The United States has long welcomed refugees fleeing persecution, war, or natural disaster. Historically, the expectation has been that immigrants and refugees would learn and adopt American values, norms, and the English language as their way of life. But this has been difficult for many people, and instead, a blend of new cultures has been the result. This idea of a "melting pot" is that the immigrants' traditions are combined with Anglo-American customs to create a new, and evolving, culture. The "Anglo-conformity" and the "melting pot" idea have not, however, resolved the ethnic tension, discrimination, and prejudice running rampant throughout American society. In ethnic relations, therefore, it is appropriate for social workers to promote "cultural pluralism," which recognizes the uniqueness of different cultures and allows immigrants to retain their beliefs, customs, and values.

With the increase in migration between 1986 and 1989, when the number of refugees entering the country nearly doubled, the number of immigrant and refugees needing social work services also rose. The social problems that immigrants and refugees most frequently encounter are alcoholism, substance abuse, child abuse, juvenile delinquency, gang activity, physical and mental health issues, care of the elderly, and family conflicts, including domestic violence. Immigrants also face problems of housing, unemployment and underemployment, and, for Asians, the pressure of being a "model" minority. Accordingly, it is imperative for social workers to learn the knowledge and skills that will allow them to maximize the uniqueness of the immigrants' culture while helping them adjust to American life.

Nationally, the cuts and changes in the health care and social welfare systems are affecting the immigrant and refugee populations. Indeed, legislation such as Propositions 187 and 209 in California is specifically aimed at discontinuing assistance to immigrants and refugees. Accordingly, the role of the social worker is expanding as immigrants and refugees feel the effects of these changes. We must remember that the new immigrants to America are extraordinarily diverse and culturally rich, and their strengths and social developments have given this country a global perspective. In fact, during the last two decades, immigrants have contributed more than $25 billion to the U.S. economy after the estimated costs of social services were deducted. In addition, the new immigrants have brought with them strong family, child-rearing, and cultural values.

This book takes an ecological perspective, examining social work practice, community work, policy issues, cultural diversity, multiculturalism, social justice, oppression, populations at risk, and social work values and ethics. The authors' primary purpose is to explore ideas, concepts, and skills that will offer both a foundation and boundaries to social workers to help them work effectively with immigrants and refugees.

The book's ecological perspective gives special attention to the relationship between individuals and their social and physical environment, implying that neither persons nor environments are inadequate but, rather, the fit between person and environment may or may not be in harmony (Rappaport 1977).

Among the many challenges of working with immigrants and refugees is the notion that Americans tend to view these people as "parasites," thereby making their adjustment even more difficult. When applying this ecological perspective to the immigrant and refugee populations, therefore, workers must be ethnically sensitive and skilled in helping these groups adapt to their environment without losing their cultural heritage. The coping and adaptation of these "new Americans" need to be seen as a dual process—learning new customs and lifestyles while retaining old traditions and values. This book is mainly about the major immigrant groups who have come to the United States since the 1965 Immigration Act. It begins with an overview of the recent immigrant groups, followed by five chapters on immigrants and refugees from Asia, Latin America, Europe, and Africa. Each chapter examines the immigrants from a particular region and how their demographic and cultural characteristics affect their adaptation to the new environment. The authors look at these groups' needs and how they could be addressed at both the micro and macro levels. Besides facing many of their predecessors' problems, the immigrants of today also have special needs with which social workers should be familiar.

This volume is designed primarily for undergraduate and graduate students in social work. But because of the topics covered and their timeliness, it should be useful as well to social work practitioners, schoolteachers, and other helping service professionals who want to learn about the new immigrant and refugee groups.

REFERENCES

Rappaport, J. (1977). *Community Psychology: Values, Research and Action*. New York: Holt, Rinehart and Winston.

ACKNOWLEDGMENTS

As an immigrant myself who arrived in the United States forty years ago, I am interested in the struggles and successes of immigrant groups, especially those arriving as a result of the Immigration Act of 1965. So when I was invited by Frederic A. Reamer, the series editor of the Foundation of Social Work Knowledge, to write a book on new immigrants, I readily accepted his offer and express my sincere appreciation to him.

I decided that the best strategy to meet my objectives for this book would be to ask social work academics with special expertise in different immigrant and refugee groups to write the various chapters. This edited volume is therefore a culmination of the insights and scholarship of social work colleagues and friends. I am extremely grateful to each of the contributors to this book.

I particularly want to thank two of my graduate students, Corinne Field and Hellen McDonald, for their help, and I also want to thank Jeannette Ingram and Cheryl Street for their tireless and generous efforts for their secretarial assistance. I am grateful, too, to the editorial and production staffs at Columbia University Press: John L. Michel, senior executive editor, for his continued support and encouragement in completing this book; and Anne McCoy, managing editor, and Margaret B. Yamashita, copy editor, for their valuable help in meeting deadlines and providing quality copyediting of this book.

I also give special thanks to my wife, Shyamala Balgopal, for her ever-ready help in locating appropriate references. "Kannu-Appape." Finally, I send my fond appreciation and gratitude to my family: Shyamala, Meena, Paul, Anita, and Anand, for their support and love.

Pallassana R. Balgopal
University of Illinois
Urbana, Illinois

SOCIAL WORK PRACTICE
WITH IMMIGRANTS AND REFUGEES

CHAPTER 1

SOCIAL WORK PRACTICE WITH IMMIGRANTS
AND REFUGEES: AN OVERVIEW

Pallassana R. Balgopal

The purpose of this volume is to examine and develop the role of social workers serving new immigrants and refugees in the United States. New immigrants are considered in this text as those immigrants who entered the United States after 1965. In the past, "old" immigrants were the first groups that settled the country, and "new" immigrants were the Eastern and Southern Europeans arriving since the nineteenth century.

Today's immigrants represent much greater diversity with regard to country of origin, race and ethnicity, spoken language, religion, and, often, different value systems. In addition to Mexico, today's arrivals come mostly from Asia, Central and Latin America, and the Caribbean. Where once there were Jewish pushcart peddlers, now there are Korean green grocers, Indian newsstand dealers, Ethiopian and Caribbean bus boys, Mexican and Central American gardeners and farmhands, Vietnamese fishermen, and Nigerian and Pakistani cab drivers. The presence of new immigrants, especially from the Asian countries, is particularly evident in the health-care and high-technology fields. In sum, the American landscape, both urban and rural, now reflects the faces and lifestyles of the new immigrants (Foner 1998).

As table 1.1 shows, the composition of the immigrant population changed between the early 1800s and 1990s, making the United States a mosaic of multiculturalism. This drastic change in the immigrants' profiles was a result of the passage of the Immigration and Nationalities Act of 1965. This act repealed the quotas for each country and instead set 20,000 immigrants per country in the Eastern Hemisphere and established a seven-category preference system based on family unification and skills. In 1976, the immigration act was amended to extend the 20,000-per-country limit to the Western Hemisphere. And in 1980, the Refugee Act was passed, establishing for the first time a permanent and systematic procedure for admitting refugees. Between 1820 and 1940, only a little more than one million immigrants came from Asia, whereas between 1970 and 1997, nearly seven million immigrants were from Asia. The number of immigrants from Mexico, Central and Latin America, and the Caribbean also dramatically increased. The highest number of immigrants continues to come from Mexico. Between 1994 and 1997, 511,763 legal Mexican immigrants were admitted. During this period, the other countries supplying great numbers of immigrants were the Philippines (209,512), China (172,323), Vietnam (163,683), and India (152,589) (U.S. INS 1999). The social welfare needs of these immigrant groups are often different from those of immigrants before 1965, so social work responsibilities have changed as well. In this text we take an ecological perspective, especially in regard to issues concerning direct and indirect practice, community work, policy, cultural diversity, social justice, oppression, populations at risk, and social work values and ethics. We systematically examine and analyze the data concerning new immigrants arriving in the United States after 1965 and explore ideas, concepts, and skills that can help social workers serving immigrant and refugee populations.

The majority of today's immigrants face many of the same problems that their predecessors encountered, as well as their own special needs, such as a focus on family closeness, on collectivism, and language barriers. For these reasons, social workers should obtain culture-specific knowledge and skills. This book includes a chapter on refugee populations and their needs to which social workers must be able to respond.

UNDERSTANDING RECENT IMMIGRANTS AND REFUGEES

Immigrants

The United States has always been a land of immigrants, with the majority coming from Europe. The first immigrants were Protestants from the northern European continent. Then gradually, more and more Southern and Eastern Europeans began to migrate to the United States, along with people from Africa who were brought over as slaves. Then came immigrants from Asia and Latin America. At first, the Southern and Eastern European immigrants—from Italy, Greece, Poland, Portugal, Armenia, and the former Soviet Union—were shunned by the

TABLE 1.1
Immigrants Admitted by Region: Fiscal Years 1820–1997

Country of Last Residence	1820	1821–1850	1851–1880	1881–1910	1911–1940	1941–1970	1971–1994	1995	1996	1997
All countries	8,385	2,455,815	7,725,229	17,729,563	10,371,451	6,782,195	16,341,228	720,461	915,900	798,378
Europe	7,690	2,191,920	6,789,643	16,346,876	7,132,647	3,070,366	2,193,839	131,914	151,898	119,898
Asia	6	226	230,457	468,347	375,890	617,919	5,641,168	259,984	300,807	265,786
America	387	107,457	645,371	827,827	2,820,414	3,068,122	8,027,383	282,270	407,813	307,488
Caribbean	164	29,663	33,663	169,656	213,825	643,029	2,049,648	96,021	115,991	105,299
Central America	2	517	701	9,145	38,789	167,746	870,319	32,020	44,316	43,676
South America	11	4,966	3,749	20,659	91,917	371,399	995,203	46,063	61,990	52,877
Africa	1	125	880	8,575	16,479	50,413	366,317	39,818	49,605	47,790

Source: Adapted from U.S. Immigration and Naturalization Service, *Statistical Yearbook of the Immigration and Naturalization Service, 1996* (Washington, DC: U.S. Government Printing Service, 1997).

dominant class of white Protestant Americans. Accordingly, passage of the Immigration Restriction Act of 1924 welcomed the Northern and Western Europeans while limiting the entry of the Southern and Eastern Europeans (Greenbaum 1974:424). But the Immigration and Nationality Act of 1965, which replaced the 1924 act, opened the doors to all. Many immigrants of various races, cultures, and countries of origin then entered the United States, and their presence has enhanced the nation. Eventually, acceptance gave way to the entrance, or attempt to enter, of the Asian and Latin American populations, such as Brazilians, Cubans, and Mexicans. Asian immigrants arrived from India, Indochina, China, the Philippines, Korea, and Vietnam, to name a few countries of origin. Table 1.1 describes the change in demographics from the 1800s to 1997. Note that in between 1971 and 1997, the number of Asian, Central and Latin American, and African immigrants greatly increased compared with their number between 1941 and 1970 and the number of European immigrants.

Refugees

Those people who have relocated to the United States for reasons different from those of the immigrants are *refugees* and *asylees*. According to the U.S. Immigration and Naturalization Service, "a refugee is an alien outside the United States who is unable or unwilling to return to his or her country of nationality because of persecution or a well-founded fear of persecution" (1997:72). Thus, refugees are persons who flee their country of origin for fear of persecution or oppression due to political, religious, or national reasons or membership in certain social groups. Refugees, however, are often discriminated against and rejected, which makes it difficult for them to become part of U.S. society. Kim's 1989 study of Southeast Asian refugees between 1975 and 1979 showed that they did not feel accepted and were concerned about their future in the United States. In addition, most of the respondents stated that they did not agree that "I feel that the Americans that I know like me" (p. 93).

The Refugee Act of 1980 (Public Law 96-212, 94 Statute 102) amended both the Immigration and Nationality Act of 1952[1] and the Migration and Refugee Assistance Act of 1962.[2] Its goal was to create a more uniform basis for providing aid to refugees. The act established specific guidelines for who could be admitted to this country, and when; whether they could bring their spouse and children; and the processes of asylum and deportation. Currently, refugees may work in the United States and may apply for permanent residency after living in this country for one year. They are eligible to receive welfare assistance immediately upon entering, unlike those legal immigrants not considered refugees, who must wait five years before becoming eligible. The number of applications for refugee status filed with the INS rose by 9 percent from 1995 (143,223) to 1996 (155,868). Most of the applicants were from Vietnam (45 percent), the former Soviet Union (25 percent), Bosnia-Herzegovina (12 percent), and Somalia (9 percent). The number of refugees arriving in the United States fell from 98,520 in 1995 to 74,791 in 1996. The main reason for this decline is the smaller number of Vietnamese refugees (U.S. INS 1997).

Asylees are refugees already in the United States when they file for protection. "An asylee is an alien in the United States who is unable or unwilling to return to his or her country of nationality because of persecution or a well-founded fear of persecution" (U.S. INS 1997:77). Only 10,000 asylees may be accepted as legal permanent residents each year; otherwise they have the same benefits as refugees. U.S. refugee and asylee laws are based on the premise that it is this country's policy to respond to the urgent needs of persons being persecuted in their countries of origin, that the United States should "provide opportunities for resettlement or voluntary repatriation, as well as necessary transportation and processing" (Miller and Miller 1996:115). In addition, the United States encourages other nations to assist refugees as much as they can. Nonetheless, certain groups of asylees are not readily admitted into the United States. For example, Miller and Miller (1996) reported that Haitians, Salvadorans, and Guatemalans have been restricted from entering the United States despite the threat of persecution in their homelands. In 1985, of the 6,000 applications by Iranians, 63 percent were granted asylum, most of whom were students already in this country. But of 668 Haitian applicants, only 0.5 percent were accepted; of 409 Guatemalan applicants, 1.2 percent were accepted; and of 2,107 Salvadoran applicants, 5 percent were granted asylum. Why are certain nationalities accepted and others are not? Perhaps the Iranian students are likely to complete their degree and to become employed. And perhaps the Haitians have fewer job skills and may be more dependent on the United States' welfare system. Are ethnicity and race important to determining who is allowed to come to the United States?

Illegal Immigrants

Illegal immigration began slowly at first in the 1870s, increased slightly by the 1920s, and peaked after passage of the Immigration Act of 1965. Currently, in order to enter the United States, one must be a relative of a U.S. citizen or a permanent resident alien or have skills, education, or job experience needed in the United States or be a political refugee. Accordingly, with so many immigrants and so few nonpreference visas available, it often seems easier to enter illegally.

Miller and Miller found that "by the mid-1970s, the problem with illegal immigrants was generally considered to be out of control" (1996:27). The U.S. Immigration and Naturalization Service (1997) reported that in October 1996, about 5 million undocumented or illegal immigrants were residing in the United States. Mexico is identified as the leading country of origin, with 2.7 million, or 54 percent, of the illegal immigrants. Indeed, more than 80 percent of illegal immigrants are from countries in the Western Hemisphere.

Illegal immigrants are those people who enter this country without proper documentation or with expired visas or passports. Such immigrants may also include those who enter the United States as migrant workers and then stay beyond their employment dates. In addition, many undocumented Salvadorans, Guatemalans, and Haitians are from lower socioeconomic classes with little education (Rumbaut 1994b:613). For people like them, the implications of the Personal Responsibility and Work Opportunity Reconciliation Act of 1996 (PRWORA) are devastating. Furthermore, the states are prohibited from offering state or local benefits to most illegal immigrants, unless the state law was enacted after "August 22, 1996 (the day the bill was enacted) that explicitly makes illegal aliens eligible for the aid" (Katz 1996:2701). However, a state may provide school lunches to children of illegal immigrants if they are already eligible under that state's law for free public education. And a state may provide other benefits related to child nutrition and emergency food assistance. Ironically, though, a state may opt not to offer prenatal care to pregnant illegal immigrants.

For example, California's Proposition 187 denies reproductive services to illegal immigrant women, as well as public education to the children of illegal immigrants. In addition, citizenship is denied to the children of illegal immigrants who are born in the United States, a reversal of the Fourteenth Amendment, which automatically grants citizenship to anyone born in the United States. According to Roberts (1996), there is a rising fear in America that the country will be overrun by darker-skinned people. Because the majority of immigrants, both legal and illegal, entering the United States are not white, limits are being set on who can get prenatal care and education in this nation. As mentioned earlier, Haitians and Mexicans are usually undocumented and usually "darker skinned," and they seem to be the ones not receiving prenatal care.

The reasons that people flee their country vary, but most of the refugees and asylees who meet the U.S. definition of a refugee or asylee are escaping a communist takeover or some other communist-related regime. For example, large numbers of people from Vietnam, Laos, and Cambodia fled the communist takeover of their countries. The INS reported that between 1981 and 1987, 465,827 refugees from this group were granted asylum and permanent residency. In addition, 38,214 persons from the Soviet Union were granted permanent residency during this same time period. Nicaraguans fled their homeland to escape the civil war against the leftist regime, and Haitians wanted to live in the United States instead of under their right-wing military regime (Portes and Rumbaut 1990:244).

The socioeconomic classes of refugees also have changed through the years. In the early to mid-1950s, the Cuban refugees escaping Fidel Castro's forces were mainly from the middle and upper classes. In fact, Miller and Miller (1996:2) estimated that "more than 50 percent of its [Cuba's] doctors and teachers" entered the United States in a two-year period. Eventually, though, most of the Cuban refugees were "boat" people, the "Marielitos," who were less well educated and from the working class."

A BRIEF HISTORY OF AMERICAN IMMIGRATION

Most of the earliest immigrants to the United States were Anglo-Saxon Protestants, whose attitude toward other immigrants was mixed. On the one hand, the immigrants were needed to develop the new country, but on the other hand, the Protestants did not welcome the impoverished Catholics from Germany, especially when they moved into the Midwest to farm their own lands, thus "taking over" a large piece of the United States.

During this time, these immigrants forced the Native Americans out of their lands and homes. Before Columbus's arrival in the New World, it is estimated that the population of Native Americans was as large as 12 million. But by 1880, after years of genocide and wars, this number had fallen to about 250,000 (Karger and Stoesz 1994). Lack of immunity to European diseases, displacement from their lands, systematic starvation, widespread killing in war, and cold-blooded murder account for this dramatic drop in the Native American population. Between 1950 and 1990, however, the Native American population again grew by 1.6 million, and by 1994, the U.S. Census Bureau estimated the population of Native Americans at 2.2 million. In addition to the natural increase are the Census Bureau's methodological improvements in the way it counts people on reservations in trust lands and Native Alaskan villages and the increase in indigenous people, including mixed Indians and non-Indian parents reporting themselves as "American Indians" (Shinagawa and Jang 1998).

The African slaves were brought to the United States to work on the expanding plantations and vast lands; they were not freed until the late 1800s. They were not permitted to vote until the early 1900s, and not until 1964 with the passage of the Civil Rights Act were they accorded the rights and privileges available to other American citizens. The most obvious difference between the early immigrants and the African slaves is that the latter group had no choice in their immigration. They were brought into this country by force to help in its development but were forbidden, for centuries to come, to reap the rewards for their efforts. In 1790 when the first U.S. census was taken, African Americans numbered about 750,000. By 1860 their number had increased to 4.4 million, but except for 488,000 counted as "freemen" and "freewomen," the majority were still slaves. By 1992 the African American population had grown to 31.4 million, and "it is projected that by year 2000 this population will be around 35 million" (Shinagawa and Jang 1998:23).

Along with the influx of immigrants, policies were passed to regulate it. Some of the laws were overtly discriminatory, while others were more subtle. The Alien Act of 1798 was the "first Federal law pertinent to immigration rather than naturalization" (U.S. INS 1997:A. 1-1). This act allowed the president to arrange for the arrest or deportation of any person who appeared dangerous to the country. It also provided that aliens arriving by ships were to be reported by the captain to U.S. Customs. In 1819, the Steerage Act required that all vessels entering the United States supply a list of their passengers to Congress, and some restrictions were placed on the numbers of people leaving or entering U.S. ports. By 1862, discrimination against the Chinese was rampant. "Coolies," as the Chinese workers were called, were prohibited from being transported by ship or boat. In 1870, although Africans and African Americans could now be naturalized, the Chinese were excluded. The U.S. Immigration and Naturalization Service's *Statistical Yearbook* reports that under the 1875 policy, permission was needed to bring in "Oriental persons" (1997:A. 1-2).

The 1882 Chinese Exclusion Act, a very restrictive piece of legislation, prevented Chinese workers from entering the United States for ten years, and those who were caught and were in the country illegally were immediately deported. Most important, those Chinese already in the United States were not allowed to become naturalized citizens.

National quotas were instituted in the 1920s. For example, Spanish immigrants were limited to a quota of 252 yearly, Greeks to 308, Portuguese to 440, and Italians to 5,000. Thus it was not only Asian and Latin American immigrants who were oppressed and discriminated against, but anyone who was not a white Anglo-Saxon Protestant.

In 1943, the Chinese Exclusion Act was repealed, and by the 1950s, the Japanese Exclusion Act of 1924 was repealed. In 1952, a ceiling of 150,000 was set for non-Western countries, with preferences for highly skilled persons. Finally, by

1965, all quotas were abolished when the Immigration Act was passed. Immigration was no longer dependent on national origin, race, or ancestry. The Immigration Act introduced a seven-category preference system by which immigrants related to U.S. citizens or permanent residents were issued visas on a "first come, first serve" basis, favoring those with occupational skills or training needed in the United States.

In 1980, the Refugee Act was passed, separating refugee admissions from immigration, with refugees offered certain medical and social services. By 1986, the Immigration Reform and Control Act (IRCA) granted amnesty to almost three million undocumented people and established new ways of regulating undocumented immigration. For example, employers were fined for hiring illegal immigrants. Then the Immigration Act of 1990 raised to 650,000 the number of immigrants permitted entry for employment and family reunification. In 1996, President Clinton signed major welfare reforms into law. The Personal Responsibility and Work Opportunity Reconciliation Act (PRWORA) does not give legal immigrants (legal permanent residents) the right to receive Supplemental Security Income (SSI) or food stamp vouchers. Rather, it states that legal permanent residents may receive such benefits if they have paid Social Security taxes and have worked in the United States for a minimum of ten years.

Underlying all this discrimination and outright prejudice, both overt and covert, is a possible explanation. Although discrimination and prejudice can never be justified, we can try to clarify or understand the theoretical foundation for what happened during the early to later years of immigration: the reason is Anglo conformity. For the major legislative milestones in U.S. immigration history, see table 1.2. From 1882 until 1924, U.S. immigration policies focused on excluding persons on qualitative grounds, such as prostitution and physical and mental illness. The first quantitative restriction was imposed in 1924. The inclusionary era in immigration policy began in 1965 and continued until 1996 when the Personal Responsibility and Work Opportunity Reconciliation Act was passed, adversely affecting both legal and illegal immigrants and refugees.

Anglo Conformity

With the arrival of the European settlers, the African slaves, and the force against the Native Americans, the Anglo-conformist viewpoint dawned in the United States. This ideology became the hopeful foundation for the "Americanization" of all future newcomers. Milton Gordon described Anglo conformity "as a broad term used to cover a variety of viewpoints about assimilation and immigration; they all assume the desirability of maintaining English institu-

TABLE 1.2
Major Legislative Milestones in U.S. Immigration History

Chinese Exclusion Act (1882): Suspends immigration of Chinese laborers for ten years; provides for deportation of Chinese illegally in United States.

Immigration Act of 1891: As first comprehensive law for national control of immigration, establishes Bureau of Immigration under Treasury; directs deportation of aliens unlawfully in country.

Immigration and Naturalization Act of 1924: Imposes first permanent numerical limit on immigration; establishes national-origins quota system, resulting in biased admissions favoring northern and western Europeans.

Immigration and Naturalization Act of 1952: Continues national-origins quota and imposes quota for skilled aliens whose services are urgently needed.

Immigration and Nationality Act Amendments of 1965: Repeals national-origins quota system; establishes seven-category preference system based on family unification and skills; sets 20,000-per-country limit for Eastern Hemisphere.

Immigration and Nationality Act Amendments of 1976: Extends 20,000-per-country limit to Western Hemisphere.

Refugee Act of 1980: Sets up first permanent and systematic procedure for admitting refugees; removes refugees as a category from preference system; defines refugees according to international, versus ideological, standards; establishes process of domestic resettlement; codifies asylum status.

Immigration Reform and Control Act of 1986: Institutes employer sanctions for knowingly hiring illegal aliens; creates legalization programs; tightens border enforcement.

Immigration Act of 1990: Increases legal immigration ceilings by 40 percent; triples employment-based immigration, emphasizing skills; creates diversity admissions category; establishes temporary protected status for those in the U.S. jeopardized by armed conflict or natural disasters in their native country.

Personal Responsibility and Work Opportunity Reconciliation Act of 1996: Adversely affects legal and illegal immigrants and refugees; makes legal immigrants ineligible for SSI and food stamps until becoming citizens.

Source: Adapted from M. Fix and J. S. Passel, *Immigration and Immigrants: Setting the Record Straight* (Washington, DC: Urban Institute, 1994), 11.

tions (as modified by the American Revolution), the English language, and English-oriented cultural patterns as dominant and standard in American life" (1978:246).

The terms *assimilation* and *Americanization* have been used interchangeably. In the early part of the twentieth century, most of the Anglo-American population wanted the new groups of European immigrants to be assimilated. In fact, except for the white Southern and Eastern European immigrants, "it was ordered—that Mexicans, Asians, and blacks would remain culturally separate" (Bouvier 1992:111). Even Presidents Theodore Roosevelt and Woodrow Wilson held anticultural pluralism attitudes. Indeed, President Wilson was recorded as saying: "Any man who thinks [of] himself as belonging to a particular national group in America has not yet become an American" (p. 111).

The Americanization movement encouraged the adoption of Anglo-conformist ideals, as the Anglo conformists apparently could not understand that the newer immigrants could adjust to their new home while at the same time preserving their cultural ethnic, religious, and linguistic background. What occurred next, therefore, was a transition from one ideological base to another, from Anglo conformity into the melting pot perspective.

The Melting Pot

The "melting pot" theory has been described as "more generous [than Anglo conformity] and [with] idealistic overtones ...[which] has its adherents and exponents from the eighteenth century onward" (Gordon 1964:249). Israel Zangwill, author of the 1908 play *The Melting Pot*, depicted a young Russian-Jewish composer who, after migrating to America, dreams of completing a symphony

> Which will express his deeply felt conception of his adopted country as a
> Divinely appointed crucible in which all the ethnic division of mankind
> Will divest themselves of their ancient animosities and differences and
> become
> Fused into one group, signifying the brotherhood of man.   (p. 251)

When this drama was written, the United States consisted primarily of white Europeans. The white immigrants from countries other than England were similar in many ways to the dominant group. Either they spoke or learned to speak English, or their customs and cultural attitudes did not greatly diverge from the Anglo-Saxon norms. But when Asians, Latin Americans, Africans, and other nonwhite and non-English-speaking immigrants came to the United States, "the great Melting Pot where all the races of Europe are melting and reforming" (Gordon 1964:251) no longer applied. This country became, and still is, the destination for people from all over the world. Europe was not the only continent of origin; Africa, Asia, and Latin America also sent their share of diversified peoples. Ramakrishnan and Balgopal stated that owing to the prevalence of Anglo conformity, it became very difficult for ethnic groups that were "ethnically and racially different, such as, the Chinese, Japanese, African American, Hispanics, and Native Americans" to "melt in the American crucible" (1995:17). The idea of assimilation thus underlay the melting pot theory. It was not easy to become "welded" to or "assimilated" into American society, as previously assumed. Although the melting pot idea promoted assimilation, in reality it was the dominant group that determined the acceptable values and customs. If minority cultural groups attempted to retain or "cling" to their traditions, they were seen as unassimilable or sometimes even deviant.

Assimilation

The melting pot ideology emphasizes assimilation and blending, and the dominant Anglo group in the new United States provided the principal value structure to which all the other groups were expected to adhere. The preservation of their ethnic and cultural heritages was not encouraged. In other words, cultural assimilation meant that members of minority groups were to adopt the cultural norms of the dominant group. Epps observed that "traditionally, American society has been willing to accept culturally different peoples if they were willing to become acculturated and reject their cultural distinctiveness" (1974:15). Despite the negative aspects of the assimilation process, it did make some positive contributions. For instance, the development and preservation of a national identity through assimilation helped create a common American culture.

Numerous scholars have defined assimilation. Walker defined it as "a more specific process, [which] consists of structural and organizations absorption of formerly autonomous institutions or members of one society by another" (1972:1). Gordon's definition of assimilation is as follows: "Assimilation is a process of interpretation and future in which persons and groups acquire the memories, sentiments, and attitudes of other persons or groups, and, by sharing their experience and history, are incorporated with them in a common cultural life" (1964:62). The acquisition of "the memories . . . and attitudes of other persons" is essential to the assimilation or "Americanization" process. In order to be assimilated or blended into a dominant group, one must be willing and able to conform and thus remove one's original cultural and ethnic background. In essence, one must be able to forget one's heritage, family, and previous lifestyle, as if in a type of "forced" amnesia. Gordon (1964) also pointed out that assimilation takes place at two levels, the structural level and the behavioral level. Behavioral assimilation (often known as *acculturation*) applies to minority persons whose behavior must conform to the dominant group's norms. In other words, their behavior becomes more like that of the dominant group because if the minority persons' behavior stands out, they are seen as different and as not belonging to the mainstream. To avoid being identified as "foreign," minority members assimilate behaviorally. Although this type of assimilation takes place on a behavioral level, it does not necessarily occur at a structural level.

In order to assimilate structurally, individuals must have equal access to membership in the society's institutions and other kinds of decision-making structures. But even if minorities do adapt behaviorally, they will not necessarily be accepted into the dominant group's institutions. For example, even if legal permanent residents have the ability or desire to assimilate behaviorally, they do not have the right to vote until they become citizens. And they cannot become citizens until they have been married for three years to a U.S. citizen or have resided in the United States continuously for five years (Morse 1994). This lack of citizenship has "contributed to the isolation of immigrants" (Morse 1994:57). Furthermore, without the right to vote, immigrants cannot be represented on local, state, and national levels.

Another example of why behavioral assimilation does not necessarily guarantee structural assimilation concerns female immigrants who are married to U.S. citizens or legal permanent residents and who are victims of domestic violence. In the past, such women were not protected and risked losing custody of their children and being deported to their home country. Now, however, the Violence Against Women Act (VAWA), part of the Violent Crime and Law Enforcement Act of 1994 (Pub. L. No. 103-322, 108 State. 1796), protects women waiting for their permanent residency. Wheeler states that according to the VAWA, such women may petition for residency if they are

(1) abused spouses and children of U.S. citizens or legal permanent residents, (2) nonabused spouses who are parents of abused children of U.S. citizens or legal permanent residents, and (3) abused spouses of U.S. citizens or legal permanent residents and their nonabused children, even if the children are not related to the U.S. citizen or legal permanent resident abuser. (1996:223)

Currently, a number of shelters for victims of domestic violence have been opened to specific ethnic groups. For example, shelters particularly for Asian American women take into account their cultural customs and lifestyles.

Behavioral and structural assimilation is especially difficult for those immigrants arriving in the United States since 1965. Immigrants from Africa, Asia, and Latin America are especially negatively affected by structural assimilation. They may be able to learn the dominant society's language, social expectations, and norms, but at the same time, they are denied advancement in the political and economic arenas because of the prevailing institutional racism. Further-more, because Asian Americans are viewed as a "model minority," they may have to endure, as Karger and Stoesz found, "heat from the white majority as well as from other minorities" (1994:102). Such tension is, for example, evident between Korean shopkeepers and African American residents in the inner cities.

These immigrants' adaptation to the mainstream expectations of public be-havior creates a different kind of conflict for them and their family members. On one hand, they are supposed to act, behave, and interact according to the dominant culture's standards, but at home, they continue to behave according to their own cultural or ethnic background. This dichotomy can cause conflict in the immigrant families. For example, immigrant children may behave like the dominant group, and their parents may feel that their children are giving up their ethnic values and lifestyle, thus creating more tension between the parents and their children. In comparison, the parents of the earlier immigrants were much more receptive and willing to become American.

Maintaining the two identities is very difficult for new immigrants. Pettys and Balgopal (1998) discussed the concept of the power of one's ethnicity— that is, maintaining one's own customs, heritage, and language. For example, when a Vietnamese adolescent raised in the United States informs her parents that she wants to date just like her American peers, her parents may become upset, as they may not approve of dating unless marriage is to be the ultimate outcome.

Based on his study (1994a) of more than five hundred children of Asian, Latin American and Caribbean immigrants residing in the San Diego and Miami metropolitan areas, Rumbaut found major differences in the eighth and ninth grades in patterns of ethnic self-identification. Gender was a significant predictor of virtually every type of ethnic self-identity. That is, compared with boys, girls were much more likely to choose additive or hyphenated identities. Perceptions of discrimination also had a profound effect on the way that chil-dren defined their ethnic identities. Rumbaut's study demonstrated that those who had experienced discrimination were less likely to identify themselves as American. The determination of dissimilative racial or panethnic self-identity seems to follow a different logic that includes the youngsters' location and na-tionality. Youths, especially blacks and Hispanics, in inner-city schools define themselves in terms of their ethnicity. The children's assimilation, moreover, is moderated by their parents' ethnic socialization, their family's social status, par-ent-child relationships, and interactions among family members.

SOCIAL WORK'S PAST EFFORTS IN HELPING IMMIGRANTS

Social work pioneers such as Jane Addams, Grace and Edith Abbott, and Sophie Breckinridge have left a legacy of dedicated and committed work with new immigrants. Settlement houses, neighborhood centers, and sectarian and other voluntary agencies have provided needed services to immigrant groups struggling to adapt to their new homeland, for example, the "citizenship classes" conducted in settlement houses aimed at enabling immigrants to become "good" citizens. The profession's efforts thus complemented the much-cherished ideal of the American past, which was the ideal of the melting pot.

Pioneers in social work assumed the roles of mediators and advocates on behalf of the immigrants in their adaptation to their new environment. Addams described these roles: "The Hull House residents sought not only to understand their immigrant neighbors but to interpret them to a public which had fears and doubts about those 'un-American types' who lived in the slums" (Addams 1915, quoted in Bryan and Davis 1990:131). Immigrants have been a special concern of social work from its inception, with the explicit aim of successfully integrating the immigrants through a planned program of resettlement (Bernard and Greenleigh 1960).

But the melting pot theory did not always work as expected. The history of race relations in America is a history of conquest, slavery, and exploitation of migrant and immigrant labor (Steinberg 1989). After Japan bombed Pearl Harbor in 1941, Japanese Americans were "hauled away" by the FBI, and all Japanese on the mainland, U.S. citizens or not, were evacuated to internment camps. Social worker Harry Kitano offered a personal account of this experience: "The first feeling of being a prisoner occurred almost immediately. After assembling and answering a roll call—we were bused to the train depot—and were herded into some old fashioned railroad cars with armed guards. They told us to pull down the shades and to obey the soldiers" (Kitano 1993:42–44). At that time, Kitano was fifteen years old, and he spent three of his adolescent years in the camp. The exclusionary tendencies of the dominant Euro-Americans toward all other ethnic and racial groups were bluntly captured by Schlesinger—"It occurred to damned few white Americans in these years that Americans of color were also entitled to the rights and liberties promised by the constitution" (1991:15).

Despite such prejudices and biased treatment of immigrants of color as well as of citizens belonging to minority groups, social workers were able to help disadvantaged and vulnerable groups. During this period of American history, the profession did a remarkable job of advocating and mediating on behalf of new immigrant groups. Work with city halls through protests and cooperation was aimed at improving the new arrivals' living conditions. Social workers teamed with trade unions and were instrumental in enacting labor legislation to improve working conditions and stopping the exploitation of the labor force, especially the immigrant women and children victimized in sweatshops (Addams 1930).

As mentioned earlier, the ideal of the melting pot, implemented through assimilation, contributed to the effectiveness of social work. Although the immigration groups from Europe were quite diverse, they were similar in regard to ethnicity and race. In addition, the socioeconomic classes, educational backgrounds, and such of different nationality groups were not unalike. Another factor smoothing the assimilation process was that the immigrant groups had little or no contact with their countries of origin. Social workers worked with different immigrant groups in their own neighborhood and environments, often serving them under the same agency structure and providing services to clients of all ages.

Immigrant Bashing and the Rise of Nativism

Discrimination against immigrants in the United States has a long history, and calls for policies restricting immigration have frequently dominated political debates. Portes and Rumbaut pointed out that paradoxically, "the most ardent advocates of this policy are often children of immigrants who wear their second-generation patriotism outwardly and aggressively" (1990:26). Furthermore, second- and third-generation Mexican, Latin American, and Asian immigrants who are also members of racial minorities stand out visually and continue to be targets of nativistic racism.

Proposition 187, a statewide initiative, was approved by California voters in 1994. It denies social services and benefits to illegal immigrants and requires that all agencies report anyone suspected to be illegal to state agencies and the U.S. Immigration and Naturalization Service. Immigrant bashing and the need for immigration reform became common themes in those states with the most new arrivals. Expressing one's anger at the changing demographics brought on by immigration and targeting anyone who appeared "foreign looking" became acceptable issues for debate in public and political arenas (Chavez 1997). A quick and easy solution was implied: getting rid of these people would solve all the problems facing the American economy, health care, and education.

California voters passed Proposition 187 under the guise of better fiscal management, a blatant expression of racism and anger directed not just at new immigrants but also at all the members of these ethnic groups who have been Americans for generations. Its proponents use war metaphors such as "unlawful immigrants represent the liberal/left foot soldiers in the next decade" and "I have no intention to being the object of 'conquest' peaceful or otherwise by Latinos, Asians, blacks, Arabs or any other groups of individuals who have claimed my country" (quoted in Chavez 1997:67–68).

The rise of nativism of the 1990s, caused by the public's growing fear that many immigrants were exploiting public services, encouraged Congress to pass the Personal Responsibility and Work Opportunity Reconciliation Act of 1996 (PRWORA), the most restrictive anti-immigration legislation passed since 1965. It adversely affected both legal and illegal immigrants and refugees. Legal immigrants were not eligible for Supplemental Security Income and food stamps until they became citizens. Based on mistaken beliefs and faulty studies, $20 billion in food stamps and medical benefits were eliminated (Hing 1998). Indeed, Mary Jo Bane, a strong opponent of this legislation, felt compelled to resign her position as assistant secretary for children and families in the Department of Health and Human Services.

Recent research has shown that despite the common belief, most immigrants do not use welfare. Overall, only 66 percent of immigrants' use welfare (Fix, Passel, and Zimmerman 1996). Accordingly, in response to active protests by citizen groups, especially in New York, New Jersey, California and Texas, and with large immigrant populations now voting in large numbers, the Clinton administration and Congress began restoring some of the benefits in 1997 and 1998. The Balanced Budget Act of 1997 brought back Supplemental Security Income for the disabled and medical benefits to 420,000 legal immigrants who were in the country before PRWORA was enacted. The Agricultural Research Act of 1998 provided food stamps for 225,000 legal immigrant children, senior citizens, and disabled individuals. In his current budget, President Clinton has proposed a $1.3 billion, five-year program to close the remaining gaps in medical and food stamp benefits for legal immigrants (Janotsky 1999). Unfortunately, great damage to the immigrant groups has already been done, and the present piecemeal attempts to restore these benefits are too late and too little.

Current Status of Immigrants in American Social Welfare System

The current status of immigrants in the American social welfare system is determined by whether an immigrant is legally or illegally in this country and what his or her educational and economic situation is. Migrant and seasonal farm workers, mainly Mexican Americans, "are among the most impoverished people in America" (Karger and Stoesz 1994:100). Often the entire family, including the children, works in the fields six to eight months of the year. Social support systems are very important to the Cubans, Central and Latin Americans, but many do not have easy access to their families in their home country. For example, Puerto Ricans have easier access to their extended families "back home" due to "relative proximity, cost of travel to the island, and legal status," whereas Cubans are the least connected to their homeland because of "political pressures and an economic blockade" Ho (1987:151).

The statistics for Asian Americans vary. Karger and Stoesz (1994) reported that only 5 percent of Japanese Americans are at the poverty level, whereas 35 percent of Southeast Asian immigrants are at the poverty level. Hmong refugees have a "dismal economic situation" compared with that of other recent immigrants (Portes and Rumbaut 1990:144). The Hmong believe that they have no opportunities in the United States because they lack goals, have no control over how to make a living, and prefer death to living without dignity. As a group, they are likely to be illiterate and have little if any education and few job skills, making it difficult to compete in an industrial society (Portes and Rumbaut 1990). In 1990, Hmong and Cambodian families in America had the highest poverty rates: 62 percent and 42 percent, respectively (Shinagawa and Jang 1998).

In contrast to the lower-paid Cambodians, Afghans, and Laotians, political refugees from Eastern Europe can be found in "preeminent and well-paid professional careers" (Portes and Rumbaut 1990:24). In the 1980s, however, "only about 3 percent of America's immigrants came from the Eastern bloc—roughly the same number that arrived from the small island of Jamaica" (Briggs and Moore 1994:88), because the United States permitted very few refugees from the Soviet Union bloc.

The majority of immigrants are in the "employable" age group. Of the 720,461 immigrants admitted into the United States by the end of fiscal year 1995, only 6.2 percent were seventy or older. Of them, 46.3 percent were male and 53.7 percent were female (U.S. INS 1997). Table 1.3 shows us that of the total number of immigrants admitted in 1995, 321.557 (35 percent) were employed. The category "No Occupation" includes homemakers, students, unemployed or retired persons, and others, not all of whom, of course, are on welfare. In fact, "immigrants earn higher incomes, contribute more in taxes, and use less of many services the longer they have been in the United States" (Briggs and Moore 1994:92). Another key factor to bear in mind is that many in the "No Occupation" category get a job soon after immigrating to the United States. Because the data on employment status at the time of immigrating can be misleading, it is important to look at the immigrants' employment status one or two years after they enter the United States.

Foner's (1998) summation of recent immigrants' background and status noted that a century ago, immigrants were usually poor, with minimal education and technical skills, but as noted in table 1.3, more than 35 percent of the immigrants admitted to the United States now are professionals and trained technicians in a variety of fields. Those immigrants who are on welfare usually are refugees and elderly people who "use welfare at disproportionate rates to their numbers." For example, elderly immigrants and refugees account for 21 percent of all immigrants, and they also constitute "40 percent of the welfare users" (Fix, Passel, and Zimmerman 1996:on-line). Nonrefugee working-age immigrants use welfare at about the same rate as do "all other" Americans. Moreover, in April 1997, the U.S. Department of Health and Human Services announced that the total number of welfare recipients had dropped by 1.2 million since PRWORA was signed on August 22, 1996. At present, therefore, immigrants contribute $25 billion more to the U.S. Treasury than they collect in benefits and services. Nonetheless, the 1996 act stopped providing services to the most vulnerable—the aged, new arrivals, women, and children (on-line: http://www.welfaretowork.com/facts/index/html).

THE CHANGING CLIMATE OF MULTICULTURAL SOCIETIES

The passage of the 1965 Immigration Act brought with it major changes regarding issues of equity, equality, acceptance of diversity, and the affirmative action. Because the Civil Rights Act of 1964 did not bring racial equality to the economic and political arenas, affirmative action was required. Basically, affirmative action is a "set of policies designed to achieve equality in admissions and employment opportunities for minorities" (Karger and Stoesz 1994:104). But the immigrant population is not necessarily benefiting from this remedy, for immigrants, as minorities, are not always evenly and equitably distributed in the job arena. When the job market is bad, women and other minorities are the most likely to be shut out. Likewise, when job opportunities are abundant and the economy is prospering, minorities have more job options. According to Beck, however, affirmative action was "never intended for immigrants." Rather, the impetus for affirmative action "was not concern for something called 'ethnic minority'; its impetus was concern for black Americans" (1996:187). Some people may disagree.

TABLE 1.3

Immigrants Admitted by Major Occupation Group and Region and Selected Country of Birth (Fiscal Year 1996)

Region/country	Total	Prof.[a]	Exec.[b]	Sales	Admin.[c]	Repair[d]	Oper.[e]	Farm.[f]	Serv.[g]	No. occ.[h]
All countries	915,900	75,261	31,850	15,317	21,618	23,867	76,843	14,675	62,126	594,357
Europe	147,581	19,308	6,429	2,159	4,044	5,187	8,122	858	8,969	92,505
Asia	307,807	33,191	16,053	5,740	7,540	6,399	16,738	7,390	16,857	197,899
America	340,540	10,247	4,594	4,298	5,647	8,369	42,715	5,542	26,267	232,863
Caribbean	116,801	5,015	1,464	2,107	5,645	4,493	13,075	1,583	11,069	75,057
Central America	44,289	1,135	567	756	1,037	1,256	6,260	224	5,361	27,693
South America	61,769	4,136	1,909	1,324	1,799	2,156	6,836	451	5,111	38,047
Africa	52,889	7,597	2,426	1,675	2,427	1,569	2,148	245	4,517	30,185

[a] Professional specialty and technical
[b] Executive, administrative, and managerial
[c] Administrative support
[d] Precision production, craft, and repair
[e] Operator, fabricator, and laborer
[f] Farming, forestry, and fishing
[g] Service workers
[h] No occupation or not reported. Includes homemakers, students, unemployed or retired persons, and others not reporting or with an unknown occupation.

Source: U.S. Immigration and Naturalization Service, Statistical Yearbook of the Immigration and Naturalization Service, 1996 (Washington, DC: U.S. Government Printing Office, 1996), 70–71.

As the United States absorbs more and more cultures and ethnic groups, it needs to create a social climate to accept this diversity. This *cultural pluralism* urges "a new type of nation in which the various national groups would preserve their identity and cultures, uniting as a world federation in miniature" (Bouvier 1992:112). Cultural pluralism is often perceived in terms of exotic foods and dress rather than diverse traditions, values, thoughts, and aspirations. But Pantoja and Perry maintain that

> cultural pluralism as a societal value and societal goal requires that the society permit the existence of multicultural communities that can live according to their own styles, customs, languages and values without penalty to their members and without inflicting harm upon or competing for resources among themselves. Cultural pluralism does not imply rigid barriers of psychological and physical separations. Since all groups are valued as one values one's own affiliations, interactions among cultural groups are valued and encouraged.   (1976:81)

Cultural diversity has often been deemed socially unacceptable and deviant. Only occasionally was such diversity tolerated as novel or exotic customs. With the advent of cultural pluralism, however, this notion is changing. Now, cultural and ethnic groups, big or small, closer to the dominant American values or drastically different, and ethnically, racially, and religiously diverse are seen to have an equal right to retain and practice their own customs. This view may be somewhat idealistic, however. For example, the U.S. Bureau of the Census (1996) revealed that California admitted 52,088 Mexican immigrants and Arizona, 4,340, of whom a significant number speak Spanish. These statistics, moreover, do not include the 1,444,000 illegal immigrants in California. Nonetheless, despite these large numbers of Spanish-speaking people, California's public schools are not required to teach courses in Spanish.

The term *cultural pluralism* was first used in 1924 by Horace Kallen, in a chapter in *Culture and Democracy in the United States*. In this text, he claimed that *cultural pluralism* was the idea that "democracy is an essential prerequisite to culture, that culture can be and sometimes is a fine flowering of democracy, and that the history of the relation of the two in the United States exhibits this fact" (p. 11). Kallen pointed out that a person automatically and involuntarily belongs to an ethnic group, whereas one volunteers to belong, or not belong, to a social club, a political party, or even a state. He emphasized that people may change their dress, get a new spouse, alter their religious beliefs, or move to another country, but they cannot change their ethnic background.

Cultural pluralism gives all groups an equal opportunity to interact on an equal footing, with an emphasis on mutual acceptance and equal opportunity to obtain society's resources. Besides an equal acceptance of one another's values, negotiation or compromise among cultural groups or traditions is necessary. Cultural pluralism facilitates the different groups' interactions and transactions. Here, interactions and transactions are behaviors both within a group and transcending the group. For example, when Korean Americans interact with African Americans, this is a transaction. From a cultural pluralism perspective, both ethnic groups should function as equal members of the larger society. In addition, they should be able to continue to practice their customs and preserve their traditions without being defensive or apologetic.

Today, the United States is struggling to convey to the global community that it is committed to ensuring basic human rights for all people around the world. Of course, it first must ensure those rights for all its own citizens. It must demonstrate that not only are the American shores open to all legal immigrants from all the parts of the world but that once they arrive, they can practice and preserve their cultural heritage, customs, norms, values, religion, and language. Unlike their predecessors, immigrants arriving after 1965 are not expected or pressured to become part of the American melting pot. But there is both an implicit and an explicit expectation for new immigrants to become "Americanized," and the sooner they do, the easier it will be for them to survive in their new home. Such pressures are institutional and formal as well as individual and informal. For example, in school, immigrant children are expected not only to learn American ways of talking, behaving, and interacting but also are discouraged from adhering to any of their cultural practices or patterns of behavior different from the prevailing ones.

Why Cultural Pluralism?

Greenbaum (1974) made five major points regarding cultural pluralism: (1) Besides encouraging respect for the United States, supporting multicultural identities also promotes "true universalism in which the merits and faults of different belief systems can be more intelligently assessed because the individual and the group deeply understand more than one culture" (p. 434). (2) There is an enormous need for humans to be self-conscious and self-aware. For this reason, ethnic groups can maintain and use their institutions and communities to their own group's advantage. (3) Cultural pluralism is supported by the awareness that Anglo conformity did not prevent inequalities among the people, especially the economically disadvantaged. (4) Pluralism can help remedy poverty and individualism. Pluralistic groups stress the interdependence of persons, families, colleagues, groups, and communities. These groups seek economic, scientific, technological, and governmental positions so that their members will be served rather than dominated. (5) Pluralism is necessary as the basis for "strong institutions and communities" (p. 435).

From a social work perspective, cultural pluralism is necessary because it recognizes the uniqueness of different cultures and allows immigrants to maintain their beliefs, customs, and values. With the increase in migration, the number of immigrants and refugees needing social work services is also expected to rise, particularly owing to the increase in poverty, domestic violence, AIDS, teen pregnancies, divorce, and other societal problems. Immigrants also face the problems of unemployment and underemployment and, for Asian Americans, the pressure of being the "model minority." Social workers must learn skills that will allow them to maximize the uniqueness of the immigrants' culture while assisting them with their needs in the American society. This supports the strength perspective which is being increasingly discussed in the profession.

This text encourages diversity as a strength and not a weakness or deviance. The new ethnic and cultural groups in the United States bring with them distinctly different values, norms, and traditions. For example, the African, Asian, and Hispanic communities emphasize dependence on families and one's kinship network. Individuals in these ethnic communities thus readily seek and accept assistance from both their immediate and their extended family. Such dependence on families is not necessarily regarded as negative or as rigid as American individualism; rather, it is seen as providing mutual support through social kinship networks. People from varying ethnic and racial backgrounds are considered unique and multitalented and as important members of and contributors to American society. In addition, they are not expected or encouraged to conform to the dominant culture.

Cultural Pluralism as Affirming Social Work Values and Ethics

With respect to social work's cardinal values, *self-determination* is actuated through cultural pluralism. That is, immigrants themselves must decide whether to adopt "Americanized" values, norms, and ways of thinking. Cultural pluralism allows them to make this choice. *Dignity and self-worth* are acknowledged by allowing each immigrant the opportunity to make responsible choices regarding their cultural heritage. For example, an American couple permits a Vietnamese couple to take care of their baby, acknowledging their particular style of discipline and upbringing.

Social workers must respect immigrants' *right to confidentiality*. This right, however, may be challenged by the new law (PRWORA 1996) that assumes that workers employed at agencies that administer Supplemental Security Income (SSI), welfare bloc grants, or housing assistance must report the addresses and names of illegal immigrants to the Immigration and Naturalization Service (INS) (Katz 1996). In addition, this new reform may also impinge on the social work value regarding individuals' *equal access to all resources*. If legal permanent residents cannot obtain SSI, Medicaid, or food stamps until they become citizens of the United States or have worked in the United States and paid taxes for at least ten years, then their accessibility to all resources is limited (Northern California Coalition for Immigrant Rights 1996).

The final cardinal social work value, *affirming the client's individuality and uniqueness*, also embraces cultural pluralism. Diversity, individuality, and uniqueness can be viewed as strengths and not as weaknesses or deviances. By recognizing and acknowledging each immigrant's cultural and ethnic heritage, including differences in lifestyles and upbringing, social workers can create a solid foundation for their right to be treated as unique beings.

ECOLOGICAL PERSPECTIVE

The Relationship Between People and the Environment

The ecological perspective is widely used in social work to formulate "preventive psychological interventions." Balgopal and Vassil defined the ecological perspective as explaining "the actions which govern how people get along" (1983:21). These actions are based on "a combination of ways in which the individuals have managed their lives in the past, and how they anticipate the future" (p. 21). In essence, then, in social work, people are seen interacting with their environment. As the environment changes, so too may the people. And as they adjust and cope with the changing environment, they can learn new skills and modify "old ones." These adjustments must be made in different areas such as language, culture, social relationships, norms, and values. But the environment may have to make adjustments as well. In other words, U.S. citizens may also have to learn to accept immigrants' differences in coping styles, language, ethnic and cultural upbringing, and general perspectives.

This diversity is apparent not only between Americans and immigrants but also among the different ethnic and racial groups in the immigrant population. As the immigrants learn the ways of their new environment, they are also expanding their competence and well-being, by adding new skills and values to their already existing supply. The positive attributes of one ethnic group thus can be copied and enhanced by another.Coping with and adapting to the new environment is a skill that may be easier for one immigrant group to learn than another. But being able to maintain the values of the home country and adjusting to the "new" ones prevailing in the United States can be quite challenging. Social workers may need to identify these issues and discuss them with their clients. The conflict of adjusting or not may impede some immigrants' growth and ability to function productively. Add to this a language barrier and conflicting ethnic customs, it becomes clear how stressful this adaptation can be.

Social Environment

To understand the context in which social workers practice, we must look at the social environment in which they must function. In practical social work situations, social workers must be aware of life patterns, including "interrelationships with *family, social networks, organizations and communities*" (Balgopal and Vassil 1983:36, italics in original).

In the family, nurturance, socialization, and education are important to the development and growth of children and adults. Each family member plays certain roles, and the expectations of these roles can "mold" the family's functioning. In the broader external environment—the neighborhood, community, town, or city—immigrants are faced with multiple issues. In the family unit, immigrant parents may attempt to teach their children their native language, apply their religious values, and reinforce their style of discipline. But when the children enter school and play at their friends' homes, the values and morals of the United States take precedence.

Extended family, neighbors, friends, and work associates form an important base for people's stability, self-worth, and support. Their social network is those other persons to whom people are linked in terms of influencing or being influenced by, supporting or being supported by, depending on or being depended on. For immigrants, it is important to locate their social network and its composition. A strong support system enables people to function efficiently.

The broader organizational environment is important as well, for the organization cannot function without the individual, and vice versa. Accordingly, much preparation and planning is necessary to accommodate and support immigrants. Studying cultural diversity and understanding the obvious and subtle differences based on language and ethnicity is a good place to start.

Finally, the quality of communities and neighborhoods influences the development of individuals. If their environment is not conducive to growth, both individual and social, its inhabitants will suffer. For example, if an immigrant is living in a community in which job opportunities and food are scarce, normative community patterns will be limited. Illness, marginal shelter, inadequate clothing, lack of weather-specific utilities (such as heat and air conditioning), nonfunctional living facilities, and inaccessible or underutilized health services are examples of dysfunctional community patterns. If such functions were present, the community would be more supportive, making easier the immigrant's adjustment to the new environment. Without such factors, however, the community's functions are stifled, thus creating more problems for immigrants and their families.

NOTES

1. The Immigration and Nationality Act of 1952, also known as the McCarran-Walter Act, was the "first codification immigration and nationality law and is still the basic code" (Morse 1994:89). The quota for immigrants from non-Western Hemisphere countries was set at 150,000, with a preference for highly skilled workers. In addition, the act allowed the attorney general to admit those refugees for up to two years whose presence would be in the best interest of the United States.

2. The main purpose of the Migration and Refugee Assistance Act of 1962 was to coordinate the movement and numbers of immigrants. Under this act, (a) refugees would be transported; (b) projects would be established to enhance employment or to update refugees' professional training; (c) aid would be given to refugees who had fled their country because of persecution based on race, religion, political concerns, and other circumstances; (d) refugees would be assisted if the president decided that doing so would contribute to the defense of the United States; and (e) contributions would be made to the United Nations High Commission for Refugees (Miller and Miller 1996).

REFERENCES

Addams, J. (1930). *Twenty Years at Hull-House.* New York: Macmillan.

Balgopal, P. R., and Vassil, T. V. (1983). *Groups in Social Work: An Ecological Perspective.* New York: Macmillan.

Bane, M. J. (1997). Welfare as we might know it. *The American Prospect* (January/ February 1997): 47–53.

Beck, R. (1996). *The Case Against Immigration: The Moral, Economic, Social, and Environmental Reasons for Reducing U.S. Immigration Back to Traditional Levels.* New York: Norton.

Bernard, W. S., and Greenleigh, A. (1960). Aliens and foreign born. In R. M. Kurtz (ed.), *Social Work Year Book*. New York: National Association of Social Workers Press.

Bird, M. Y., Fong, R., Galindo, P., Nowicki, J., and Freeman, E. M. (1996). The multicultural mosaic. In P. Ewalt, E. M. Freeman, and A. Kirk, and D. L. Poole (eds.), *Multicultural Issues in Social Work*. Washington, DC: National Association of Social Workers Press.

Bouvier, L. F. (1992). *Peaceful Invasions: Immigration and Changing America*. Lanham, MD: University Press of America.

Briggs, V. M. Jr., and Moore, S. (1994). *Still an Open Door? U.S. Immigration Policy and the American Economy*. Washington, DC: American University Press.

Bryan, M. C., and Davis, A. E. (1990). *100* Years at Hull-House. Bloomington: Indiana University Press.

Chavez, L. R. (1997). Immigration reform and nativism: The nationalist response to the traditionalist challenge. In J. F. Perea (ed.), *Immigrants Out!* New York: New York University Press.

D'Innocenze, M., and Sirefman, J. P. (eds.) (1992). *Immigration and Ethnicity: American "Melting Pot" or "Salad Bowl"?* Westport, CT: Greenwood Press.

Epps, E. G. (ed.). (1974). *Cultural Pluralism*. Berkeley, CA: McCutchan.

Ewalt, P. L., Freeman, E. M., Kirk, S. A., and Poole, D. L. (eds.). (1996). *Multicultural Issues in Social Work*. Washington, DC: National Association of Social Workers Press.

Fix, M., and Passel, J. S. (1994). *Immigration and Immigrants*. Washington, DC: Urban Institute.

Fix, M., Passel, J. S., and Zimmermann, W. (1996). The use of SSI and other welfare programs by immigrants. In *Summary of Facts About Immigrants' Use of Welfare*. On-line. Available at http://www.urban.org/immig/borjas.htm.

Foner, N. (1998). New immigrants: The transnationals. *Natural History* 34–35 (March).

Glazer, N. (1987). *Affirmative Discrimination: Ethnic Inequality and Public Policy*. Cambridge, MA: Harvard University Press.

Goldberg, D. T. (ed.). (1994). *Multiculturalism: A Critical Reader*. Cambridge, MA: Blackwell.

Gordon, M. M. (1964 and 1978). *Assimilation in American Life: The Role of Race, Religion, and National Origins*. New York: Oxford University Press.

Greenbaum, W. (1974). American in search of a new ideal: An essay on the rise of pluralism. *Harvard Educational Review* 44 (3): 411–440.

Haines, D. W. (ed.). (1989). *Refugees as Immigrants: Cambodians, Laotians, and Vietnamese in America*. Totowa, NJ: Rowan and Littlefield.

Hing, B. O. (1998). Don't give me your tired, your poor: Conflicted immigrant stories and welfare reform. *Harvard Civil Rights: Civil Liberty, the Law Review* 33 (1): 159–182.

Ho, M. K. (1987). *Family Therapy with Ethnic Minorities*. Beverly Hills, CA: Sage.

Janotsky, M. (1999). Legal immigrants would regain aid in Clinton's plan. *New York Times* (January 25): A1, A19.

Kallen, H. M. (1924). *Culture and Democracy in the United States: Studies in the Group Psychology of the American Peoples.* New York: Boni and Liveright.

Karger, H. J., and Stoesz, D. (1994). *American Social Welfare Policy: A Pluralist Approach.* 2d ed. White Plains, NY: Longman.

Katz, J. L. (1996). Welfare overhaul law. *Congressional Quarterly* 54: 2696–2705.

Kay, A. E. (1997). Impact of the new law on immigrants. *India Abroad* 27 (March 7): 23.

Kim, Y. Y. (1989). Personal, social, and economic adaptation: 1975–1979 arrivals in Illinois. In D. W. Haines (ed.)., *Refugees as Immigrants.* Totowa, NJ: Rowan and Littlefield.

Kitano, H. H. L. (1993). *Generations and Identity: The Japanese American.* Needham, MA: Ginn Press.

Lucinai, G. (ed.). (1993). *Migration Policies in Europe and the United States.* Norwell, MA: Kluwer Academic.

Miller, E. W., and Miller, R. M. (1996). *United States Immigration: A Reference Handbook.* Denver: ABC-CLIO.

Morse, A. (ed.). (1994). *America's Newcomers: An Immigrant Policy Handbook.* Washington, DC: National Conference of State Legislators.

Northern California Coalition for Immigrant Rights. (1996). Immigrants and the new welfare law. On-line. Available at ncci@igc.org.

Pantoja, A., and Perry, W. (1976). Social work in a culturally pluralistic society: An alternative paradigm. In M. Sotomayor (ed.), *Cross-Cultural Perspectives in Social Work Practice and Education.* University of Houston, Graduate School of Social Work.

Perea, J. F. (ed.). (1997). *Immigrants Out!* New York: New York University Press.

Pettys, G. L., and Balgopal, P. R. (1998). Multigenerational conflicts and new immigrants: An Indo-American experience. *Families in Society* 79 (4): 410–423.

Portes, A., and Rumbaut, R. G. (1990). *Immigrant America: A Portrait.* Berkeley and Los Angeles: University of California Press.

Powers, M. G., and Macisco, J. J. Jr. (eds.). (1994). *The Immigration Experience in the United States: Policy Implications.* New York: Center for Migration Studies.

Ramakrishnan, K. R., and Balgopal, P. R. (1995). Role of social institutions in a multicultural society. *Journal of Sociology and Social Welfare* 22 (1): 11–27.

Roberts, D. E. (1996). Who may give birth to United States citizens? *Women's Right Law Reporter* 17 (93): 273–278.

Rumbaut, R. G. (1994a). The crucible within: Ethnic identity, self-esteem and segmented assimilation among children of immigrants. *International Migration Review* 28 (4): 748–794.

Rumbaut, R. G. (1994b). Origins and destinies: Immigration to the United States since World War II. *Sociological Forum* 9 (4): 583–621.

Schlesinger, A. Jr. (1991). *The Disuniting of America: Reflections of Multicultural Society*. Knoxville, TN: Whittle Direct Books.

Shinagawa, L. H., and Jang, M. (1998). *Atlas of American Diversity*. Walnut Creek, CA: Altmira Press.

Simcox, D. E. (ed.). (1988). *U.S. Immigration in the 1980s*: Reappraisal and Reform. Boulder, CO: Westview Press.

Steinberg, S. (1989). *The Ethnic Myth: Race, Ethnicity, and Class in America*. Boston: Beacon Press.

U.S. Bureau of the Census. (1996). *Statistical Abstract of the United States*. 116th ed. Washington, DC: Hoover Business Press.

U.S. Department of Health and Human Services Administration for Children and Families (1997).{{Au: Title??}} On-line. Available at http://www.welfareto work.com/facts/index.html.

U.S. Immigration and Naturalization Service. (1997). *Statistical Yearbook of the Immigration and Naturalization Service, 1995*. Washington, DC: U.S. Government Printing Office.

U.S. Immigration and Naturalization Service. (1999). *Annual Report Legal Immigration, Fiscal Year 1997*. Washington, DC: U.S. Government Printing Office.

Walker, D. E. Jr. (1972). *The Emergent Native Americans*. Boston: Little, Brown.

Wheeler, C. (1996). New protections for immigrant women and children who are victims of domestic violence. *Clearinghouse Review* 30 (3): 222–229.

Williamson, C. Jr. (1996). *The Immigration Mystique*. New York: Basic Books.

CHAPTER 2

SOCIAL WORK PRACTICE WITH ASIAN IMMIGRANTS

Jayashree Nimmagadda and Pallassana R. Balgopal

Asians are the fastest-growing immigrant group in the United States, representing different ethnicities, cultures, socioeconomic classes, and generations. This diverse group is made up of Chinese, Japanese, Filipinos, Koreans, Vietnamese, Asian Indians,[1] Cambodians, Hmong, Laotians, and Thais, along with "other Asians," "Pacific Islanders," and "other Pacific Islanders." Hawaiians, Samoans, and Guamanians are referred to as Pacific Islanders. People from Tonga, Tahiti, Fiji, the Northern Mariana Islands, and Palau are the "other Pacific Islanders," and Bangladeshis, Burmese, Indonesians, Malaysians, Pakistanis, and Sri Lankans are classified as "Other Asians" (U.S. Bureau of Census 1992).

In the 1990 census, the Asian or Pacific Islander (API) category had the following options: Chinese, Filipino, Hawaiian, Korean, Vietnamese, Japanese, Asian-Indian, Samoan, Guamanian, and other API, but in 1997 the U.S. Office of Management and Budget (OMB) recommended that federal statistics separate Asians and Pacific Islanders. In addition, the OMB has recommended that the 2000 census allow individuals to choose more than one race. This change will identify Asian Americans who have a non-Asian parent or grandparent or whose parents come from different Asian ethnic groups, and it will also mean that individuals are not obliged to choose one identity over another. This option, of course, will further complicate the task of determining who the Asian Americans are (Lee 1998).

BRIEF IMMIGRATION HISTORY

The immigration of Asians was made possible by the passage of the Immigration Act of 1965, which became fully operational in 1968. Between 1970 and 1980, the overall population of the United States increased by 11 percent, but Asian Americans increased by 141 percent, and between 1980 and 1990, the total population of the United States increased by 10 percent and that of Asian Americans rose by 99 percent (Barringer, Gardner, and Levin 1993), a number that should double again by 2010. The estimated 9.6 million Asian Americans in 1997 made up around 4 percent of the total U.S. population (Lee 1998).

After the Immigration Act of 1965, immigrants poured in from the Philippines, China, Taiwan, Hong Kong, India, Korea, and Vietnam. Prominently absent were the Japanese, mostly because of Japan's economic prosperity. Those people who immigrated immediately after the Immigration Act tended to be well qualified and highly trained, the best in their country. Over the last three decades, however, this pattern has changed, and the more recent immigrants are not as highly skilled as the earlier ones.

Like other immigrant groups, Asians and Pacific Islanders have a long history of struggle and hardship in making the United States their new home. They have frequently been attacked and brutalized because of racism and prejudice. Both local ordinances and national policies and laws were enacted to withhold from them the same treatment offered to their European counterparts. But these hardships and brutal treatment did not deter Asians from coming to this country or stop them from helping build the United States of today.

> Unlike European immigrants Asians were victimized by laws and policies that discriminated on the basis of race. . . . The laws determined not only who came to America, but also who could become citizens. The Naturalization Law of 1790 had specified that naturalized citizenship was to be reserved for "whites." This law remained in effect until 1952.   (Takaki 1989:13)

Asian Americans have been in this country for more than 150 years, yet very little is known about their history and the struggles they have had to endure. They are given hardly any credit for their contributions to our country's development. American history books give only cursory attention to the people of Asian ancestry and their hard work and role in building this nation. (Some of the major events of Asian Americans' chronological history are listed next. For a more extensive account of these events, see Chan 1991 and LEAP 1998.)

Brief Chronology

1763	First settlement of Filipino Americans in Louisiana bayous is recorded.
1790	First arrival of an Asian Indian in the United States is recorded.

1835   Americans establish first sugar plantation in Hawaii.

1848–52 Discovery of gold at Sutter's Mill, CA, draws Chinese immigrants to West Coast to mine gold. Many arrive as indentured servants.

1853   California levies Foreign Miner's Tax, which forces Chinese to pay a tax not required of U.S. citizens.

1854   Law forbids Chinese to testify in court against whites.

1859   Exclusion of Chinese from public schools in San Francisco.

1868   Japanese contract workers arrive in Hawaii to work on sugar plantations.

1869   Chinese laborers built most of western section of transcontinental railroad.

1870   During anti-Chinese riots in Los Angeles, twenty Chinese are killed.

1882   Chinese Exclusions Act suspends immigration of Chinese laborers for ten years, thereby excluding Chinese from citizenship by naturalization.

1892   Geary Act prohibits Chinese immigration for another ten years.

1893   When a Japanese man applies for naturalized U.S. citizenship, Massachusetts circuit court declares him ineligible for naturalization.

1898   The Philippines becomes a U.S. protectorate.

1903–04 Seventy-eight hundred Koreans go to Hawaii to work on plantations.

1906   Korean children are prohibited from attending public schools.

1907   Asian Indians are subjected to racial violence in Bellingham, WA, and seven hundred farm and timber mill workers are driven into Canada.

1908   Japan and the United States reach a "gentlemen's agreement" whereby Japan stops issuing passports to laborers wanting to emigrate to the United States.

1917   Aspiring Asian Indian immigrants are prevented from disembarking in Vancouver.

1923   *U.S. v. Bhagat Singh Thind* declares Asian Indians ineligible for naturalized citizenship.

1924   Immigration Act declares no one ineligible for citizenship may immigrate to the United States, thereby ending Asian immigration completely.

1925   Legislative Act makes Filipinos ineligible for citizenship unless they have served three years in U.S. Navy.

1929–30 Anti-Filipino riots and murders take place on West Coast.

1942   Executive order 9066 puts 112,000 Japanese (primarily U.S. citizens) in ten internment (concentration) camps.

1943   Magnuson Act repeals Chinese Exclusion Act of 1882.

1946   All concentration camps are closed.

1952   McCarran-Walter Act makes Japanese eligible for citizenship.

1956	California repeals its alien land laws; Dalip Singh Sound from California is elected to Congress.
1959	Hawaii becomes fiftieth state; Daniel K. Inouye and Hiram Fong are elected to represent Hawaii in Congress.
1962	Daniel K. Inouye becomes U.S. senator from Hawaii.
1964	Patsy Takemoto Mink becomes first Asian American woman elected to serve in Congress from Hawaii.
1965	Immigration law abolishes national-origins quota system.
1975	The fall of Saigon signals arrival of large numbers of refugees from Vietnam, Cambodia, and Laos.
1982	Vincent Chin, a Chinese American, is clubbed to death in Detroit.
1987	Navoroze Mody an Asian Indian is killed by gang in New Jersey.
1988	Civil Liberties Act is passed, apologizing and offering redress and reparations to thousands of Japanese Americans denied their civil and constitutional rights by U.S. government during World War II.
1990	President George Bush proclaims May as Asian Pacific Heritage Month.

DEMOGRAPHICS

In 1970 the Asian American population of the United States was 1.5 million; in 1980 this number had almost doubled, to 3.7 million; and in 1997 the estimate was 9.6 million Asian Americans, of which 95 percent were Asian and 5 percent were Pacific Islander (U.S. Bureau of Census 1988, 1992). By 2030 this population should grow to 20 million (Barringer et al. 1993, Ong and Hee 1993). Asians and Pacific Islanders are the only group whose net international migration (201,000) added more people than the natural increase (134,000) (U.S. Census Bureau homepage, January 1997).

The Chinese (24 percent) and Filipinos (21 percent) are the two largest Asian groups, followed by the Asian Indians (13 percent), Vietnamese (11 percent), Japanese (10 percent), Koreans (10 percent), other Southeast Asians (e.g., Vietnamese, Cambodians, Laotians, Thais, and Hmong), and the Pacific Islanders (Lee 1998). The actual number of each group is shown in figure 2.1. Unlike most other Asian Americans, many Southeast Asian Americans are involuntary migrants who were forced to leave their homes in Vietnam, Cambodia, Laos, and the Hmong communities for fear of persecution after the U.S. military left Southeast Asia. Between 1975 and 1984, more than 700,000 Vietnamese and 500,000 Cambodian and Laotian refugees were resettled in the United States (Lee, 1998).

The median family income of Asian Americans in 1990 was estimated to be $35,900, higher than the national median of $34,200 (U.S. Bureau of Census, cited in Gall and Gall 1993). But these figures do not reflect the differences among

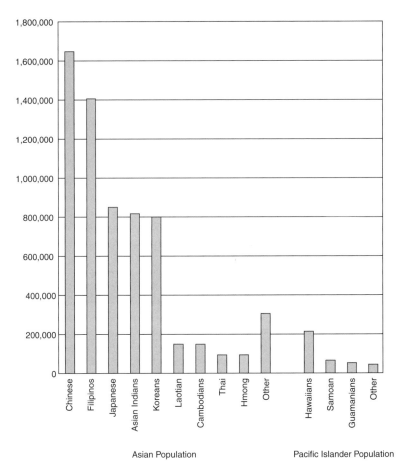

Total Asian and Pacific Islander Population in United states = 7,273,662

FIGURE 2.1 Breakdown of 1990 Asian American and Pacific Island American Populations
Source: U.S. Bureau of the Census. (1992) *1990 Census of population—General population characteristics.* Washington, DC: U.S. Government Printing Office.

the various groups in this category. Gould (1988) correctly argued that these statistics were misinterpreted, that in fact the incomes of many Asians and Pacific Islanders were below the median U.S. income. In March 1991, 8.7 percent of Asian and Pacific Islander immigrants were estimated to be living below the poverty level (U.S. Bureau of Census, cited in Gall and Gall 1993). Then, between 1994 and

1995, although the number of whites and blacks living in poverty had decreased significantly, there was no significant change for Asians and Pacific Islanders (U.S. Census Bureau homepage, January 1997). Furthermore, their unemployment rate in 1990 was 3.5 percent, which was lower than the national average of 6.8 percent. The different groups' median incomes and percentages of families and persons living below the poverty level are shown in table 2.1.

Asians and Pacific Islanders speak many different languages, and figure 2.2 gives the percentages of Asian and Pacific Islander immigrants who speak a language other than English at home.

Fifty-three percent of Asians and Pacific Islanders have employer-provided health insurance. Estimates in 1989 showed that 80 percent of this population had insurance, compared with white non-Hispanics (85 percent); black non-Hispanics (84 percent); and Hispanics (68 percent) (cited in Gall and Gall 1993). Even though the number of Asians and Pacific Islanders living in poverty is lower than that of the other groups, the percentage of this population having adequate health insurance coverage is smaller than that of the other groups.

In 1990, Asians and Pacific Islanders made up the highest percentage (76 percent) of the U.S. population living in married-couple families (U.S. Bureau of Census 1990). Not surprisingly, the divorce rate among these ethnic groups was 4.0 percent, which was less than that of the total population (8.1 percent) and of whites (8.0 percent) (cited in Gall and Gall 1993).

GEOGRAPHIC SETTLEMENT

The first waves of Asian immigrants tended to settle in clusters on the East or West Coast, such as in the Chinatowns that can be found in cities all over the country. The states with the most Chinese are California (704,850), New York (284,144), Hawaii (68,804), Texas (63,232), New Jersey (59,084), Massachusetts (53,792), Illinois (49,936), Washington (33,962), Maryland (30,868), and Florida (30,737). Japanese are most numerous in California (312,281), Washington (34,366), and Illinois (21,831), as well as in New Jersey, Texas, Oregon, Colorado, and Hawaii (one-fourth of whose population are Japanese Americans) (Murase, 1995). The five states with the highest Asian Indian population are California (159,973), New York (140,985), New Jersey (79,440), Illinois (64,200), and Texas (55,795) (U.S. Bureau of Census 1990). Although Southeast Asians have settled primarily in California and Texas (U.S. Bureau of Census 1990) and in small numbers across the United States, especially in Massachusetts (Howe 1991, Silka and Tip 1994). Koreans, Filipinos, and Taiwanese can be found all over the coun-

TABLE 2.1

Median Income, Percentage of Families and Persons Below Poverty Level for
Asian and Pacific Islander Population

Group	Median Income Household	Percent Families Below Poverty	Percent Persons Below Poverty
All persons	$30,056	10.0	13.1
Asian and Pacific Islander	$36,784	11.6	14.1[b]
Asian	$37,007	11.4	14.0[b]
Chinese	$36,259	11.1	14.0[b]
Taiwanese	$42,316	11.2	13.7[b]
Filipino	$43,780	5.2	6.4
Japanese	$41,626	3.4	7.0
Asian Indian	$44,696	7.2	9.7
Korean	$30,184	14.7	13.7[b]
Vietnamese	$29,772[a]	23.8	25.7[b]
Cambodian	$18,837[a]	42.1	42.6[b]
Hmong	$14,276[a]	61.8	63.6[b]
Laotian	$23,019	32.2	34.7[b]
Thai	$31,632	10.8	12.5
Indonesian	$28,597[a]	19.9	25.2[a]
Pakistani	$33,520	12.2	15.1[b]
Pacific Islander	$31,980	15.0	30.7[b]
Polynesian	$32,626	15.3	28.5[b]
Hawaiian	$34,830	12.7	14.3[b]
Samoan	$27,511[a]	24.5	38.2[b]
Tongan	$26,440[a]	20.6	23.1[b]
Micronesian	$29,327[a]	14.4	17.6[b]
Guamanian	$30,786	12.3	15.3[b]
Melanesian	$31,450	8.5	9.5

[a]Median income below national median

[b]Age of people below poverty higher than national average

Source: U.S. Department of Commerce, Economics and Statistics Administration, Census of Population: Asian and Pacific Islanders in the United States, 1990 CP-3-5 (Washington, DC: U.S. Government Printing Office, 1990), 141–175, table 5.

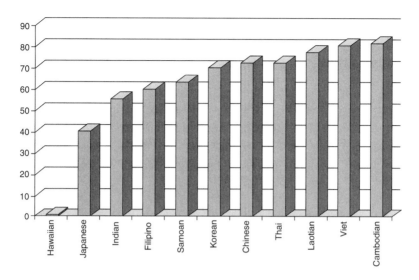

FIGURE 2.2 Home Language by Asian Ethnicity. Percent of Asian/Pacific Islanders by ethnic group who speak a language other than English at home, 1989.
10.2% overall population average
Source: Asian American Health Forum, Inc. (San Francisco, CA, April 1989).

try. About 44 percent of the Pacific Islanders were living in Hawaii in 1990, 30 percent in California, and 4 percent in Washington. Most Hawaiians live in Hawaii, Samoans and Guamanians in California, and Tongans in Utah (U.S. Bureau of Census 1991, cited by Barringer et al. 1993). (The distribution of Asian American groups in the different states is shown in figure 2.3.) In 1990, Asians made up 2+ percent of the population of just twelve states, but in 1996, this number dramatically rose to twenty-nine states. These increases are likely to be repeated in the 2000 census (Lee 1998). The U.S. Census Bureau projects that between 1995 and 2025, the Asian population will grow the fastest in the West, with an increase of 7 million, and in the Northeast, with an increase of 2 million.

SALIENT CULTURAL FACTORS

The principal differences among the various Asian and Pacific Islander groups are based on the part of Asia from which they have immigrated, how long they have been in the United States, where in the United States they are living, their

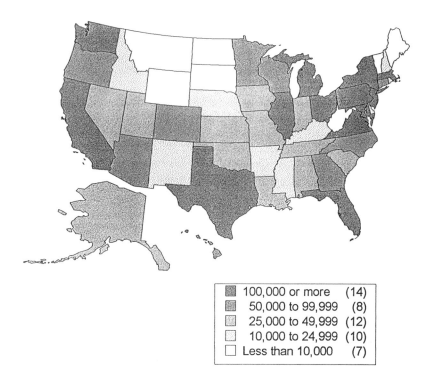

100,000 or more   (14)
50,000 to 99,999   (8)
25,000 to 49,999   (12)
10,000 to 24,999   (10)
Less than 10,000   (7)

FIGURE 2.3   Number of Asian Americans, by state, 1994.

social class, and so on. Fong (1994) also differentiated between those immigrants who are struggling to preserve their traditions and the American-born Asians who have different problems, such as maintaining their ethnic identity.

Many of Asian Americans' traditional values can be traced to their religion. For example, Chinese, Japanese, Korean, and Vietnamese traditions have their roots in Confucianism and are based on two important principles—filial piety and loss of face (Fong 1994). Confucian philosophy and ethics emphasize the specific roles of and proper relationships with different people. *Oyakōkō*, the Japanese version of filial piety toward one's parents encompasses children's obligation and loyalty to their parents and the broader family. *Giri*, "obligation," governs Japanese family roles. The concept of shame *tiu lien* in Chinese families is used to reinforce familial expectations and proper behavior both within and outside the family (Ho, 1990). And according to Kim and Kim (1992), Koreans are highly motivated, and competitive in regard to individual and family success. "They are overly concerned about personal as well as family grace and celebrity or *che-myum*—an internalized reaction to the probably externally imposed social, psychological and behavioral prescriptions" (Kim and Kim 1992:236). Filipino American families are very closely knit, and family members depend on one another for financial and emotional support. Smooth and caring interpersonal relationships within the extended family create a system of support and cooperation and are maintained through "*utang ng loob* (reciprocal obligation), *Liya* (shame), *amor proprio* (self-esteem), and *pakikisma* (getting along with)" (Agbayani-Siewert 1994:430).

For Asian Indians, dharma is the law of being, the orderly fulfillment of an inherent nature of destiny. *Dharma*, loosely translated as "duty," is based on the righteousness or moral order of the world. It is been extensively discussed in the Bhagavad Gita, the holy book of the Hindus. According to Rangananthananda, "Dharma is social ethics; it is the integrating principle between man and man in society" (1971:361). He added, "Dharma in human life, is an eternal value. It cannot be molded and shaped to suit the human convenience" (p. 273). Buddhists conceive of dharma as a wheel, and human life, collective as well as individual, as a cart on wheels. The concept of dharma is accepted not only by Hindus but, because of its Buddhist influence, by Asians in general.

Each human being has an individual, personal dharma that is determined by (1) the *karmas*, both good and bad, from past lives and (2) the three dharmas of this life—universal, human, and social. For Asian Indians, karma is another key concept and refers to any voluntary action with a particular effect, either bad or good according to the action. The Bhagavad Gita explains how to attain selflessness in work and how to perform tasks selflessly, without attachment and desires and without incurring their fruits or bondage. Karma is also associated with rebirth, the path to ultimate liberation (Desai 1946).

The Meaning of Self

To understand Asian cultures, you must understand the meaning of self. For Asians, the self is defined in the context of family and relatives, not individual ideals, goals, and achievements. Rather, individual achievements bring praise and credit to the family as a whole and not to an individual member. Instead of autonomy and independence, Asian families emphasize subordination to and solidarity with the group. Interdependence is encouraged, and self-serving behavior is discouraged. Thus, in Asian cultures, group and family needs are more important than individual needs. Conversely, individualism, which is a Western concept, means that one must be responsible for one's own actions and behave independently. Collectivism, in contrast, means cooperation with the group and the group's social norms instead of individual preferences (Triandis 1994). For instance, in Filipino families, the individual's interests, desires, and relationships outside the family are less important than the family's needs. For Filipinos, *pakikisma* means going along with others even if doing so contradicts one's own desires and needs (Agabayani-Siewert 1994). Asians in the United States must constantly battle this conflict between living in an individualistic culture and maintaining collectivistic values. In such an environment, interpersonal conflicts that disrupt group harmony are avoided (Balgopal 1995, Mokuau 1991, Segal 1991).

FAMILY ROLES AND EXPECTATIONS

Asian cultures tend to be patriarchal and patrilineal, and so are the relationships among family members to a large extent. Males hold all the authority, and the father is the head of the household. Females listen to their father when they are growing up, to their husband when they are married, and to their sons when they are widowed. The relationships within the immediate family, extended family, and the larger community are defined by authority and hierarchy. Elders have more authority and are revered. Males, especially fathers, hold the power in the family, and their authority is unquestioned. The hierarchy within the family is determined by the husband's sibling order in the family; thus the wife of the eldest son has greater status than the wife of a younger son.

In South Asia, marriage is a union between two families, not between two individuals. In this system, the woman is the repository and guardian of her family's honor. She must observe strict codes of privacy and protect the family from public shame, including the shame of a broken marriage. It is therefore the women's duty to make marriage work, often with the result that Asian women must endure all kinds of atrocities and violence committed by their husbands and extended family members. The role of the mother is another important facet of a woman's identity. If she leaves even a dysfunctional family, she will be accused of causing shame and will be at least figuratively disowned by both her natal and affinial families as well as her ethnic group.

The details of the collective family structure and patriarchy differ in each Asian group. For the Chinese, the belief in filial piety, in which obligation to the family and interdependence are emphasized, is paramount (Kim 1995, Lum 1996). And as discussed earlier, for Asian Indian families, the roles and expected behavior of all members are guided by the two concepts of dharma and karma. The Japanese are guided by *oyakōkō* (filial piety) and *giri* (an obligation to be fulfilled) (Murase 1995). The Laotians, Vietnamese, and Cambodians also value filial piety and obligation (Duong Tran and Matsuoka 1995). Samoan and Guamanian elders have a higher status than the young, and men over women (Mokuau and Chang 1991, Untalan 1991).

For all Asians, the family is the basic unit. Extended families are common, and often two or more generations live together. Sons stay with their parents even after they marry. In immigrant families, the grandparents often act as baby-sitters. Asian families often host and help other families from their community even if they are not related by blood. It is common, therefore, for new immigrants to be taken care of (including financial support) by not only their immediate family but also their extended family or their community.

Children and Child Rearing

"Spare the stick and spoil the child" may seem outdated, but it still does subtly influence Asian American child-rearing practices. The Vietnamese have a common proverb that links love to punishment: "When we love our children, we give them a beating; when we hate our children, we give them sweet words" (Freeman 1989:28). In one of the Indian languages, Tamil, there is a proverb that says, "Only the hand that beats will also hug (*adikera kai thaan annaikum*)." These two proverbs illustrate the vast differences in child-rearing practices among the Asian Pacific group.

Ima and Hohm (1991) noted that the Cambodians and Laotians were surprised that the Americans would not trust an eight-year-old to take care of a two-year-old. The Cambodians and Laotians believed that it was all right to leave the children unattended in the apartment grounds and that it was not necessary to watch their children closely. Researchers have linked this casualness to the Buddhist belief that one's current life is the result of one's previous lives. According to the same study, the Vietnamese do supervise their children closely and administer few physical punishments, despite the proverb mentioned earlier. This tendency, in turn, is attributed to the more Confucian emphasis in the Vietnamese belief system that places responsibility on the parent to shape the child's character (Ima and Hohm, 1991). Morrow (1989) discussed how shame and loss of face in Southeast Asian child-rearing patterns are used to ridicule and induce guilt in order to produce acceptable behavior.

Asian Indian families view children as the culmination of their lifetime of work (Durvasula and Mylvaganam, 1994). For Hindus, one of the aims of marriage is progeny. Durvasula and Mylvaganam observed that in Asian Indian families, the goal of parenting is "not to provide the children with sufficient skills to leave the family but to instill a sense of obligation and duty through which they may achieve higher spirituality" (1994:99). Therefore, children are raised in their family according to collectivist norms, but they still have to strive for independence and individualism in mainstream America, which can create conflict between parents and children (Segal 1991).

Religion

Asians practice a variety of religions. Some Asians—for example, Filipinos, Koreans, Chinese, and Asian Indians—are Christians. Immigrants from Pakistan, Bangladesh, Indonesia, Malaysia, and a number from India are Muslims, but Confucianism, Taoism, Buddhism, and Hinduism are the principal Asian religions. Many of the cultural beliefs related to filial piety, obligation to the family, loyalty, and the emphasis on the family are rooted in Confucianism (Dunn 1975). However, although the Korean culture and lifestyle are greatly influenced by both Confucianism and Buddhism, more than 80 percent of Korean Americans claim to be Christians, usually Protestants. At the present time Korean Americans have established churches in many communities that help maintain Korean ethnicity (Kim and Kim 1992, Min 1995). The majority of Filipino Americans are Catholic, though they hold rather liberal Catholic beliefs, especially with regard to gender roles, which are becoming increasingly egalitarian (Agbayani-Siewert 1994). A few Filipinos are Protestants. Buddhism is the largest Asian religion. Most of the immigrants from Thailand, Cambodia, and Laos are Buddhist. Buddhists stress two virtues, *khanti,* "patience" or "endurance," and *caga,* "open-mindedness." These two virtues stress tolerance and the acceptance of diversity. This means not losing one's temper, refraining from finding fault in others, and "keeping a respectful silence." Buddhists should free themselves from desires, adopt an acceptable lifestyle, and practice meditation. Canda and Phaobtong (1992) discuss in detail the role of the Buddhist monks in helping Southeast Asian refugees in the U.S. Midwest. On the West Coast, especially in California and Hawaii, Buddhist temples are numerous, and in recent years, new temples have been built, primarily by Thai immigrants.

Hinduism is the predominant religion of Asian Indians, although some Asian Indians are Christians, Muslims, Sikhs, or Jains. Despite Hindus' various ritual practices, attitudes, and thinking, a single ideology prevails at a deeper level, with universality, nonaggressiveness, and humanism the three essential values underlying this spirituality (Ranganathananda 1971). Immigrants from Pakistan, Bangladesh, Indonesia, and Malaysia are Muslims.

Marriage

Because the Asian tradition of marriage is based on the philosophy of "marry first and then fall in love," arranged marriage versus love marriage is a source of conflict for many Asian Americans. Parents still hold considerable influence over the selection of mates for their children, but increasingly their sons and daughters are gaining more control over whom they marry (Balgopal 1995, Ho 1990, Nambiar 1993).

Probably one of the main fears of South Asian immigrants is the issue of "outmarriage"—that is, their children marrying a person outside their ethnic community. Among Asian Indians, Segal (1997) writes, this fear is twofold, first, because the parents fear that their children will lose their cultural heritage and, second, because of the belief that most American marriages end in divorce. For nearly all Asians, dating is a cause of conflict between parents and children, because in most Asian communities, dating is often equated with sexual activity, which is unacceptable before marriage. Thus, the recent immigrants do not tolerate dating, which is further complicated if their children go out with individuals of other ethnicities, especially non-Asians.

Intermarriage or outmarriage patterns for the various Asian groups differ significantly. "Intermarriage is much higher among native-born than foreign-born Asian Americans. In 1990, 40 percent of married U.S.-born Asians had a spouse of another race or Asian ethnic group, up from 35 percent in 1980. The percentage was notably lower among foreign-born Asians, 17 percent" (Lee 1998:22).

Help-Seeking Behaviors

Asians encourage harmony, so negative emotions are usually suppressed in favor of willpower and self-control. Because of this emphasis on endurance and tolerance, Asians also tend to believe that mental illness is caused by a character flaw (Fugita et al. 1991). Harmony between people is also extended to the natural and the social environment, in accordance with Confucian, Buddhist, and Hindu beliefs, and it is internalized as a part of Asians' culture (Chung 1992).

Cultural meanings of health and ill-health also play an important role in determining Asians' health-seeking behaviors, and Lin-Fu (1994) described at length what she refers to as ethnocultural barriers to health care. Asians' belief in folklore and traditional healers may be what leads them to seek alternative forms of health care. As mentioned earlier, not expressing negative emotions makes it difficult for Asians to discuss their emotions, so they instead express them physically. The stigma attached to mental illness stems from these beliefs.

Based on a study of forty-nine Asian community–based agencies delivering mental and physical health services in four cities on the West Coast, Murase (1992) reported that mental health services were successful when members of the family were made part of the therapy team and symptomatic relief could be obtained through short-term treatment. Furthermore, Asian clients preferred a medical model of treatment, so physical and mental health services need to be integrated.

EMERGING PROBLEMS

Child Abuse

The idea that child abuse does not exist in Asia may be a myth. To find out, a few researchers have addressed the cultural relativity of child abuse and have questioned whether child abuse laws should be applied to all immigrant groups in the United States (Ima and Hohm 1991)

Rao, DiClemente, and Ponton (1992) studied ethnic differences in child abuse and, in particular, compared Asian families with other populations. In their analysis of sixty-nine Asian families in San Francisco who had been accused of child sexual abuse they found that the victims were older than comparable non-Asian victims, had suffered a less physically invasive form of sexual abuse, were more likely to be living with both parents, were more likely to have been abused by a male relative, and, finally, were more likely to be immigrants. Furthermore, Asian families were less likely than non-Asian families to report the abuse or even to believe that it had occurred, and of all the populations studied, they were the least supportive of the victim. Research by Wong (1987) revealed similar findings, that Southeast Asian parents did not believe that child sexual abuse was a problem in their community. Although these findings are preliminary and cannot be generalized, this information could be used to design culturally sensitive prevention and counseling programs. Rao, DiClemente, and Ponton (1992) suggested that victims be advised that their family would not believe them. In addition, reporting child sexual abuse is closely related to the cultural issue discussed earlier of bringing shame to family—

many victims might not report the abuse because they would give their family a "bad name."

Child abuse and neglect is also an issue related to child rearing. For example, the Southeast Asian practice of rubbing hot coins on the skin leaves burn marks that might be interpreted as child abuse (Yeatman and Viet 1980). Whether parents who do this should be prosecuted has been a source of controversy (Feldman 1984, Nguyen 1985). In their 1991 exploratory study of Asian and Pacific Islander child abuse cases in San Diego, Ima and Hohm found that 53 percent of the reported cases were physical abuse, 4.9 percent sexual abuse, 6.0 percent emotional abuse, and 36.1 percent neglect. Compared with the general U.S. population, the Asians and Pacific Islanders had significantly fewer sexual abuse cases. Not included were Japanese, Asian Indians, Chinese, and other Asians. Moreover, since the study sample was drawn from an agency serving Asians and Pacific Islanders not fluent in English, the accuracy of these findings is questionable (Ima and Hohm 1991).

Domestic Violence

Marital and domestic violence has received unprecedented attention in the past decade and is now viewed as one of the more serious problems facing the Asian communities (U.S. Commission on Civil Rights, cited in Rhee 1997). As discussed earlier, Asian women are socialized by their culture to be subordinate, and their behavior is based on patriarchal norms. When they immigrate to this country, they face a conflict with the values of the mainstream culture which advocates equal rights for both sexes. Since the 1980s, many organizations that address the needs of Asian women have been established all over the country. An example is the South Asian Women's Organization (SAWO), which caters to South Asian women from India, Pakistan, Bangladesh, Sri Lanka, Bhutan, and Nepal. Many abused women are forced to remain in the abusive relationship because of poor language skills, inadequate training, visa problems (especially issues related to their green card), lack of support in the United States, and lack of financial security.

The incidence of domestic violence among South Asians is at least as high as that in the general U.S. population, which is 4 percent of women over eighteen years of age (Lawrence 1994). Apna Ghar, a shelter for battered Asian women, estimated that in 1994 one out of two, or around 100,000 Asian women, in the Chicago area alone could be a victim of domestic abuse (Balgopal and Biswas 1996). Chun (1990) reported that according to the Los Angeles District Attorney's Office, among Asians, Koreans had the highest number of cases of domestic violence.

Domestic violence committed against South Asian women is closely associated with the custom of arranged marriages. When parents arrange the match in India, for example, they have difficulty doing a background check on the prospective bridegroom, which usually includes his character, lifestyle, and the like. Coupled with this, the dowry system causes additional tension in the marriage. The stories of these women have been so horrifying that the U.S. Immigration Service has often granted asylum to women who have been prosecuted in their home country (Wu 1994). Example are Chinese women who may be forced to be sterilized because of their country's one-child policy or Pakistani women who have been raped and are pregnant and will be prosecuted under Pakistan's Hudud ordinances for illegal sexual relations unless her assailant confesses or four Pakistani men testify as witnesses of the sexual act (Wu 1994).

The Elderly

Since ancient times, the family has dominated Asian cultural values and beliefs. But Asian families have changed in recent years as the problem of what to do with aging family members has risen to the fore. Most elderly Asians have few or no means of support and must rely on their family (Gulati 1995). According to Ramanathan and Ramanathan (1994), in India, this stage of the life cycle is seen as a period of rightful dependency, with the person's security assured by the extended family, especially the sons. The children's caregiving is a product of cultural expectations, duty, love, and an extraordinary sense of caring and positive regard for their elderly family members. These values are similar to traditional Chinese culture, in which parents live with their children, and society promotes support and respect for the elderly (Cheung 1989).

Japanese family values related to the elderly are obedience to rules, roles, and controls; obligations to the family; a sense of fatalism; strong dependency needs; family reciprocity and filial piety; indirect methods of communication; and modesty (Kitano 1990). In their 1997 analysis of Japanese Americans' help-seeking behavior, Yamashiro and Matsuoka found that it was greatly influenced by Buddhism, which teaches that all life is subject to suffering. Adherence to this doctrine is reflected in a number of Japanese beliefs such as *gaman* (endurance), and *shikata ga nai* (whatever has happened cannot be helped).

In Asian American immigrant families, the burden of elder care is complicated by cultural, social, and economic barriers. Informal caregiving has traditionally fallen on wives, daughters, and sisters who, in the past, were not employed outside the home. In recent years, however, these caregivers have entered the workforce and are now faced with balancing or choosing between a career and their aging parents. Another barrier faced by the immigrant population is access to formal care services, which is restricted by their immigrant status (Liu 1986). With the passage of the Personal Responsibility and Work Opportunity Reconciliation Act of 1996, many legal elderly immigrants, especially permanent residents, lost their eligibility for Supplemental Security Income and food stamps until they became citizens. Because many elderly Asian Americans were directly affected by this law, they are scrambling to change their status from permanent resident to citizen. Their biggest hurdles are the ability to pass an English fluency test and the expensive lawyer fees for changing their immigrant status.

For most older immigrants, the hardest time was when they first moved to the United States. These people immigrated in 1965 or later and have grown old in the United States. Another immigrant group is the elderly who came here because their children immigrated here. They arrived in the United States much later in life, hoping to be taken care of by their children. This group is more likely not to speak English and has more difficulty assimilating.

The elderly face several problems—conflict with the younger generation who may not accord them the traditional respect and want them to live in nursing homes, financial insecurity, and difficulty obtaining services. Cheung (1989) described several of these problems among the Chinese elderly and recommended culturally appropriate services—peer groups in Chinatowns, adequate health care, services delivered in an accessible area, attention to housing and financial needs, cultural events, and social services to help them adjust to their environment. Korean elderly seem determined to maintain their independence and are reluctant to ask for help from sources outside their family (Kim and Kim 1992). Although the Filipino and Hawaiian cultures emphasize respect for their elderly, this does not mean authority. Thus grandparents are indulged and respected but are not perceived as authority figures and do not have the final say in family matters (Agbayani-Siewert 1994).

A life expectancy study conducted in 1980 in Hawaii revealed that the life expectancy of Japanese (eighty years), Chinese (eighty-one years), and Filipinos (seventy-eight years) was higher than that of whites (seventy-two years) (U.S. General Accounting Office, cited in Gall and Gall 1993). In addition, elderly Chinese American and Japanese American women have the highest suicide rate of all racial and ethnic groups, including European Americans (Chin 1991). In a study of suicide among Asian Americans, the older population, particularly women, showed a marked contrast to the white population. In 1985, the number of suicide deaths per 100,000 population aged eighty and older was much higher for Asian Americans (Office of Minority Health Resource Center, cited in Gall and Gall 1993).

Boult and Boult (1995) studied the service utilization patterns of older Asian-Americans in the U.S. county with the second largest Hmong community. They found that the Hmong rarely went to see a physician, owing to several obstacles, namely, difficulty with the English language and with making appointments; unfamiliarity with Western medicine, payment methods, and the concept of preventive care; their reliance on traditional healing practices; and the stigma of mental illness. Lee, Balgopal, and Patchner (1988) found that Asian American elderly were reluctant to seek services from non-Asian agencies, as they felt these agencies were unable to address their specific needs and did not understand their culture.

Physical and Mental Health

Asians and Pacific Islanders have been stereotyped as a model minority in regard to physical and mental health. In an attempt to debunk this myth, Chen and Hawks (1995) examined federal government publications related to the health status of Asians and Pacific Islanders and found that the stereotype was undeserved because (1) the population growth rate has been unusually rapid and recent; (2) data regarding the health status are inadequate because the current databases have only small Asian and Pacific Islander samples; (3) Asian and Pacific Islander populations are heterogeneous with respect to demographic factors and risk factors, and (4) their risk-factor and mortality data suggest that the number of certain preventable diseases, namely, tuberculosis, hepatitis B, liver cancer, and lung cancer, may be higher than those of other racial and ethnic populations. Petzold (1990) looked at sudden unexplained death syndrome (SUDS) among the Southeast Asian refugees and argued that it was caused by extreme stress.

Similar trends are evident in mental health research. Sue and Morishima (1982) contended that based on statistical data, Asian Americans have a low divorce rate, high socioeconomic status, high educational attainment, and a low crime rate. The popular belief thus is that they are socially well adjusted, although there are no well-documented epidemiological studies of the prevalence of mental health disorders in this group. Treatment outcomes have also not been systematically documented. What has been documented consistently is that Asian Americans tend to underutilize mainstream mental health services (Sue 1993, Sue et al. 1994).

A 1987 study of 2,800 Southeast Asians conducted by the California State Department of Mental Health showed that 95 percent needed psychological help, compared with 33 percent of the general population, and federal studies revealed as much as a 300 percent increase in the suicide rate among Asian American children. Despite the increasing use and abuse of alcohol and other drugs by Asian Americans, there are few reliable data on the exact prevalence and incidence of this problem (Zane and Sasao 1992). The increase in alcohol and drug use is reflected, however, in the higher rates of domestic violence and child abuse and in the emergence of gangs. In one of the few documented studies, in 1987 the U.S. Department of Health and Human Services reported that the Asian American population accounted for only 0.6 percent of alcohol and substance abuse treatment services (cited in Gall and Gall 1993).

ADAPTATION AND COPING

Prejudice and Civil Rights

During the early years of immigration, Asian Americans were considered to be an inferior race and thus faced numerous discriminatory practices in the United States (Balgopal 1995, Kitano 1987, Murase 1977). For example, antimiscegenation laws prohibited interracial marriages, and antialien land laws prevented them from owning property. Later in the century, as the immigration laws changed and many successful Asian Americans were allowed to immigrate, they began to be seen as hardworking, patient, and courteous people (Kitano 1969, Kitano and Sue 1973).

This refurbished image led to the myth of Asian Americans as the model minority, with their low rates of drug abuse, juvenile delinquency, divorce, and mental illness. On the positive side, this image has helped these groups be accepted, especially by the employers and educational institutions, as conscientious people who do not make waves. But on the negative side, Asian Americans are seen as needing no special assistance or help from public programs. According to Crystal, "the 'Model Minority' myth has obscured many serious problems in the Asian community and has been used to justify omitting Asian Americans from federal funding and some minority programs" (1989:405). Although some Asian Americans have done considerably better than the general population in education and employment, it is not correct to assume that such is the case with the entire group. As Min pointed out, "Asian ethnic groups individually and as a whole fare well in terms of median family income when compared to white

Americans. However, Asian and Pacific Islander Americans as a whole and three Asian groups—Vietnamese, Koreans, and Chinese—in particular show higher proportions of families at the poverty level than white Americans" (1995:27). According to the 1993/1994 data of the U.S. Bureau of the Census, the median family income of white Americans was $37,152, and 7 percent of the families in this group lived at the poverty level. The median family income of Koreans was $33,909, with 14.7 percent living below the poverty level. However, the Vietnamese median family income was $30,550, with 23.8 percent living below the poverty level (Min 1995:28).

After the 1965 Immigration Act abolished the quota system and established the preference system, many of the new Asian immigrants arriving in the 1970s were well educated and professionals, and in addition, the families of the new arrivals provided support and took care of one another. This is what gave rise to the myth of Asian Americans as the model minority. By the 1980s, when the model minority thesis and its negative impact were being felt, structural barriers were recognized not only by Asian American scholars but also by activists, including social workers. Min (1995) refers to this as the "revisionist critique of the model minority thesis." Revisionists argue that Asian Americans do not receive economic rewards commensurate with their education and professional training. Indeed, it has been shown that workers in this group receive fewer economic rewards for their education and training than do their white counterparts. This means that Asian Americans need more education and training just to maintain economic parity with white Americans (Min 1995). "The primary labor market is characterized by high wages, fringe benefits, job security, unionization and opportunity for promotion, the secondary labor market has the opposite characteristics" (Min 1995:40). Regardless of their education and professional training, new immigrants of color such as Asian Americans are trapped in the secondary labor market.

Revisionists also contend that Asian Americans' high median family income compared with that of whites is not a valid indicator of their socioeconomic status, for three reasons. First, Asian Americans have more wage-earning workers per family; second, their family incomes do not accurately reflect their standard of living because a large number of them live in San Francisco, Los Angeles, and Honolulu where living expenses are much higher; and finally, family income is misleading because Asian Americans are socioeconomically polarized (Min 1995).

The model minority image is also misused by the public and private agencies and institutions. By playing up the success of the Asian Americans, these agencies have made life worse for other ethnic minority groups, such as African Americans and Hispanics, by implying that they do not work and try as hard as Asians do (Crystal, 1989). Such comparisons in turn widen the interethnic conflicts.

In his essay on Asian American activism from the 1960s to the 1990s, Omatsu (1994) analyzed Asian Americans' struggles, which helped spawn numerous grassroots and student organizations and Asian American studies classes. According to Omatsu, the Asian American movement did not coincide with the civil rights movement but, rather, with the demand for black liberation. The goal of the Asian American activists was not to assert racial pride but to reclaim the struggles of earlier generations, with an emphasis on the issues of oppression and power. Omatsu also suggested that along with other movements, the Asian American movement disintegrated mainly because of the rise of the New Right and the devastating corporate offensives. The 1980s was a period of ambiguity for Asian Americans. On the one hand, increasing numbers of Asian Americans—especially refugees from Southeast Asia—became impoverished; more and more racist hate crimes were directed toward Asian Americans of all ethnicities and income levels; and the class polarization in the communities sharpened, with a widening gap between the very rich and the very poor (p. 38). David and Lin (1997) examined the history of institutionalized discrimination against Asian Americans and the more recent issues affecting this group in public and higher education, the workplace, and voting rights. In public education, bilingual education and limited-English proficiency, as well as interethnic tensions, are issues that need attention. In the 1980s, the top universities began restricting the number of Asian American students they admitted. The U.S. Commission on Civil Rights (1992) finally intervened and made some policy changes. Similarly, at the workplace, there is a glass ceiling for Asian Americans promoted to upper management positions.

Acculturation, Assimilation, and Ethnic Identity

All Asian Americans must assimilate both their own and American cultural values. *Acculturation* and *assimilation* describe the process by which they blend their home country's cultural values with American values. *Ethnic identity* refers to the preservation of the home country's cultural values within the dominant culture. To illustrate, Kitano and Maki (1996) created the following heuristic model of acculturation and ethnic identity:

In this model, the authors identified four types of immigrants: Type A, who

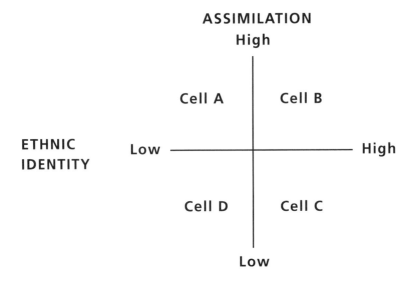

(Kitano and Maki (1996), p. 141).

are high in assimilation and low in ethnic identity (individuals who have been Americanized); Type B, who are high in assimilation and high in ethnic identity (individuals who subscribe to two cultures); Type C, who are high in ethnic identity and low in assimilation (newly arrived or older individuals who have had little contact with the mainstream society); and Type D, who are low in ethnic identity and low in assimilation (individuals who are alienated from both cultures, who have difficulty integrating either of the two cultures). This model is useful in determining Asian Americans' stage of assimilation and retention of their ethnic identity.

Some scholars have argued that acculturation is at the heart of many of the struggles in the Asian American community (Chambon 1989, Nicassio 1985, Silka and Tip 1994). Teenagers typically belong to Type A; the culture of their home country is primarily applicable to their parents and not to them. They are more immersed in the dominant culture and have been Americanized, which of course creates conflicts with their parents. Persons who have recently arrived in the United States in accordance with family reunification immigration laws (e.g., the elderly) are Type C individuals, and they may have limited contact with the dominant culture. Adolescents who belong to gangs and abuse alcohol and drugs also feel rejected and alienated from their own culture as well as the dominant culture; they belong to Type D.

Maintaining Connections

Maintaining close connections with their country of origin is extremely important to Asian Americans. Staying in contact helps them not only maintain their
cultural heritage but also adapt to their new environment. There are several
routes by which these intimate ties are maintained, including visits to their
home country, phone calls, e-mail, letters, newspapers, magazines, social and
cultural events involving artists from their home country, movies, and visits
from close relatives. Another important way in which Asian Americans remain
connected is through their religious institutions and, often, festivals celebrated
at these religious sites.

STRENGTHS

Family and Community Support

The support of the family is a crucial source of strength for Asian American
families, who turn to their family first for help with any problem (Lum 1996).
Indeed, Asian Americans seek help from outside agencies only when family
support is not adequate or available (Fong 1994, Ho 1992, Shon and Ja 1982).

Religious Ties

Religion is closely interwoven with the transmission of culture and values, and
when trying to adjust to living in the United States, Asian Americans use it as a
force to keep their group together. Segal (1997) identified three ways in which
religion is used to transmit culture: through the family and at home, where
there is strict adherence to cultural practices; by joining religious organizations
that meet regularly, for example, the Korean church or the Hindu temple; and
through formal education.

THE ROLE OF SOCIAL WORKERS

In a process model of multicultural social work practice relevant to working
with Asian American clients, Dungee-Anderson and Beckett proposed eight
steps based on simple communication principles that could help in culturally
sensitive communications: "(1) acknowledge cultural differences, (2) know self,

(3) know other cultures, (4) identify and value differences, (5) identify and avoid stereotypes, (6) empathize with persons from other cultures, (7) adapt rather than adopt, and (8) acquire recovery skills" (1995:463).

Asian Americans nurture interdependence and solve most of their problems though the immediate family, the extended family, and then community leaders, in that order of preference. Filipino families use relatives, or "go-betweens," as mediators to resolve family conflicts (Agbayani-Siewert 1994). They rarely go to an outsider for help, so when social workers have Filipino clients, they should be aware of the difficulty in asking for professional help. Furthermore, since Asians are likely to seek professional help only as a last resort, the problem may well be serious, such as a full-blown psychosis. Often they are hesitant and not forthcoming early in the sessions, since seeking help from a professional might be perceived as dishonorable or shameful and open to social stigmatization and ostracization (Nakanishi and Rittner 1996). Murase, Egawa, and Tashima (1985) observed that building rapport is dependent on how social workers can project themselves as helping persons. In addition, social work interventions and programs need to ensure anonymity and accessibility (Rhee 1997).

The Initial Phase

Establishing rapport is closely associated with establishing trust. Asian clients need to develop trust in the social worker needs special attention. Often, they may not be fluent in English, so an interpreter may be useful. Or transportation may be difficult. Nakanishi and Rittner (1996) suggested that the initial focus on obtaining concrete services like interpreters, transportation, financial assistance, housing assistance, connections with other agencies, and applications for job training are ways of building trust that would help clients share their emotional and personal issues.

Asian Americans rarely seek help alone, but usually are accompanied by family members. For social workers, this poses a problem—should they include everybody in the session, and what about violations of confidentiality? Lee (1982) believes that it is important to involve both the entire family and significant members of the community, based on Asian Americans' familiarity with holistic approaches using interactions and contextual perspectives in the assessment and treatment (Nakanishi and Rittner 1996). Social workers also should be careful to maintain the hierarchy of family members or people from the community when addressing and talking to them.

Similar to focusing on concrete issues, to encourage these clients to continue in treatment, it is important to set a goal in the first meeting (Ho 1990). Kim

Berg and Miller (1992) and Ho (1990) pointed out that since Asian Americans tend to terminate therapy early, it is necessary to use problem-solving approaches to issues. Because Asian Americans tend to be task oriented, a brief approach based on problem solving is effective (Ramakrishnan and Balgopal 1992). Also, if instructions seem to work well, they may be appropriate (Allen and Nimmagadda 1999).

Another important issue is the relationship between the social worker and the client. It may be difficult for Asian clients to accept an equal status in the relationship (Marsella 1993), as they regard the social worker as the one with authority and power and thereby to be addressed as somebody with a higher status than themselves. The social worker also must be comfortable with the issue of self-disclosure. Since Asian Americans are hesitant to discuss their personal problems with strangers, they will ask the social worker personal questions about himself or herself, and it is important that the social worker not become defensive (Tsui and Schlutz 1985). Although these clients view the social worker as an authority figure, they also want to please him or her. Thus it is not uncommon for clients to bring gifts and food and invite the worker to their home.

It is crucial for the practitioner to establish credibility with the clients and/or their family right from the beginning. Sue and Zane (1987) offered three ways that might help foster credibility—conceptualizing the problem in a manner consistent with the client's belief system; suggesting solutions that are culturally consistent; and setting goals that agree with the client's expectations.

The Assessment and Exploration Phase

Because of their cultural emphasis on self-control and remaining calm, Asian Americans have difficulty expressing their feelings. Instead, they manifest their emotional distress through bodily symptoms, such as headaches or backaches. Therefore, during the assessment, if the social worker asks various questions related to the distress that focus on past symptoms, history of mental problems, and psychosocial stressors, the Asian client will tend to become confused and would lead the discussion back to his or her physical symptoms (Nakanishi and Rittner 1996). This is the reason that family physicians also should evaluate these clients.

According to Kim Berg and Miller (1992), the following techniques are culturally effective: (1) identifying the exceptions to the presenting problem, thereby helping the client "save face" and also taking a "strengths" perspective in therapy; (2) asking questions about the client's relationships, thus elucidating the client's interactions and resources; (3) asking the client to state a miracle that would solve the problem and would help set goals and also would remove self-blame, since it is based on the future; (4) asking the client to tell stories about previous coping strategies, which might help in empowerment, highlight strengths, and offer reassurance. Asian clients often expect advice and want to be told what to do, which directly contradicts the social work principle of self-determination. Unfortunately, when clients ask for advice, they may be perceived as resistant and defensive. The Asian cultural emphasis on fate and destiny is often regarded by Westerners as another form of resistance to change. But a belief in fate and destiny helps Asians accept adversity and motivates them to get back on track.

Kim Berg and Jaya (1993) recommend mediation or negotiation as a culturally appropriate strategy to use with Asian Americans. To be credible, the practitioner should focus on efforts that are culturally sensitive; for example, asking a son to assert his rights with his father or an elderly uncle may not be appropriate, and negotiation may be better. Providing immediate benefits also is useful (Sue and Zane 1987). Sue and Zane found that explanations of future benefits to the clients may not be adequate motivation, so they use the phrase *gift giving* (p. 42) to symbolize helping the client experience immediate benefits from sessions and related activities. Asian clients, they argue, need a demonstration of the immediate benefits of an activity and a reduction of the distress. The following are possible gifts: normalization (supportive therapy), stress relief procedures, reassurance, hope, and the establishment of concrete assistance.

Working with the Family

Working with any Asian American client will probably involve the family as well, since the support systems are always called in when there is a problem. Indeed, Asian American clients might not be agree to be treated unless the family is involved (Nakanishi and Rittner 1996, Tsui and Schultz 1985). Furthermore, Kim Berg and Jaya found that Asian families respond better to mediation and negotiation than to confrontation. For example, banishing a child from the family is considered the ultimate punishment. Thus, after a son marries, his wife moves in, and they live with his parents. Every family also has a hierarchy that must be maintained, even in therapy. For example, it may not be appropriate to ask the daughter-in-law for information about her father-in-law (Kim Berg and Jaya 1993, Nimmagadda and Cowger 1999). It is important also to accord proper respect to elders and those high in the hierarchy. In fact, several Asian languages contain words of respect that are used to address elders. It is helpful if the therapist can maintain this respect, order, and hierarchy (Kim Berg and Jaya 1993).

Fong (1994) discussed keeping the family together in child welfare practice with Asian families. She also talked about the concept of empowerment and shared partnership in the context of Asian American culture and how this might conflict with immigrants' values: "Empowering Asian immigrant and refugee families involves (1) developing coping abilities in families, groups, and communities; (2) increasing their connectedness or bonding with other social systems; and (3) strengthening their ability to create relationships" (p. 336).

Termination

Termination is a sensitive time in any practitioner-client relationship. The relationship may be ended because the client decided not to show up or because the client has improved. Asian American clients, however, often terminate the therapy prematurely, deciding that he or she does not want to be a burden (Ho 1988). Practitioners should be aware of this possible outcome and be prepared to help their clients understand the need for therapy.

Because a relationship has been established with the practitioner, the client and the family perceive the practitioner as a family member (Ho 1988). Therefore, they will want to stay in touch with the practitioner and so may invite him or her to participate in family celebrations or even express their appreciation by giving gifts. Applying Western notions of "separation anxiety" to this dependency may not be helpful, as Asian Americans believe that a good relationship is one that is treasured for life (Ho 1988). Instead, the practitioner should try to understand these cultural dynamics and help the family make this transition as smooth as possible.

Dhooper (1997) summarized the following points for effective intervention at the micro level: (1) Social workers should help clients maintain their ethnic and cultural pride; (2) help them understand and believe in the American political and legal systems; (3) help them maintain hope despite their discouraging experiences; and, finally, (4) help them reduce their sense of powerlessness by teaching them language and interpersonal communication skills, as well as skills marketable in the workplace.

At the macro level of practice, it is important to recognize that Asian Americans are reluctant to seek help, especially from non-Asian agencies. Lee, Balgopal, and Patchner (1988) listed five factors necessary for the effective development, delivery, and utilization of services by Asian Americans: (1) having Asian Americans as professional staff, (2) having bilingual staff available, (3) providing outreach activities that use Asian languages, (4) offering specific programs for the unique cultural needs of Asian American clients, and (5) locating services near Asian American communities.

Chow's 1999 study reported that for the effective delivery of social services, the agencies must be multiservice or comprehensive, "one-stop service shopping." Immigrant Asian American communities are receptive to services that are designed to meet the normative needs of the general population, like language and job skills.

Asian Americans and Pacific Islanders—initially subject to much discrimination and then, in last two decades, having to cope with the myth that they are the model minority—have struggled to survive in an alien culture. This group's main concerns are a rise in alcoholism and drug use and abuse, domestic violence, problems of the elderly, low service utilization, and thus issues related to physical and mental health and child abuse and neglect. This group struggles against discrimination and attempts to assimilate into the majority culture while maintaining their own cultural customs and practices and connections with their homeland. Indeed, their cultural heritage seems to be a buffer against adversity from the "outside" world, and their strong family and community support and religious commitment help them cope and adapt. To be effective, therefore, social work must adjust its interventions to the vast diversity of this group and to their many cultural differences.

NOTE

1. Asian Indian refers to immigrants from the Indian subcontinent who identify themselves as Indian. This group is also referred to as South Asians, East Indians, or Indo-Americans. Immigrants of Indian ethnicity from the Caribbean nations also are included in this category.

REFERENCES

Agbayani-Siewert, P. (1994). Filipino American culture and family: Guidelines for practitioners. *Families in Society* 74 (September): 429–438.

Allen, R., and Nimmagadda, J. (1999). Asian Indian women and feminism: A double-edged sword? *Asian Pacific Journal of Social Work* 9 (1): 26–41.

Balgopal, P. R. (1995). Asian Americans overview. In R. L. Edwards (ed.), *Encyclopedia of Social Work.* 19th ed., vol. 1. Washington, DC: National Association of Social Workers Press.

Balgopal, P. R., and Biswas. K. (1996). Domestic violence in Asian Indian families in the U.S. Unpublished manuscript, University of Illinois.

Barringer, H. R., Gardner, R. W., and Levin, M. J. (1993). *Asians and Pacific Islanders in the United States: The Population of the United States in the 1980s.* New York: Russell Sage.

Boult, L., and Boult, C. (1995). Underuse of physician services by older Asian-Americans. *Journal of the American Geriatrics Society* 43 (4): 408–411.

Canda, E. R., and Phaobtong, T. (1992). Buddhism as a support system for Southeast Asian refugees. *Social Work* 37: 61–67.

Chambon, A. (1989). Refugee families' experiences: Three family themes—Family disruption, violent trauma, and acculturation. *Journal of Strategic and Systematic Therapies* 8: 3–13.

Chan, S. (1991). *Asian Americans: An Interpretive History.* Boston: Twayne.

Chen, M. S., and Hawks, B. L. (1995). A debunking of the myth of healthy Asian Americans and Pacific Islanders. *American Journal of Health Promotion* 9 (4): 261–268.

Cheung, M. (1989). Elderly Chinese living in the United States: Assimilation or adjustment? *Social Work* 34: 457–461.

Chi, L. K., and Schneiderman, L. (1992). Policy implications for factors associated with economic self-sufficiency of Southeast Asian refugees. In S. M. Furoto, R. Biswas, D. K. Chung, K. Murase, and F. Ross-Sheriff (eds.), *Social Work Practice with Asian Americans.* Newbury Park, CA: Sage.

Chin, S. (1991). Asian health: A special prescription. *San Francisco Chronicle*, July 7.A, 1:1.

Chow, J. (1999). Multiservice centers in Chinese American immigrant communities: Practice principles and challenges. *Social Work* 44 (1): 70–81.

Chun, E. (1990). The Korean battered spouse: Where to go for help. *Korean American Journal* 1 (3): 22–23.

Chung, D. K. (1992). Asian cultural commonalties: A comparison with mainstream American culture. In S. M. Furoto, R. Biswas, D. K. Chung, K. Murase, and F. Ross-Sheriff (eds.), *Social Work Practice with Asian Americans.* Newbury Park, CA: Sage.

Crystal, D. (1989). Asian Americans and the myth of the model minority. *Social Casework* 70 (7): 405–413.

David, G., and Lin, J. (1997). Civil rights and Asian Americans. *Journal of Sociology and Social Welfare* 24 (1): 3–24.

Desai, M. (1946). *The Gospel of Selfless Action on the Gita According to Gandhi.* Ahmedabad: Navajivan.

Dhooper, S. S. (1997). Poverty among Asian Americans: Theories and approaches. *Journal of Sociology and Social Welfare* 24 (1): 25–40.

Dungee-Anderson D., and Beckett, J. O. (1995). A process model for multicultural social work practice. *Families in Society: The Journal of Contemporary Human Services* 76: 459–468.

Dunn, L. P. (1975). *Asian Americans: A Study Guide and Source Book*. Laguna Beach, CA: Reed.

Duong Tran, Q., and Matsuoka, K. (1995). Asian Americans: Southeast Asians. In R. L. Edwards (ed.), *Encyclopedia of Social Work*. 19th ed., vol. 1. Washington, DC: National Association of Social Workers Press.

Durvasula, R. S., and Mylvaganam, G. A. (1994). Mental health of Asian Indians: Relevant issues and community implications. *Journal of Community Psychology* 22: 97–107.

Feldman, K. (1984). Pseudoabusive burns in Asian refugees. *American Journal of Diseases of Children* 138: 768–769.

Fong, R. (1994). Family preservation: Making it work for the Asians. *Child Welfare* 73: 331–341.

Freeman, J. M. (1989). *Hearts of Sorrow: Vietnamese-American Lives*. Stanford, CA: Stanford University Press.

Fugita, S., Ito, K. L., Abe, J., and Takeuchi, D. T. (1991). Japanese Americans. In N. Mokuau (ed.), *Handbook of Social Services for Asian and Pacific Islanders*. New York: Greenwood Press.

Gall. S. B., and Gall, T. L. (eds.). (1993). *Statistical Record of Asian Americans*. Detroit: Gale Research.

Gould, K. (1988). Asian and Pacific Islanders: Myth and reality. *Social Work* 33: 142–146.

Gulati, L. (1995). Women and family in India: Continuity and change. *Indian Journal of Social Work* 56 (2): 133–154.

Ho, M. K. (1988). *Family Therapy with Ethnic Minorities*. Newbury Park, CA: Sage.

Ho, M. K. (1990). *Intermarried Couples in Therapy*. Springfield, IL: Thomas.

Ho, M. K. (1992). *Minority Children and Adolescents in Therapy*. Beverly Hills, CA. Sage.

Howe, P. J. (1991). State portrait: Census data show gains in people of color. *Boston Globe* (March 6): 1, 18.

Ima, K., and Hohm, C. F. (1991). Child maltreatment among Asian and Pacific Islander refugees and immigrants: The San Diego case. *Journal of Interpersonal Violence* 6: 267–285.

Kim, P. K., and Kim, J. (1992). Korean elderly: Policy, program, and practice implications. In S. M. Furoto, R. Biswas, D. K. Chung, K. Murase, and F. Ross-Sheriff (eds.), *Social Work Practice with Asian Americans*. Newbury Park, CA: Sage.

Kim, Y. (1995). Cultural pluralism and Asian Americans: Culturally sensitive social work practice. *International Social Work* 38: 69–78.

Kim Berg, I., and Jaya, A. (1993). Different and same: Family therapy with Asian American families. *Journal of Marital and Family Therapy* 19 (1): 31–38.

Kim Berg, I., and Miller, S. (1992). Working with Asian American clients: One person at a time. *Families in Society: The Journal of Contemporary Human Services* 73: 31–38.

Kitano, H. H. L. (1969). *Japanese Americans: The Evolution of a Subculture*. New York: Prentice-Hall.

Kitano, H. H. L. (1987). Asian Americans. In A. Minahan (ed.), *Encyclopedia of Social Work*. 18th ed., vol. 1. Silver Spring, MD: National Association of Social Workers Press.

Kitano, H. H. L. (1990) Values, Beliefs and practice of the Asian American elderly: Implications for geriatric education. *Minority Aging*. Washington, DC: U.S. Department of Health and Human Services.

Kitano, H. H. L., and Maki, M. T. (1996). Continuity, change, and diversity: Counseling Asian Americans. In P. B. Pedersen, J. G. Draguns, W. J. Lonner, and J. E. Trimble (eds.), *Counseling Across Cultures*. Thousand Oaks, CA: Sage.

Kitano, H. H. L., and Sue, S. (1973). The model minority. *Journal of Social Issues* 29 (2): 1–9.

Lawrence, L. A. (1994). Brave and battered: Abuse turns South Asian women's lives upside down in the U.S. *Far Eastern Economic Review* 157: 48–49.

LEAP. (1998). A leadership education for Asian Pacifics Inc. Los Angeles.

Lee, E. (1982). A social systems approach to assessment and treatment for Chinese-American families. In M. McGolrick, J. Pearce, and J. Giordano (eds.), *Ethnicity and Family Therapy*. New York: Guilford Press.

Lee, J. J., Balgopal, P. R., and Patchner, M. A. (1988). Citizen participation: An effective dimension for serving the Asian American elderly. In D. S. Sanders and J. Fischer (eds.), *Visions for the Future*. Honolulu: University of Hawaii, School of Social Work.

Lee, S. H. (1998). Asian Americans: Diverse and growing. *Population Bulletin* 53: 2.

Lin-Fu, J. S. (1994). Ethnocultural barriers to healthcare: A major problem for Asian and Pacific Islander Americans. *Asian American and Pacific Islander Journal of Health* 2 (4): 290–298.

Liu, W. (1986). Health services for Asian elderly. *Research on Aging* 8 (1): 165–175.

Lum, D. (1996). *Social Work Practice and People of Color: A Process-Stage Approach*. Pacific Grove, CA: Brooks/Cole.

Marsella, A. (1993). Counseling and psychotherapy with Japanese Americans: Cross-cultural considerations. *American Journal of Orthopsychiatry* 63: 200–208.

McInnis-Dittrich, K. (1992). The economic well-being of Asian/Pacific Islander female-headed households: Implications for social welfare policy. In S. M. Furoto, R. Biswas, D. K. Chung, K. Murase, and F. Ross-Sheriff (eds.), *Social Work Practice with Asian Americans*. Newbury Park, CA: Sage.

Min, P. G. (1995) (ed.) *Asian Americans*. Thousand Oaks, CA: Sage.

Mohan, B. (1997). Notes toward a theory of secondary integration: Aporias of a lost paradigm. *Journal of Sociology and Social Welfare* 24 (1): 113–117.

Mokuau, N. (ed.) (1991). *Handbook of Social Services for Asian and Pacific Islanders*. Westport, CT: Greenwood Press.

Mokuau, N., and Chang. N. (1991). Samoans. In N. Mokuau (ed.), *Handbook of Social Services for Asian and Pacific Islanders*. Westport, CT: Greenwood Press.

Morrow, R. D. (1989). Southeast Asian child rearing practices: Implications for child and youth care workers. *Child and Youth Care Quarterly* 18 (4): 273–287.

Mui, A. C. (1996). Depression among Chinese immigrants: An exploratory study. *Social Work* 41: 633–645.

Murase, K. (1977). Minorities: Asian Americans. In J. Turner (ed.), *Encyclopedia of Social Work*. 17th ed. Washington, DC: National Association of Social Workers Press.

Murase, K. (1992). Model of service delivery in Asian American communities. In S. M. Furoto, R. Biswas, D. K. Chung, K. Murase, and F. Ross-Sheriff (eds.), *Social Work Practice with Asian Americans*. Newbury Park, CA: Sage.

Murase, K. (1995). Asian Americans: Japanese. In R. L. Edwards (ed.), *Encyclopedia of Social Work*. 19th ed., vol. 1. Washington, DC: National Association of Social Workers Press.

Murase, K., Egawa, J., and Tashima, N. (1985). Alternative mental health services models in Asian/Pacific Communities. In T. C. Owan (ed.), *Southeast Asian Mental Health*. Washington, DC: U.S. Department of Health and Human Sevices.

Nakanishi, M., and Rittner, B. (1996). Social work practice with Asian Americans. In D. F. Harrison, B. A. Thyer, and J. S. Wodarski (eds.), *Cultural Diversity and Social Work Practice*. Springfield, IL: Thomas.

Nambiar (1993). Love with a proper stranger. *Washington Post* (November 7): C1, C4.

Nguyen, D. (1985). Culture shock: A view of Vietnamese culture and its concepts of health and disease. *Western Journal of Medicine* 142: 409–412.

Nicassio, P. M. (1985). The psychological adjustment of the Southeast Asian refugee: An overview of empirical findings and theoretical models. *Journal of Cross-Cultural Psychology* 16 (1): 53–173.

Nimmagadda, J., and Cowger, C. (1999). Cross-cultural practice: Social worker ingenuity in the indigenization of practice knowledge. *International Social Work* 42(3): 261–276.

Omatsu, G. (1994). The "four prisons" and the movement of liberation: Asian American activism from 1960s to 1990s. In K. Aguilar-San Juan (ed.), *The State of Asian America*. Boston: South End Press.

Ong, P., and Hee, S. J. (1993). The growth of the Asian Pacific American population. In LEAP Asian Pacific Public Policy Institute and UCLA Asian American Studies Center (eds.), *The State of Asian Pacific America*. Los Angeles: LEAP Asian Pacific American Public Policy Institute and UCLA Asian American Studies Center.

Petzold, J. E. (1990). Southeast Asian refugees and sudden unexplained death syndrome. *Social Work* 35: 387.

Ramakrishnan, K. R., and Balgopal, P. R. (1992). Linking task-centered interventions with EAPs. *Families in Society* 73 (8) (October): 488–494.

Ramanathan, C. S., and Ramanathan, P. N. (1994). Elder-care among Asian Indian families: Attitudes and satisfactions. *Community Alternatives* 6 (1): 93–112.

Ranganathananda, S. (1971). *The Message of the Upanishads*. Bombay: Bhartiya Vidya Bhavan.

Rao, K., DiClemente, R. J., and Ponton, L. E. (1992). Child sexual abuse of Asians compared with other populations. *Journal of American Academy on Child Adolescent Psychiatry* 31 (5): 880–886.

Rhee, S. (1997). Domestic violence in the Korean immigrant family. *Journal of Sociology and Social Welfare* 24 (1): 63–78.

Segal, U. (1991). Cultural variables in Asian Indian families. *Families in Society* 72: 233–242.

Segal, U. (1997). Asian Indians. In C. H. Mindel, R. Habenstein, and R. Wright (eds.), *Ethnic Families in America* (4th ed.). New York: Prentice-Hall.

Segalman, R., and Basu, A. (1981). *Poverty in America: The Welfare Dilemma*. Westport, CT: Greenwood Press.

Shon, S., and Ja, D. (1982). Asian families. In M. McGoldrick, J. Pierce, and J. Giordano (eds.), *Ethnicity and Family Therapy*. New York: Guilford Press.

Silka, L., and Tip, J. (1994). Empowering the silent ranks: The Southeast Asian experience. *American Journal of Community Psychology* 22: 497–529.

Sue, S. (1993). The changing Asian American population: Mental health policy. In LEAP Asian Pacific American Public Policy Institute and UCLA Asian American Studies Center (eds.), *The State of Asian Pacific America*. Los Angeles: LEAP Asian Pacific American Public Policy Institute and UCLA Asian American Studies Center.

Sue, S., and Morishima, J. (1982). *The Mental Health of Asian Americans*. San Francisco: Jossey-Bass.

Sue, S., Nakamura, C. Y., Chung, R. C., and Yee-Bradbury, C. (1994). Mental health of Asian Americans. *Journal of Community Psychology* 22: 61–67.

Sue, S., and Zane, N. (1987). The role of culture and cultural techniques in psychotherapy. *American Psychologist* 42: 37–45.

Takaki, R. (1989). *The Asian American Experience*. New York. Chelsea House.

Triandis, H. C. (1994). *Culture and Social Behavior*. New York: McGraw-Hill.

Tsui, P., and Schultz, G. (1985). Failure of rapport: Why psychotherapeutic engagement fails in the treatment of Asian clients. *American Journal of Orthopsychiatry* 55: 561–569.

Untalan, F. (1991). Chamorros. In N. Mokuau (ed.), *Handbook of Social Services for Asian and Pacific Islanders*. Westport, CT: Greenwood Press.

U.S. Bureau of Census. (1988). *The Asian and Pacific Islander Population in the United States: 1980*. Report no. PC80-2-1E. Washington, DC: U.S. Government Printing Office.

U.S. Bureau of the Census. (1990). *The Asian and Pacific Islander Population in the*

United States: March 1991 and 1990. Current Population Reports nos. 20–459. Washington, DC: U.S. Government Printing Office.

U.S. Bureau of the Census. (1992). *1990* Census of the Population—General Population Characteristics. Washington, DC: U.S. Government Printing Office.

U.S. Commission on Civil Rights. (1992). *Issues Facing African Americans in the 1990s.* Washington, DC: U.S. Commission on Civil Rights.

Westermeyer, J. (1987). Prevention of mental disorder among Hmong refugees in the U.S.: Lessons from the period 1976–1986. *Social Science Medicine* 25: 941–947.

Wong, D. (1987). Preventing child sexual assault among Southeast Asian refugee families. *Child Today* 16: 18–22.

Wu, I. (1994). Grounds for refuge: Women benefit as U.S., Canada ease asylum Policy. *Far Eastern Economic Review* 157: 24–25.

Yamashiro, G., and Matsuoka, J. K. (1997). Help seeking among Asian and Pacific Americans: A multiperspective analysis. *Social Work* 2 (2): 176–186.

Yeatman, G. W., and Viet, V. D. (1980). Cao gio (coin rubbing): Vietnamese attitudes toward health care. *Journal of the American Medical Association* 244: 2748–2749.

Zane, N., and Sasao, T. (1992). Research on drug abuse among Asian Pacific Americans. *Drugs and Society* 6 (3 and 4): 181–209.

CHAPTER 3

SOCIAL WORK PRACTICE WITH
LATINO AMERICAN IMMIGRANTS

John F. Longres and Davis G. Patterson

(Ed) P. R. Balgopal (2000).
Social work practice
with immigrants + refugees
NY: Columbia University
Press.

The 1990 census recorded more than 22 million persons designated as Hispanic.[1] This represents a huge increase, since as recently as 1982 the Census Bureau estimated this population at only 14 million. Because of rising immigration rates, it is projected that Latinos, who now represent 8 percent of the labor force, will represent 12 percent by the year 2010 (Fix and Passel 1994). By the year 2020, they are projected to be the largest ethnic minority group, surpassing the number of African Americans.

The purpose of this chapter is to lay the foundation for competent social work practice with Latino American individuals, families, and communities. We build this foundation on three central points: First, we believe that there is no one Hispanic or Latino community. Indeed, when working with clients, social workers may find the terms Latino and Hispanic highly inappropriate. Instead, most Latinos identify with a particular Latin American nation. Mexican-origin people make up the largest number, yet there are vast generational and regional differences among them. Puerto Ricans, Cubans, and people from an additional twenty-odd distinct Central and South American nations also comprise this group. Although most people believe that the term Latino refers only to immigrants from Spanish-speaking countries, although some include non-Spanish-speaking immigrants from Brazil and other parts of Central and South America (Castrex 1994). Second, we believe that social workers must understand the larger societal context of their practice. To work with Latinos is to enter into the politics of immigration, race relations, and ethnic stratification, that is, the quest for social and economic security against the obstacles posed by

U.S.[2] society and institutions. It is therefore essential to be familiar with the public issues surrounding immigration, for these provide the background for understanding the needs of Latinos and prepare us to advocate on their behalf. Third, we believe that culture must be understood in dynamic terms. Accordingly, Latino cultures cannot be reduced to a list of unified, timeless, and unchanging values and characteristics. Latino-origin groups are diverse and riddled with internal tensions and conflict. Their cultures are constantly emerging as Latinos deal with old conflicts in the context of the new realities produced by migration. Social workers therefore should be wary of any attempt to simplify Latinos or gather them together in a homogenous mass. In this chapter, then, we are trying to contribute to culturally competent social work practice by describing the complex reality of Latino immigration and settlement; immigration policies and issues; demographic and cultural characteristics; acculturation processes; and service needs, issues, and community resources.

LATINO IMMIGRATION AND SETTLEMENT PATTERNS

Latinos have entered the United States in many different ways: through conquest, legal and illegal immigration, temporary labor programs, and as refugees and asylees. A culturally competent social worker should be able to distinguish among these modes of entry and understand their implications for socioeconomic success, acculturation conflicts, and social service needs.

Annexation Through Conquest

Although we are focusing here on recent immigrants, we should note that the origins of Mexicans and Puerto Ricans in the United States are rooted in coercive modes of entry (Cortes 1980, Fitzpatrick 1982). Almost all the southwestern part of the United States, stretching from Texas to California and as far north as Colorado and parts of Wyoming, once belonged to Mexico. Except for New Mexico and California, this area was not heavily populated and therefore was vulnerable to takeover by the United States. In Texas, U.S. settlers immigrating into the territory quickly outnumbered the Mexican population and rebelled against the Mexican government. In spite of the U.S. loss at the Alamo, the newcomers were eventually victorious and created the Lone Star Republic, which then became a U.S. state in 1845. Later, when the Mexican government refused to part with other lands in the Southwest, the U.S. army attacked, marching through New Mexico and toward California, which already was in the process of separating from Mexico and joining the union. After U.S. forces captured Mexico City in 1848, Mexico ceded much of the Southwest to the United States. The Treaty of Guadalupe Hidalgo gave Mexicans living in the newly conquered areas the right to remain where they were or to return to Mexico within two years. Those who stayed were given the option of becoming U.S. citizens. It is estimated that fewer than fifty thousand Mexicans became citizens at that time. All rights to property belonging to Mexicans were to be guaranteed, but little by little, the Mexicans who stayed behind lost their lands to U.S. settlers who laid claim to them, often in devious and criminal ways.

In many ways, Puerto Ricans who come to the U.S. mainland from the island may be considered voluntary immigrants. Yet ignoring the social relationship between the island of Puerto Rico and the government of the United States is a serious error (Maldanado-Denis 1972). During the Spanish American War, U.S. armed forces invaded Puerto Rico and proclaimed it a U.S. territory. The conquest was institutionalized under the Treaty of Paris, which settled the war. Although there was no insurrection against the U.S. troops, and even a certain amount of support for them, there also was no referendum to allow Puerto Ricans to choose their own political destiny. Many who supported the U.S. invasion believed that Puerto Rican independence would follow, but this has not happened.

Before the annexation of Puerto Rico, the United States had never had overseas territories. It was necessary, therefore, to clarify the use of the term *territory* with respect to Puerto Rico. All previous continental territories had the right to statehood if they had been incorporated and established a provisional or territorial government. But in *Downes v. Bidwell* (1905), the U.S. Supreme Court ruled that overseas territories were not incorporated and therefore were not eligible for statehood. The rationale for this decision was rooted in the open racism of the era, and as a racially mixed society, Puerto Rico and other territories could not become part of the United States.

Supported by the Forracker Act of 1900, Puerto Ricans were removed from power; English became the language of public school instruction; direct trade between Puerto Rico and other nations was forbidden; and Protestant missionaries came in large numbers to convert the island's largely Catholic population. Eventually, these oppressive policies were eliminated or altered, and Puerto Ricans were granted U.S. citizenship in 1917 with all rights except the right to vote in federal elections. A program of economic development was initiated in the 1940s under the leadership of the first freely elected Puerto Rican governor, Luis

Muñoz Marín. In 1952, Puerto Rico adopted a new constitution and became a commonwealth of the United States. The exact meaning of commonwealth is unclear, however, and although Puerto Ricans constantly debate their status, with some wanting independence and others wanting statehood, commonwealth status has prevailed.

The colonization of the Southwest and the annexation of Puerto Rico form a background for understanding the minority status of Puerto Rican and Mexican Americans. Being conquered peoples, their history in the United States is shrouded by a higher level of prejudice and discrimination not experienced by European immigrants. Accordingly, social workers should not be surprised that as a result of their forced entry and lingering minority status, many Mexicans and Puerto Ricans feel ambivalent toward the United States. Although they welcome the opportunities available, they doubt that they will ever be allowed to take advantage of some that other Americans enjoy.

Legal Immigration

Immigrants from Latin America have long been visible in the United States. As far back as 1860, laborers from Mexico, Chile, and Peru were recruited to work in the mines and on the railroads of the West (Edmonston and Passel 1994). Immigration into the United States began to be regulated by government policy only in the late nineteenth and early twentieth centuries. The early immigration policies, however, did not affect immigration from the Western Hemisphere. In theory, anyone from Latin America could immigrate, and many people did come. Massey (1995) pointed out that Latin American immigration represented a major source of immigration throughout the twentieth century, often rivaling that of Europeans.

Between 1924 and 1965, a quota system based on national origins dominated immigration policies. That is, numerical quotas were allotted to specific countries, with the largest share going to northern and western European nations. Then the Immigration and Nationality Act of 1965 repealed the quota system, providing a twenty-thousand-per-country ceiling on immigrant visas for countries from the Eastern Hemisphere and placing a general ceiling on immigration from the Western Hemisphere. Under the Immigration and Nationality Act Amendments of 1976, the twenty-thousand-per-country ceiling on immigrant visas was extended to countries in the Western Hemisphere. At present, therefore, the same limits that apply to the rest of the world now apply to immigration from Latin American and Caribbean nations.

Even before the passage of the 1965 legislation, the number of immigrants from Latin America was beginning to surpass that of immigrants from other parts of the world (Massey 1995). During the 1950s, 40 percent of all immigrants came from Latin America, and throughout the 1960s, 52 percent of all immigrants came from Latin America. Since that time, the percentage entering from Latin America has remained relatively stable, at about 50 percent.

Throughout the twentieth century, Mexicans have comprised the largest proportion of Latino immigrants. During the 1960s, Cubans entered in very large numbers, and more recently, the Dominican Republic and El Salvador also joined the ranks of the top ten countries sending immigrants. In 1996, people from Mexico, Cuba, El Salvador, and the Dominican Republic made up 32.5 percent of the total number of foreign-born residents of the United States (U.S. Bureau of the Census 1996).

We should point out that Puerto Ricans moving from the commonwealth to the states are not included in statistics on immigration, since they are natural-born citizens. Their migration to the mainland is similar to transnational migration because of the geographic, social, cultural, and linguistic barriers that Puerto Ricans must cross. Puerto Ricans began to move to the continent in large numbers during the 1940s, and since that time, they have represented a significant number of the "foreign born." In 1990, 53 percent of the almost three million Puerto Ricans living on the continent were born in Puerto Rico (Campos 1995). If the number of Puerto Ricans living in the United States but born in Puerto Rico were included in the figures on immigration, the percentage of Latino immigrants would be significantly higher.

Illegal Immigration

With the regulation of immigration from the Western Hemisphere, illegal immigration began. Nonetheless, with all the attention given to illegal immigration, it is important to stress that only 13 percent of all migrants enter illegally. Owing to the countries' proximity, it is not surprising that about two-thirds of all illegal or undocumented immigrants come from Mexico, Central America, South America, and the Caribbean (Fix and Passel 1994).

Data on illegal immigration are difficult to obtain, and data based on border apprehensions are unreliable, since many immigrants are counted two, three, or more times as they attempt to enter and reenter. Similarly, significant numbers of undocumented entrants return to Mexico without settling permanently. For that reason, researchers try to measure illegal "stock," that is, undocumented aliens in continuous residence (Rolph 1992). It was estimated, for instance, that the population of illegal immigrants was growing by about 200,000 a year through the early 1980s (Bean, Edmonston, and Passel 1990). About half were of Mexican origin, and about half lived in California. By 1986, it was estimated that three million to five million undocumented aliens lived in the United States. To discourage illegal immigration, Congress enacted the Immigration Reform and Control Act (IRCA) of 1986. IRCA provided opportunities for amnesty and legal settlement for those who could prove they had lived continuously in the United States since 1982. The act also called for increased border patrols and for employer sanctions for knowingly hiring undocumented aliens. To make sure that legal residents were not harmed, the law also stipulated that discrimination in hiring, firing, and recruiting on the basis of national origin was an unfair, immigration-related, employment practice.

Many social service agencies offered programs to help undocumented aliens obtain temporary resident status. Those who received temporary status became eligible for permanent residence status if, after eighteen months, they could demonstrate an adequate proficiency in English and knowledge of citizenship. However, IRCA also made it difficult for the new residents to receive federally funded health, welfare, and educational services. Although state and local governments and public service agencies could be compensated for the costs of providing services, reimbursement from the federal government came slowly, demonstrating federal reluctance to support immigrants in the process of adjustment (Rolph 1992).

As a result of IRCA, significant numbers of Latinos became legal immigrants. Fully 88.2 percent of all those gaining legal status were from Mexico, Central America, or the Caribbean, with another 3.4 percent from South America (Rolph 1992). The profile of those receiving legal status, however, surprised officials, since it did not conform to the expected profile of undocumented aliens. Undocumented aliens are often assumed to be young, relatively uneducated men who are either single or whose family has remained in the home country. Although those obtaining legal status were relatively uneducated, 43 percent were women, 40 percent were married, and the median age was only a few years younger than that of the United States–born population.

IRCA succeeded, for a time, in significantly reducing the number of illegal immigrants settling in the United States, but since 1989 the stock of illegal immigrants has increased to about the same rate as in the early 1980s (Fix and Passel 1994). It is believed the IRCA failed to reduce the flow of illegal immigration largely because it was difficult to enforce employer sanctions (Fix and Passel 1994) and because it was based on flawed knowledge about the causes of immigration (Massey and Espinosa 1997). This latter point will be explained further in a subsequent section.

Temporary Labor Programs

Many Mexican Americans trace their entry into the United States to *bracero* (laborer) programs established as a result of labor shortages brought on by World War II and the Korean War (Cortes 1980). Under the terms of a 1942 executive agreement, Mexican laborers entered the United States as short-term contract workers, primarily in agriculture and transportation. By 1947, when the first program ended, some 200,000 *braceros* worked in twenty-one different states, with the largest number in California. In 1951, the program was resurrected and continued until 1964. At its peak year of 1959, 450,000 braceros entered the country, and by 1960, *braceros* represented 26 percent of the nation's seasonal agricultural labor force (Cortes 1980). Many of the *braceros*, including César Chávez, remained in the United States and contributed greatly to the development of civil rights initiatives on behalf of Mexican Americans and other Latinos.

Latino Refugees

Refugees and asylees are distinguished from other immigrants in that they leave their home country for fear of political and religious persecution. Although they are considered legal immigrants, their entry is not governed by immigrant quotas, and they are entitled to federally subsidized health, education, and welfare services to facilitate their transition into the United States.

There have always been refugees in the Latino immigrant stream. For instance, many Mexican immigrants entered as refugees fleeing political persecution during the Mexican revolution of 1910 and the Cristero revolution of 1926–1929 (Cortes 1980). The first laws governing refugees, however, date from the end of World War II when refugees from the newly formed socialist states of Eastern Europe escaped into the West. Because of this migration, "displaced persons" laws served as a tool in the cold war being fought between the free-market ideology of Western nations and the planned-market ideology of East European and other socialist nations. Initially, displaced persons were allowed to obtain visas under the national quotas allotted to their home country. Subsequently, special quotas were instituted for refugees, separate from those for other kinds of immigrants. It was not until the passage of the Refugee Act of 1980, however, that the United States developed a clear and nonideological policy on refugees.

The Refugee Act provided the first permanent and systematic procedure for the admission of refugees and established comprehensive programs for their domestic resettlement. It created two categories of entrants. According to the act, refugees are those persons who hold a "well founded fear of persecution in their home country" (Rolph 1992:15). Refugees petition for entry from outside the United States and are entitled to permanent resident status after one year of residence. They are eligible for a broad variety of social service benefits, including relocation support. Asylees must also fear persecution and may file for entry from either outside or inside the United States. Like refugees, asylees can be granted work permits, but these are temporary, and they are not eligible for federally funded benefits. The law did not set limits on the number of allowable asylees per year, but it did include procedures for allowing five thousand asylees a year to convert to permanent resident status. The Immigration Act of 1990 increased this number to ten thousand per year.

Among recent Latino immigrants, primarily Cubans and Nicaraguans have entered the United States as refugees. With the fall of the pro-West regime of Fulgencio Batista in 1959 and the rise of the socialist regime of Fidel Castro, some 10 percent of the Cuban population fled the island. For most, the United States became the first country of asylum (Vazquez-Jimenez 1995). Among the first wave of Cubans were a large number of the country's political and economic elite. The next wave of refugees continued the "brain drain" of mainly well-educated and upper-middle-class urban professionals. University-age children, unaccompanied younger children, and married women without their husbands also left, the majority believing that Castro's revolution would fail and they soon could return to their homeland. By the end of the 1970s, however, the waves of refugees came from less affluent sectors of pre-Castro Cuba. The Marielitos, some 125,000 Cubans who were boat-lifted from the coastal town of Mariel, Cuba, to Key West, Florida, in 1981, with the approval of the Cuban government, included many considered socially undesirable in Cuba. These were people with criminal records, lesbians and gay men, patients from mental hospitals, and practitioners of Santería, a religion with many African elements (Vazquez-Jimenez 1995). Not incidentally, about 45 percent of Mariel Cubans were of African descent (Pedraza-Bailey 1985). Although Cubans have settled in many states, the largest concentration is in South Florida, where they have developed an economic and social enclave that has helped smooth the transition of Cubans into the United States.

The exodus of Nicaraguan refugees also resulted from the overthrow of a capitalist-oriented government and the rise of a socialist, Sandinista, state. Nicaraguans also tended to settle in South Florida and to build an economic enclave. Beyond this, however, there are significant differences between Cubans and Nicaraguans. Nicaraguans entered in the 1980s during a time of economic downturn. As a group, they were less educated and less wealthy than the initial wave of Cubans, had more difficulty establishing their right to refugee status, and faced more obstacles in obtaining job permits (Gil and Vega 1996).

Reasons for Immigrating

In discussing labor programs, refugees, asylees, and the like, we have provided an implicit answer to the question of why Latinos—legal as well as undocumented—voluntarily come to the United States. The simple answer often given is the lure of America. Although U.S. citizens often feel ambivalent about immigrants, most believe that the success of U.S. political and economic institutions draws immigrants to its borders. Historical analysis does not altogether deny the pull of the United States, but it is clear that immigration is largely driven by two common push factors: overpopulation and industrialization (Kennedy 1996). During the nineteenth century, these two factors accounted for wave after wave of European immigration. In the twentieth century as well, these social forces are again providing the push for legal and illegal immigration from Latin America.

Overpopulation and rapid industrialization are abundantly evident in Latin America. Since World War II, for instance, the population of Mexico has nearly tripled, increasing at a faster rate than even that of nineteenth-century Europe. Simultaneously, the Mexican economy has rapidly industrialized and, despite periodic troubles, has grown at double the average rate of the U.S. economy. As in nineteenth-century Europe, most migration has been internal, from the countryside of Mexico to its large metropolitan areas. Whereas some five million Mexicans have entered the United States since 1970, double that number have moved to Mexico City alone (Kennedy 1996).

The process of industrial expansion needs to be understood in an international context. Expansion is fueled not just by conditions in immigrant sending countries but also by factors in an increasingly global economy. Some economists, building on the ideas of Wallerstein (1974), call attention to the inherently disruptive need for capitalist development, which acts to displace people from traditional, usually agriculturally related livelihoods and forces them into transitional labor markets. In contemporary societies, these disruptions often come about by the infusion of foreign investment across international borders, thereby speeding the rate of industrialization and promoting the possibility for immigration. Thus, contemporary immigration is likely to come from nations or regions like Latin America, where international investment has helped establish an infrastructure of roads, schools, and banks. Massey and Espinosa (1997) report, for instance, that Mexican immigrants are significantly more likely to come from towns with banks and with roads that provide easy access to the outside world.

At the individual level, a number of factors promote immigration. Most economists believe that migration is driven by its potential rewards. That is, when people in one nation perceive the likelihood of higher wages and more secure employment in another, they are more likely to emigrate. This in fact is the case, as studies have demonstrated that the level of emigration from Mexico and other Latin American countries (including Puerto Rico) generally goes up as wage rates rise in the United States (Massey et al. 1994). Although wage rates appear to determine the underlying propensity to migrate, employment trends account for most of the year-to-year fluctuation in immigration to the United States. When unemployment is low in the United States relative to that of Latin America, immigration increases.

Despite the importance of wage and employment incentives, contemporary immigration from Latin America is more heavily influenced by what economists call "social capital" formation (Massey and Espinosa 1997): the more people who migrate, the more friends and family they will have—social capital—to ease the difficulties of legal and illegal migration. The odds that Mexicans will immigrate for the first time, for instance, are significantly increased if they have parents or siblings in the United States and if they are from communities from which substantial numbers of people have immigrated. Once in the United States, immigrants often acquire additional social capital—spouses and children—that keeps them interested in staying or, should they go back to Mexico, returning to the United States. In addition to social capital, immigrants also acquire human capital, in that once gaining experience in urban skilled or unskilled occupations, they are more likely to return to the United States. Massey and Espinosa (1997) concluded that after fifty years of continuous development, the processes of social and human capital formation are deeply entrenched and largely self-sustaining. They pointed out that national surveys show that half of all adult Mexicans are related to someone living in the United States. National surveys also reveal that one-third of all Mexicans have been in the United States at some time in their lives. The more experience that Mexicans have in the U.S. workforce, the more likely they are to have friends and relatives living in the United States. In short, the processes of human and social capital formation are widely diffused throughout the Mexican population and make it unlikely that immigration from Mexico will slow any time soon.

THE ENVIRONMENTAL REPERCUSSIONS OF LATINO IMMIGRATION

The Response of U.S. Society

Native-born U.S. citizens—including Latinos—are clearly conflicted in their attitudes toward immigration. On the one hand, during the past three decades, multiculturalism has been celebrated for the vitality it brings to American life. Supported by progressive Americans, cities across the country have organized parades, festivals, and community gatherings to celebrate Latino culture and traditions. On the other hand, negative attitudes are evident as well. Some native-born U.S. citizens fear that their way of life is evaporating and that new immigrants are stealing jobs and causing their taxes to rise because of overuse of health, welfare, and educational benefits. Anger and frustration have been vented at Latinos in general and particularly at immigrant Latinos.

The Labor Market Impact of Latino Immigration

A major reason for the growing hostility toward Latino immigrants is the perceived relationship between immigration and the socioeconomic well-being of native-born U.S. citizens. Indeed, since 1945, an attitude of wanting fewer immigrants has been closely correlated with the actual level of employment in the United States: as unemployment increases, negative attitudes toward immigrants also increase (Espenshade 1996/97). But what is the reality? Does immigration—and, in particular, immigration by Latinos—hurt the fortunes of native-born U.S. citizens?

This is a difficult question to answer, in part because studies often do not separate out the impact of Latino immigrants from all others, nor do they distinguish the impact of different modes of entry. Studies have shown, however, that immigration has little effect on professional and managerial positions, which are not likely to be filled by Latino immigrants (Wilson and Jaynes 1996/97). Borjas (1994, 1996) argued that those immigrants with little education, most of whom are from Latin America—especially Mexico, El Salvador, Guatemala, and the Dominican Republic—are partly responsible for a decline in the wages of native workers. After reviewing the research, Fix and Passel (1994) agreed that on balance, immigration has contributed somewhat to the declining fortunes of low-skilled native workers. They also found that immigration has had a negative impact on blue-collar African American workers living in high immigration areas with stagnant economies. On the other hand, Wilson and Jaynes (1996/97) found that although immigration does negatively influence employment, it positively influences the wages of blue-collar workers. Despite some consensus, a definitive answer is difficult because researchers acknowledge severe limitations in their ability to clearly identify effects. Furthermore, Fix and Passel (1994) noted that studies have not yet factored in the benefits that immigrants bring to the U.S. economy in the form of job creation and consumer spending.

The Fiscal Impact of Latino Immigration

Data from the 1980 and 1990 censuses suggest that immigrants are more likely to use welfare services than non-foreign-born U.S. citizens. This conjures up images of slovenly Latino immigrants being drawn to America by the promise of easy welfare benefits. In an era when lawmakers are especially concerned about balancing budgets and reducing the scope of the health and welfare safety net, the apparent rise in the use of welfare benefits has fueled anti-immigrant sentiment and led to several attempts to discourage legal and illegal immigration. Census data, however, can be misleading unless country of origin and mode of entry are taken into account and unless differences in the use of particular welfare programs are addressed (Fix and Passel 1994).Although the point is often ignored, illegal and legal immigrants pay local, state, and federal taxes. Thus, we need to consider both the benefits and the costs of accepting immigrants into the United States. With this in mind, studies suggest that immigrants generate a net surplus for the federal government, mixed costs for state governments—depending on the state and on the responsibilities assumed—and a large fiscal burden for local governments (Borjas 1996, Fix and Passel 1994). It is important to stress, however, that many studies of local government outlays underestimate the revenue obtained from immigrants while overestimating their costs. Furthermore, studies of local government often obscure the fact that native-born U.S. citizens also create a large fiscal burden (Fix and Passel 1994). Local governments are in difficult economic straits regardless of their residents' immigrant status.

Immigrants do incur costs when they use health and welfare benefits; however, not all immigrants are entitled to use them. Except for emergency Medicaid and maternal and child health nutrition programs, undocumented aliens are not eligible for public assistance. Immigrants legalizing under IRCA, as noted earlier, were also blocked from using welfare benefits for five years. Legal permanent residents are effectively barred from receiving many welfare benefits during their first three years in the country, since sponsors must assume responsibility for their economic independence. The Personal Responsibility and Work Opportunity Reconciliation Act of 1996 (PRWORA) has lengthened this period of sponsor responsibility to five years.

The statistics on welfare use among immigrants reflect the effectiveness of these barriers to service use. The two overlapping populations whose welfare use is significantly higher than that of native-born U.S. citizens are the elderly—largely Asian—and refugees who have arrived since 1980 (Fix and Passel 1994). The use of services by refugees is expected, since as noted previously, entitlement to services is built into the legislation controlling their entry into the United States.

Bean, Van Hook, and Glick (1994/95) looked more closely at welfare use by immigrants by comparing 1979 and 1989/90 rates and controlling for mode of entry, type of service use (AFDC and SSI), nativity, and a number of eligibility criteria. In doing so, they discovered much about the use of services by Latinos, in particular native-born Mexican Americans and immigrants from Mexico, El Salvador, and Guatemala. It should be noted, however, that they did not take into account the large number of Latinos who were granted amnesty under IRCA and who were therefore ineligible for welfare services during the period they studied. Nevertheless, they found no relative increase in the use of AFDC and a relatively small increase in the use of SSI by Latino immigrants in 1990 compared with 1979. They did find a significantly higher use of SSI by Asian refugees, however. They concluded that although refugee policies and procedures for enforcing SSI eligibility may need revision, immigration policy overall may not.

Recent Attempts to Curtail Immigration

Persistent immigration in a time of economic restructuring has led to three major attempts to curtail immigration, particularly illegal immigration: the already mentioned Immigration Reform and Control Act of 1986 (IRCA); Proposition 187, the victorious 1994 California anti-immigration referendum; and the Personal Responsibility and Work Opportunity Reconciliation Act of 1996 (PRWORA). All three were guided by the idea that if the costs of immigration are raised, illegal immigration will subside. In addition to providing amnesty for undocumented aliens living in the United States, IRCA attempts to discourage immigration further by increasing border patrols and prosecuting employers who knowingly hire undocumented aliens. Proposition 187 withholds state-funded social welfare programs from undocumented residents. PRWORA reinforces preexisting sanctions against the use of health and welfare benefits by illegal aliens and, in addition, denies benefits to certain "unqualified" legal immigrants for five years. Since the passage of the Social Security Act of 1935, legal permanent residents have had the same rights as U.S. citizens with regard to receiving federal insurance and public assistance. The passage of PRWORA, therefore, represents the first attempt to curtail the rights of legal immigrants.

With regard to IRCA, we have already pointed out that it has had little effect on illegal immigration. Massey and Espinosa (1997) found that employer sanctions and detention efforts along the border have actually increased the likelihood of illegal immigration. Based on their survey of more than four thousand Mexican households, they argued that prospective migrants interpreted the border crackdown as evidence that more stringent policies would follow and thus encouraged them to enter while they still could. Likewise, employer sanctions have encouraged working undocumented migrants to hang onto their jobs for fear of not being able to find one at a later time. Furthermore, by having granted amnesty to those who could prove they had lived continuously in the United States since 1982, the act increased the amount of social capital available to prospective migrants. Massey and Espinosa (1997) found that being from a household where someone had become legal under IRCA greatly increased the odds of a person's taking a first illegal trip to the United States.

Proposition 187 sought to end illegal immigration by restricting the use of health, education, and welfare services by undocumented aliens. Massey and Espinosa (1997) reported, however, that there was no correlation between having immigration documents and using medical benefits. They also discovered that with documentation, the use of educational resources increased significantly but the use of welfare benefits decreased significantly. They concluded that the implementation of Proposition 187 will have little overall influence on illegal immigration.

Because PRWORA is just beginning to be implemented, we have no data on its effects. The political controversy created by PRWORA is also forcing reconsideration of many of its particulars, such as it is no longer clear just which aspects of the act will or will not be implemented. As passed, however, the act distinguishes between *qualified* and *nonqualified* aliens. *Qualified* aliens are legal permanent residents, most often refugees, who may continue to receive health and welfare benefits. *Unqualified* aliens are all the remaining legal immigrants who are ineligible for federal government contracts, loans, grants, and commercial or professional licenses. They are ineligible for benefits for retirement, welfare, health, disability, public or assisted housing, postsecondary education, food assistance, and unemployment when the assistance is provided by a federal agency or when federal funds are appropriated to pay the assistance. The most severely affected by these cutbacks will likely be the nearly half-million elderly and disabled who need SSI, food stamps, and Medicaid. Currently, 23 percent, 16 percent, and 11 percent, respectively, of noncitizens receive SSI, food stamps, and Medicaid (Primus 1996/97). Also likely affected will be families in need of temporary assistance and other means-tested programs like school lunch, foster care, Head Start, and job training. Although the law bans all new immigrants from receiving services for five years, under the law's "deeming provisions," this period will likely last longer. Those who sponsor legal immigrants will also be required to accept responsibility for all their expenses, including medical care. The immigrants' income and resources will also be counted in establishing eligibility for federally supported services. It is this last provision that is likely to curtail immigration, since sponsors must be willing to assume far greater responsibility than in the past.

Latino Immigration and Ethnicity in the United States

Massey (1995) suggested that immigration—its effect on the economic well-being of natives and the fiscal impact on government budgets—is not necessarily driving anti-immigrant bias. Rather, he located the cause of the bias in the fear that the traditional cultural milieu of America is being lost as large numbers of non-English-speaking, non-European immigrants become more visible.

Regardless of opinions about the melting pot, it is clear that European ethnic-group members have successfully amalgamated into an undifferentiated "white" mass. Today we take this blending for granted, but it was not predicted back at the turn of the twentieth century. "Native Americans," as those from northern and eastern European nations called themselves, feared racial mongrelization by southern and eastern Europeans and fought successfully to introduce discriminatory immigration legislation. Southern and eastern Europeans, in turn, developed ethnic enclaves and social and political associations as a way of exerting their ethnic independence. And yet they intermixed. Can we expect the same fusion between natives and Latino immigrants?

A number of factors suggest that if Latino blending does occur, it will take longer than European blending (Kennedy 1996, Massey 1995). First, European integration took place during a long period when relatively few immigrants were entering the United States, whereas immigration today has been continuous since the 1960s and is projected to remain so indefinitely. Latino ethnic identity is likely to survive as long as large numbers of Latinos keep entering the country. Second, contemporary Latino immigration is highly concentrated geographically. Large Spanish-speaking communities are visible in New York, Los Angeles, Houston, and Chicago, and in Miami they have become the majority (Massey 1995). This makes the Spanish language and cultural traditions easier to sustain. Third, the European melding took place after the Great Depression of the 1930s and during a period of strong and continuing economic growth. Until the past few years, contemporary immigration has taken place during a long period of relative economic decline for working-class people. Real wages have not risen since 1973, and economic inequality has worsened considerably as continual downsizing and restructuring have led to the loss of high-paying jobs for skilled and unskilled labor. The economic opportunities that allowed the sons and daughters of relatively uneducated and unskilled European immigrants to do better than their parents are not as readily available today. If Latino children become mired in the economic insecurity of their immigrating parents and are forced to remain in ethnic enclaves, Latino identity and antiassimilation attitudes will continue to be strong.

Not only do structural circumstances point to relatively slower fusion, but this process also is likely to exact greater cultural changes in non–Hispanic Americans. The melting pot has always been a fluid, multidirectional process. As Europeans intermingled, they created a blended culture. Although still dominated by the English language and traditions, U.S. culture has been developing its own special characteristics reflective of its many immigrant strands. Because of the large numbers of Latino immigrants congregating in a relatively few states and large cities, it is possible, however, to envision a more bilingual society in which Spanish achieves a second-language status and Latinos themselves are able to exact concessions unimaginable by European immigrants (Kennedy 1996, Massey 1995). Kennedy imagines the possibility of a Mexican *reconquista*:

> Mexican-Americans will have open to them possibilities closed to previous immigrant groups. They will have sufficient coherence and critical mass in a defined region so that, if they choose, they can preserve their distinctive culture indefinitely. They could also eventually undertake to do what no previous immigrant group could have dreamed of doing: challenging the existing cultural, political, legal, commercial, and educational systems to change fundamentally not only the language but also the very institutions in which they do business.   (p. 68)

We should not, however, overestimate the coherence of Latin American–origin people.

DEMOGRAPHICS AND CULTURAL CHARACTERISTICS

Latino Identity

Latinos trace their origins to a wide range of Spanish-speaking countries, primarily in the Western Hemisphere. Those whose origins are in Mexico comprise about 64 percent of the aggregate (see table 3.1). Americans whose origins are in Puerto Rico, Cuba, or Central and South America make up 29 percent. "Other Hispanics," people who identify with Spain or with more generalized Spanish-speaking roots, make up the remaining 7 percent. The percentage of Latinos from Central and South America is growing significantly. People of Mexican origin, however, have consistently made up the majority of Latinos and, given their recent increased immigration, are likely to continue to be the single largest Hispanic national-origin group in the United States.

Latinos are mainly an urban population, and recent immigrants conform to this pattern: the majority of new legal and illegal immigrants are settling in large metropolitan areas (Fix and Passel 1994). Although they live in every state, the states of California, Texas, and New York have the largest concentrations, followed by Florida, Illinois, New Jersey, New Mexico, Arizona, and Colorado. California has the largest number, with some 30 percent of its population identified as Hispanic, followed by Texas, with some 28 percent (Kennedy 1996). A number of states not associated with large concentrations have nevertheless shown more than a 100 percent increase over the last decade. These include Washington, Oregon, Idaho, West Virginia, Virginia, Pennsylvania, South Carolina, and most of the New England states.

Hispanics share a historical connection with Spain and the Spanish language. This connection, however, is filtered through the proud heritage of separate nations, each of which is in turn heterogeneous. It is only as people from different Spanish-speaking groups become part of the United States that the need for a general term to describe them arises. Like other highly diverse groups (e.g., European Americans, Asian Americans, and Native Americans), we may be witnessing the emergence of a new ethnic group unique to the United States.

TABLE 3.1
National Origin of U.S. "Hispanic" Population (%)

Mexico	64.1
Puerto Rico	10.4
Cuba	4.2
Central or South American countries	14.0
Other	7.3
Total U.S. Hispanic population	26,646,000

Source: U.S. Bureau of the Census, *Hispanic Population from the 1994 Current Population Survey* (online: http://www.census.gov/population/www.socdemo/).

Not surprisingly, the proper term for describing this multiethnic population is open to debate. The names used to describe people come about through social and political processes taking place within and outside the groups themselves. The United States government has used a wide range of official terms, including Spanish-origin, Spanish-surnamed, and Spanish-speaking. More recently, the designation Hispanic, either white or nonwhite, has been applied. Individuals in this multiethnic group, however, are apt to identify themselves according to their national origin (de la Garza et al. 1992).

It is usually when members of different national-origin groups join together—for social, self-help, or political purposes—that they use a panethnic term to define themselves. This is what Padilla (1985) refers to as a *situational ethnic identity*. Whether the term Hispanic or Latino is used to designate the group depends on a number of factors, including regional customs and simple force of habit. Some believe, however, that political ideology is an important factor determining preference (Shorris 1992). Those concerned principally with issues of equality and who espouse activism are thought to prefer the term Latino. Those who are more interested in advancing social and cultural goals are thought to prefer Hispanic. Yet there is little evidence on this point, and personal observation suggests that the two terms continue to be used interchangeably.

Since it is common for people from Spanish-speaking nations to form and use panethnic organizations and services, perhaps in some future time a situational identity will no longer apply, though this appears to be a long way off. Data from a representative sample (de la Garza et al. 1992) indicate that the majority of Mexican, Puerto Rican, and Cuban Americans prefer their national-origin identity to a panethnic one. They also report having little or no contact with individuals outside their own national-origin group and believe that their group is "not very similar" to other Latino groups. Furthermore, Mexican, Puerto Rican, and especially Cuban Americans are likely to express greater closeness to Anglos and to marry Anglos rather than other Hispanics (de la Garza et al. 1992).

Not only is a panethnic Latino identity problematic, but consensus is lacking on national-origin identity. By calling attention to the diversity found among Latinos, we do not mean to imply that Latinos lack unity and cohesion. Indeed, the various groups often pull together to meet common, shared interests. This unity, however, is highly situational and not automatic. Class, generation, ideology, and racial diversity mark all Latino national-origin groups. Within each group, one is likely to find a wide range of attitudes toward assimilation and acculturation into the U.S. melting pot. Latinos who trace their origins to Mexico are a good example because of their long history of immigration. Within this group, self-defining labels such as Mexican, Mexican American, and Chicano give evidence of internal differences (Massey 1995). Similar kinds of diversity are found in other Latino groups. Pedraza-Bailey (1985) described the inverse correlation between date of departure and social class among Cuban refugees. Earlier refugees tended to come from professional, technical, and managerial occupations, whereas later refugees tended to have working-class, semiskilled, and unskilled occupations. Likewise, well over 90 percent of the early refugees were white Cubans, but only 65 percent of the 1980 refugee Cubans were white. Ideology and generation also divide Cubans between those who continue to be vigilantly antisocialist versus those who are more interested in adopting U.S. culture and institutions (Pedraza-Bailey 1985).

There also are differences between recent immigrants and U.S.-born Latinos that are complicated by attitudes toward illegal immigration. Not all Latinos favor increased immigration, and many are wary of illegal immigrants. In the 1996 California elections, for instance, 25 percent of voting Latinos voted for Proposition 187, which places severe restrictions on illegal immigrants (Pachon and Wilhelm 1996). Similarly, Hondagneu-Sotelo (1994) observed that interactions between Chicanos (U.S.-born Mexican Americans) and immigrants were minimal, even when they lived in the same community.

Given such wide diversity, it is difficult to predict whether a panethnic identity will ever be accepted, let alone whether the term Hispanic or Latino will become the desired way of expressing that unity. For the moment, culturally competent social workers should expect large individual differences among Latinos. They should also refrain from assuming or imposing on them a panethnic identity or even a particular national-origin identity. In fact, it would be better for them not to refer to their clients as Hispanic or Latino but, rather, to use the term used by the individuals, families, or communities with whom they work.

Language

As a fundamental binding force and, perhaps more than any one factor, the basis for any future panethnic Latino identity, the language(s) that Latinos speak deserve special attention. The Spanish spoken in the various homelands, though different in accent, vocabulary, and occasionally grammar, is nevertheless mutually intelligible. The importance of a common language, however, is as much symbolic as real. Recent immigrants and refugees are generally Spanish dominant, and many report that they do not speak English or do not speak it well. Nevertheless, second- and later-generation Latinos are likely to be English dominant and, in some instances, are unable to communicate effectively in

Spanish. Not surprisingly, everyday communication among Latinos is often in English or in some mix of English and Spanish. For instance, 63 percent of Mexican Americans, 50 percent of Puerto Ricans, and 31 percent of Cubans report speaking mostly English in their homes. Similarly, among those born in the United States, approximately two-thirds of Mexican, Puerto Rican, and Cuban Americans report greater proficiency in English than in Spanish (de la Garza et al. 1992).

These findings should not obscure the fact that many Latinos—especially those born outside the United States and those who have lived largely in Spanish-speaking enclaves or *barrios*—are not English dominant and are likely to need services in Spanish. To give an indication, the 1990 census reported that well over seventeen million Latinos over the age of five spoke Spanish in their homes (U.S. Bureau of the Census 1990). These figures should also underscore the symbolic importance of Spanish—events celebrating the history and traditions of Spanish-speaking people, songs and posters in Spanish, foods associated with Spanish-speaking homelands, and so forth—that make even English-dominant Latino people feel welcomed and accepted in U.S. society.

Phenotype

Although ethnic groups differ in phenotypic characteristics, these are not easily grouped into discrete or pure races. For this reason, definitions of race are best seen as cultural inventions rooted more in social and political processes than in biological fact.

In the United States, races are separate, "either-or" categories. To be "white" means that a person is 100 percent European in ancestry. Once racial mixing takes place, offspring have no claim to whiteness; they are Asian, black, or Indian, and identification with a racial group is a central feature of everyday life. Following this logic, the U.S. Bureau of the Census treats Hispanics as a group that is divisible into discrete races: "persons of Hispanic origin may be of any race" (U.S. Bureau of the Census 1997).

Among Latino immigrants, however, race is often not considered a relevant demographic characteristic. The Commonwealth of Puerto Rico, for instance, collects no data on the racial characteristics of its population. This is not to say that Latinos are not color conscious but merely that racial characteristics are understood in continuous terms and that racial identification is a far less significant aspect of daily life. People of mixed ancestry, unless they are very dark complexioned, tend to claim European ancestry. Thus, most racially mixed people in Spanish-speaking nations think of themselves as white or as some intermediary designation such as *mestizo* (European/indigenous) or *mulatto*, *trigueño*, or *moreno* (all variations on African/European ancestry). Most Latino immigrants, therefore, consider themselves white.

Following official U.S. definitions, Latinos are an ethnic, not a racial, group; they are included among whites unless individual Latinos choose to indicate otherwise. But this was not always the case. In the 1930 census, persons of Mexican background were designated among the "other races" (U.S. Bureau of the Census 1932). They were "returned as white" in the 1940 census (U.S. Bureau of the Census 1943) and have been so classified ever since. Similarly, throughout the 1950s, census interviewers identified the race of respondents and, applying United States criteria, overcounted the number of "nonwhite" Puerto Ricans living in Puerto Rico (U.S. Bureau of the Census 1955). Since 1960, however, census counts in Puerto Rico no longer categorize the population by race. There was some discussion about converting Latinos from an ethnic to a racial group for the 1990 census, but this was abandoned, as Latino leaders were not comfortable with the implications of being classified as nonwhite (Rodriguez 1989:81–82).

Regardless of self- and official designation, many Latinos in the United States have phenotypes associated with what is considered mixed racial ancestry. Latino national-origin groups, in fact, may be divided into three categories, depending on the type of racial mixing most common in them. One set of countries—those largely in the Caribbean Islands, Panama, and northern South America—have large populations of mixed European and African ancestry. Another set—Mexico, most of Central America, and western South American nations—have large populations that are of mixed European and indigenous (Indian) ancestry. A third set of countries—for example, Argentina, Uruguay, and, to a lesser extent, Chile—are composed almost entirely of people who are European in ancestry. These differences create interpersonal difficulties both between Latinos and non-Latinos and among Latinos.

The way Latinos think about themselves differs from the way non-Latinos think of them. Thus, many whites treat Euro-African Latinos as black. Rodriguez points to one study that found that non-Hispanic white "interviewers" defined Puerto Ricans differently than Puerto Ricans defined themselves, and another study found that Puerto Ricans sometimes were forced into a black-white dichotomy in their interactions with other Americans (Rodriguez 1989). Denton and Massey (1989) found that black and racially mixed Caribbean Latinos lived segregated from non-Hispanic white Americans. A similar phenomenon may be hypothesized in the way that whites treat Euro-indigenous Latinos. Montalvo (1991) reported that darker Mexican Americans were acutely aware of their skin color and the negative influence it had on their lives.

Phenotype also has implications for the way Latinos treat one another. Although some have claimed that racism is not evident among Latinos, such is not the case (Betances 1972, 1973; Montalvo 1991). Harsh forms of racism like neighborhood and friendship segregation are not readily discerned in Latin nations, yet subtle forms of racism are (e.g., ideas about beauty). Most Latinos are ambivalent about race, being comfortable with the fact of race mixing yet inclined to value European heritage over any other.

In the United States, this ambivalence inclines Latinos to internalize white racial norms and leads to interpersonal barriers among Latinos. For instance, Mariel Cubans, those refugees who came around 1980 and who in general were darker and of lower socioeconomic status than earlier waves, reported that other Cubans discriminate against them (Pedraza-Bailey 1985). Likewise, Caribbean Latinos of mixed racial ancestry displayed a low degree of residential segregation from white Latinos but a high degree of segregation from black Latinos and from non-Latino blacks (Denton and Massey 1989). In addition, Massey and Denton (1992) discovered that male Mexican Americans living in suburban areas were likely to have a higher income and a white spouse and to choose "white" as their race. They also reported that although light-skinned Mexican Americans seldom thought about skin color as an issue in their lives, they did admit that few of their friends and dates were dark and could recall being showered with attention as children because of their fair complexion.

Socioeconomic Well-Being

Hispanics often share the same socioeconomic circumstances in the United States. On average, each national-origin group fares worse than do non-Hispanics on such important indicators as household income (see table 3.2), labor force participation and occupational attainment (table 3.3), and educational attainment (table 3.4). Furthermore, negative differences have persisted across several census counts.

The interpretation of these differences is being debated. Many see in them evidence that Hispanics are systematically disadvantaged by prejudice, discrimination, and limited opportunities. Proponents of this view in turn support affirmative action as a necessary step in overcoming minority status. Others explain away the difference by calling attention to the need to control for age, immigration status, and other relevant variables (Chavez 1991). They in turn assert that special government policies are not needed to help Hispanics achieve the American dream. The truth lies somewhere in between.

TABLE 3.2
Percentage of Households by Ethnicity Earning More Than $50,000 and Less Than $10,000

Ethnicity	% households < $10,000	% households > $50,000
Hispanic	20.4	15.5
Mexican	18.4	14.0
Puerto Rican	31.2	12.9
Cuban	19.8	24.5
Central and South American	18.1	21.7
Other Hispanic	22.3	21.2
Non-Hispanic white	11.9	30.0

Source: U.S. Bureau of the Census, *Hispanic Population from the 1994 Current Population Survey* (online: http://www.census.gov/population/www.socdemo/).

TABLE 3.3
Percentage of Selected Ethnic Populations Age 16 and over Unemployed, in the Professions, and in the Trades

Ethnicity	Unemployed		Operators, Fabricators, Laborers		Professionals, Managers	
	Male	*Female*	*Male*	*Female*	*Male*	*Female*
Hispanic	11.2	11.0	30.1	13.5	11.3	15.6
Mexican	10.9	11.7	31.7	14.0	8.8	14.6
Puerto Rican	15.9	12.0	25.9	9.0	14.5	23.0
Cuban	8.3	5.0	24.4	12.5	22.6	20.7
Central and South American	11.7	10.7	29.4	17.0	14.1	10.7
Other Hispanic	8.8	9.2	23.7	9.3	18.3	20.2
Non-Hispanic white	6.2	5.0	18.1	6.2	29.3	31.1

Source: U.S. Bureau of the Census, *Hispanic Population from the 1994 Current Population Survey* (online: http://www.census.gov/population/www.socdemo/hispanic.html).

TABLE 3.4

Percentage of Selected Ethnic Populations Age 25 and over with Less Than a
Fifth-Grade Education and Bachelor's/Advanced Degrees

Ethnicity	% < Fifth Grade	% Bachelor's/ Advanced Degree
Hispanic	10.8	9.1
Mexican	13.3	6.3
Puerto Rican	7.5	9.9
Cuban	5.4	16.2
Central and South American	8.3	12.7
Other Hispanic	5.6	16.8
Non-Hispanic white	0.8	24.3

Source: U.S. Bureau of the Census, *Hispanic Population from the 1994 Current Population Survey* (online: http://www.census.gov/population/www.socdemo/hispanic.html).

On average, Hispanics are younger than non-Hispanics, and thus it is not fair to compare people generally at the beginning stages of labor force participation with people who are nearer the peak of their earning power. For instance, the median age for non-Hispanics is 33.5 but is only 24.1 for Mexican Americans. Cubans, however, are actually older on average than non-Hispanics, and so it is not surprising that their employment status and level of income compare more favorably than do other Hispanic national-origin groups with non-Hispanics.

Owing to the strength of recent immigration, first-generation immigrants and refugees make up a sizable percentage of Hispanics. In addition, large numbers, especially of immigrants, have little education, minimal skills, and limited ability in English. The immigrants' mode of entry appears predictive of their educational background and income. For instance, Fix and Passel (1994) compared the educational backgrounds of immigrants from Mexico, El Salvador, and Guatemala (the countries of origin of most illegal immigrants) with those from refugee-sending countries (including Cuba and Nicaragua) and with immigrants from other countries (including South America and the Caribbean). Although their data are likely to distort the reality of Latino immigrants and refugees, they successfully demonstrate the low education and incomes of illegal immigrants. Table 3.5 shows that the vast majority of immigrants from Mexico, El Salvador, and Guatemala enter with less than a high school education. Similarly, table 3.6 shows that the average incomes of Mexican, Salvadoran, or Guatemalan households in the United States are considerably lower than the household incomes of immigrants from refugee countries and immigrants from other countries.

Given the recent influx of such newcomers, the persistence of higher poverty and high unemployment rates are to be expected. It is unclear, however, what the long-term economic prospects are for Latino immigrants. As the general level of education and language competence rises, however, Hispanic immigrants should be expected to do as well as native-born Hispanics and non-Hispanics, and there is evidence that this might be occurring. Stolzenberg (1990) found that occupational achievement among white Hispanic males who spoke English very well and had completed at least twelve years of education was very close to that of non-Hispanic white males in the same geographic area and with similar schooling and English-language proficiency. But there is considerable concern that the long-term prospects of Latino immigrants may not be quite so positive. Neidart and Farley (1985) showed that the occupational returns from educational attainment among third- and higher-generation Mexican American men lags significantly behind European and Asian Americans of the same generation. More recently, Borjas (1994) reached the same conclusion. By examining the socioeconomic well-being of immigrant male cohorts, Borjas demonstrated that successive cohorts of immigrants entering between 1950 and 1959 were less likely to obtain parity with pre-1950 immigrants and native-born men. He also showed that immigrants from Latin America generally do less well in

TABLE 3.5

Education by Country of Birth and Type of Immigration, 1980–1990 Immigrants

Country of Birth	% < High School Education	% College Degree or More
Illegal immigrant sending countries (Mexico, El Salvador, Guatemala)	75.4	4.6
Refugee sending countries	46.1	16.2
All other countries	26.5	33.3

Source: M. Fix and J. S. Passel, Immigration and Immigrants (Washington, DC: Urban Institute, 1994), figure 11.

TABLE 3.6
Average Household Income, by Country of Birth, 1990 (in $)

	Year Entered		
Country of Origin	1980–1990	Before 1980	U.S. Born
Illegal immigrant sending countries	23,900	28,000	37,300
Refugee sending countries	27,700	39,100	37,300
All other countries	34,800	43,200	37,300

Source: M. Fix and J. S. Passel, Immigration and Immigrants (Washington, DC: Urban Institute, 1994), figure 13.

catching up to native-born U.S. citizens than do immigrants from Africa, Asia, and Europe. For instance, in 1990 only pre-1980 Latin American immigrants from Argentina and Peru had surpassed the average income of native-born U.S. citizens. But by 1990, the great majority of pre-1980 immigrants from Africa, Asia, and Europe had already surpassed the average income of native-born U.S. citizens. The data used by Borjas also show that mode of entry, coupled with educational and occupational background, explains a good deal of the inequality among Latino immigrants. The differences between Latino countries sending illegal immigrants, refugees, and legal immigrants are striking. For instance, pre-1980 immigrants from El Salvador, Guatemala, and Mexico earned 20 to 32 percent less than did native-born U.S. citizens. Pre-1980 refugees from Cuba earned on average 5 percent less, and refugees from Nicaragua 11 percent less than native-born U.S. citizens. Pre-1980 immigrants from Argentina, Panama, and Peru, however, had, on average, a higher socioeconomic status than did native-born U.S. citizens.

Similarly, many researchers recognize that the situation of Puerto Rican continentals is particularly bad and fear they are becoming part of a permanent underclass (Falcon and Santiago 1992). Migration from Puerto Rico changed in important ways after 1974, when the United States' minimum wage laws were applied to Puerto Rico. Although those moving to the United States have continued to be from the less-skilled, less-educated sectors of Puerto Rico, those Puerto Ricans moving back are frequently skilled and educated (Massey et. al. 1994). As a result of this return migration, Puerto Rican continentals as a group experienced a sharp deterioration in economic well-being between 1975 and 1985, and it is unclear whether their circumstances are improving (Tienda 1989).

Explanations for the persistence of relatively low socioeconomic levels once age, language ability, and immigration status are taken into account range from conservative to liberal. The conservative position holds that the high number of single-mother families among Hispanics and particularly among Puerto Ricans is a major factor. In addition, they believe that welfare programs aimed at supporting such families should be eliminated and every effort made to rebuild the nuclear family (Chavez 1991).

Liberal explanations focus on racism and structural factors in the labor market. With regard to racial discrimination, Rodriguez (1989) reported that intermediate- and dark-skinned Puerto Ricans do less well than do their light-skinned counterparts. Codina and Montalvo's (1993) analysis of depression suggests a similar consequence for darker-skinned Mexican Americans. There are some indications, though, that racism may not be an issue in economic well-being. Puerto Ricans who identify themselves as "black" actually do better economically than do those who identify themselves as "Spanish" and almost as well as those who identify themselves as "white" (Rodriguez 1989). Likewise, Dominicans and Mariel Cuban Americans, two recently arrived groups with large numbers of intermediate- and dark-complexioned individuals, appear to be doing well economically (Chavez 1991, Maldonado 1989).

In addition to racism, labor market factors have also been used to explain the persistent economic disadvantage of Hispanics and especially Puerto Ricans. Tienda (1989) discovered that for male Puerto Ricans, the labor market instability began in the early 1970s and was influenced by their concentration in geographic areas experiencing severe economic dislocation, which in turn brought about rapidly falling employment opportunities in jobs in which Puerto Ricans traditionally have worked. While the evidence is suggestive, she decided that a healthy economy was a necessary, albeit insufficient, condition for reducing inequality.

Adaptation and Coping Within the Mainstream

This discussion of differences—in language, ethnicity, and social class—leads one to wonder how well Latinos have been able to adjust to living in a dominant culture that, at its best, tries to understand and accommodate differences and, at its worst, treats outsiders with hostility and violence. The extent to which Latinos experience psychological debilitation as a result of immigration is thought to be associated with the type of adjustment made to U.S. society by immigrants and their children. Researchers have advanced three hypotheses: (1) The acceptance of U.S. ideals (high acculturation) leads to well-being because it represents a healthy adaptation to a new society; (2) the rejection of U.S. ideals (low acculturation) leads to well-being because it protects against alienation and isolation and supplies a buffer against discrimination; and (3) biculturalism, representing the complete integration of two systems of cultural value, promotes adaptability and, therefore, enhances well-being (Rogler, Cortes, and Malgady 1991). The research evidence, however, suggests that no one hypothesis consistently predicts well-being (Gil and Vega 1996).

Social workers should be ready to assess a number of conflicts identified with adaptation and coping within the mainstream (Gil, Vega, and Dimas 1994). *Language conflict* may be expected as immigrants and their children struggle with the need to get along in English and to master it in school and the workplace. Even those living in ethnic enclaves or working with other Spanish-speaking people cannot meet all their everyday needs without English competence. *Acculturation conflict*, that is, conflict related to choosing between U.S. and Hispanic-origin cultural traditions, is also commonplace. For young people, this can be seen in intergeneration conflicts, as the desire to become acculturated competes with expectations to conform to parental customs and traditions. Actual *intergeneration conflict* may occur as well when children quarrel or become alienated from their parents as they struggle for their own identity. *Perceived discrimination* is another common type of conflict experienced by immigrants. Latinos are likely to struggle with real and perceived rejection by U.S. society. Rejection may be felt in terms of ethnicity but also very likely in terms of phenotype. This may be especially true for darker-skinned Dominicans, Panamanians, Puerto Ricans, Mexicans, and Cubans who are likely to experience disorientation as they confront the U.S. construction of race (Paulino 1994). When confronted by discrimination, Latinos may perceive a closed society; that is, they may struggle with the relative absence of opportunities for socioeconomic success. In addition to these difficulties, Latinos are likely to experience conflict and stress directly related to the immigrant experience. Refugees who have had to leave quickly, often leaving loved ones behind, may regret their lack of preparation for entry into U.S. society, and illegal immigrants are likely to live with the considerable stress associated with being caught and deported.

Acculturation studies, those focusing on issues of coping and adaptation, usually examine the degree to which immigrants lose Hispanic cultural ideals. There is evidence, for instance, that with each succeeding generation, Spanish language use and other traditional, culturally aware behaviors diminish. In fact, Rogler, Cortes, and Malgady (1991) noted that the loss of Spanish is the primary measure of acculturation. But ethnic pride and loyalty are not related to language use and do not appear to diminish across generations (Keefe and Padilla 1987). Acculturation need not be thought of as only the process of leaving cultural traditions behind; it may also be thought of as acquiring U.S. ideals, a process that may be independent of the loss of Hispanic ideals. For instance, as we will explain in greater detail later, Latina Americans often gain a sense of equal partnership with their husbands, take part in larger social networks, and begin using social-scientific knowledge of child development in raising their children, as opposed to Latino folk wisdom (Negy and Woods 1992).

In addition to focusing on the loss of Hispanic cultural ideals, most research has been on the potentially debilitating effects of acculturation, such as the relationship between acculturation and alcohol and drug use among Latino adolescents. In general, researchers found that as acculturation increases, so does the likelihood of abusing alcohol and drugs (Gil et al. 1994, Wagner-Echeagaray et al. 1994). Yet the research results are not consistent on this issue. Caetano (1987) reported that drinking behavior is gender specific and, especially among Latino men, is highly dependent on age, education, work status, and other variables. With regard to other forms of psychological debilitation, including anxiety and stress disorders, affective disorders, impulse control, self-esteem, phobias, and career conflict, there is little consensus. Three recent reviews of the literature point to a highly complex association between acculturation and psychological well-being (Moyerman and Forman 1992, Negy and Woods 1992, Rogler et al. 1991). Research has less often focused on understanding the strengths that may be gained through acculturation. For instance, few studies examine the relationship between acculturation and such things as gender and sexual orientation equality, intellectual achievement, and socioeconomic success.

Part of the difficulty in understanding the effects of acculturation resides in the many different ways by which well-being has been measured. Rogler, Cortes, and Malgady (1991) observed that most studies use measures of well-being derived from U.S. understandings of psychological disorders and functioning. They suggested therefore the need for developing scales that avoid the "category fallacies" usually associated with such scales. But part of the difficulty has also been the simplistic theories generated by the researchers. As critical thinking and research sophistication improve, more complex theories appear to be evolving. Likewise, research on the effects of acculturation on well-being is limited by a tendency to see acculturation as an external event, something that originates outside and forces adaptation by the Latino population. Rogler, Cortes, and Maldagy (1991) argued that acculturation may also be endogenous, that is, induced by internal, culturally driven perceptions as they interact with external realities. Thus, the mere interaction between a Hispanic client and a U.S.-trained social worker may set up a dynamic that alters the way Hispanic clients understand their own psychological states. Rogler and colleagues call for more research on the role of culture in shaping internal understanding.

The effects of acculturation on Latinos' psychological well-being appear to depend on a wide range of factors. One is national origin, which in turn is related to mode of entry and subsequent reception into U.S. society. Immigrants from Mexico show significantly less stress than do those from Central America (Cervantes, Padilla, and Salgado de Snyder 1990; Salgado de Snyder 1987). The stresses related to legal compared with illegal immigration may therefore be quite different and have different effects. Even among refugees, contextual differences may have varying effects. Gil and Vega (1996) demonstrated that differences in the way Cuban and Nicaraguan refugees were received led to greater acculturation-related conflicts among Nicaraguans than among Cubans.

In addition to national origin, mode of entry, and reception by U.S. society, socioeconomic status and the existence of social support are important variables that cannot be overlooked when assessing the effects of acculturation on Latinos. It is becoming abundantly clear that socioeconomic status is extremely important to mediating the relationship between acculturation conflicts and psychological debilitation (Moyerman and Forman 1992, Rogler et al. 1991). The higher the socioeconomic status is, the more likely social support will be available, and the less likely there will be conflict associated with acculturation.

SOCIAL SERVICE ISSUES AND NEEDS

Changing Family Life Traditions

Any consideration of social service needs and solutions must take into account the traditions and household characteristics of Hispanics in the United States. Hispanics have traditionally been drawn together by a commitment to strong family attachments. Although nuclear households prevail, family life ideals espouse the goal of male-headed, tightly knit, extended, heterosexual units. Latinos wish to create ties that solidify marriage, bind siblings, reach across generations, and incorporate relatives and godparents or fictive relatives. Most Hispanics see this commitment to family life, or "familism," as a source of strength.

There is indeed evidence that Latinos place more emphasis on family life than do non-Hispanics. Delgado and Humm-Delgado (1982) describe it as the primary natural support system found across Latino communities. Although 80 percent of all Hispanic households are families, only 70 percent of non-Hispanic households are families (see table 3.7). The percentage of divorced Hispanics also tends to be lower than that of non-Hispanics (Frisbie, Optiz, and Kelly 1985). Likewise, table 3.7 shows that Hispanic families are generally larger: the mean number of persons in a non-Hispanic family is 3.13, while among Hispanics the figure is 3.80. In addition, Hispanic elderly are less likely to live in a home for the aged and more likely to live in a multigeneration family than are non-Hispanic elderly (Cubillos with Prieto 1987). Furthermore, this probably can be attributed to cultural values rather than to life expectancy or geographic and economic accessibility (Eribes and Bradley-Rawls 1978). Survey evidence also suggests that Hispanics, especially Mexican Americans, are more likely to be integrated into extended kin networks than are Anglos, regardless of generation, and to turn to family rather than friends for emotional support (Keefe, Padilla, and Carlos 1979). Survey data also suggest that Hispanics attribute more importance and have more of their psychological well-being tied up in family relations than do non-Latino whites (Raymond, Rhoads, and Raymond 1980).

Although male-headed, nuclear households with strong extended kin ties are the ideal, it is not always reached or sought. Hispanic families are quite heterogeneous, so cross-group differences in family life are better understood as continuous rather than either/or differences. And although cultural values contribute to differences, external realities and internal contradictions create change and conflict in those values. As a result, in many ways, the modern Hispanic family resembles the modern non-Hispanic family. Accordingly, the percentage of divorced individuals in some Hispanic national-origin groups is as high or higher than among non-Hispanics, and the percentage of female-headed, no-husband-present families is actually higher in all Hispanic national-origin groups than among non-Hispanics. Hispanic elderly are also increasingly being found in nursing homes.[3] With respect to social support, attitudes toward the desirability of turning to family for support is mixed (Keefe et al. 1979), and the availability, actual use, and satisfaction with the support given by family and friends may not be all that different between Latino and Anglo-Americans (Vega and Kolody 1985). Furthermore, conflict in attitudes toward such things as male-female status/role expectations, parental authority, and the rearing of children and in attitudes toward sexual conduct and the acceptance of gay and lesbian relationships is common within and between generations (Becerra 1988, Sanchez-Ayendez 1988, Soriano 1991, Szapocznik and Hernandez 1988).

The harsh external realities confronted by many Hispanic families often act

TABLE 3.7
Household Characteristics by Ethnicity

Characteristic	Hispanic	Mexican	Puerto Rican	Cuban	Central and South American	Other Hispanic	Non-Hispanic White
% Family households[a]	80.7	83.7	74.1	74.6	81.6	72.8	69.3
% Married-couple households	54.8	60.1	38.3	54.2	54.0	45.5	57.8
% Female householders (no husband present)	20.4	17.0	32.2	18.2	22.3	23.7	9.0
% Male householders (no wife present)	5.6	6.7	3.6	2.2	5.3	3.7	2.6

[a] Family households are those with two or more adults related by birth, marriage, or adoption. They may or may not include a nuclear family.

Source: U.S. Bureau of the Census, Hispanic Population from the 1994 Current Population Survey (online: http://www.census.gov/population/www.socdemo/hispanic.html).

as a spur to change. Griswold del Castillo (1984) noted that familism itself and the incorporation of fictive relatives through the institution of *compadrazgo* (godparenting) were responses to the need for economic survival and the reality of a short life expectancy. Similarly, the search for employment amid limited opportunities has made female-headed households and relatively egalitarian male-female relations a common reality of Hispanic families in the United States since the nineteenth century (Graebler, Moore, and Guzman 1970; Griswold del Castillo 1984).

There is also strong evidence that contemporary legal and illegal immigration patterns contribute to changes in household patterns, especially gender relations. Legal Mexican immigrants are likely to reside in neolocal, two-parent or single-parent families, regardless of how long they have been in the United States (Chavez 1985). The household patterns of illegal immigrants can be quite different. Chavez (1989) believes that the continued growth of illegal immigrants from Mexico and Central America represents "an act of defiance" against limited economic opportunities and political marginalization. In a study of some six hundred undocumented aliens in Dallas and San Diego, he demonstrated that they do not live chaotic, disorganized lives. Although the percentages between Mexican and Central American immigrants and between those living in Dallas and San Diego differ, Chavez (1989) found that about half lived in simple family households (couples with and without children and single parents and children); about 20 percent lived in nonfamily households (unrelated friends or sibling coresidence); about 15 percent lived in extended family households (sometimes with unrelated friends); another 15 percent in multiple family households; and around 8 percent lived alone either as a boarder or at work.

In sum, although the family life patterns of Latinos are likely to be different from those of non-Latinos, social workers should not expect these differences to overwhelm the similarities. Changes taking place in Latin America, coupled with the effects of acculturation, are creating strains in Latino families and reshaping them. Social workers will therefore find that Hispanics are struggling with issues of child rearing, care of the elderly, gender, and sexuality in much the same way as non-Hispanics are.

Elderly Hispanics

Hispanic women over age fifty are three times as likely to immigrate to the United States than are older men, often to care for grandchildren (Guendelman 1987). National origin appears related to the age at which most Hispanic elderly immigrated: elderly Puerto Ricans are more likely to have immigrated to the continent in middle adulthood, whereas Cubans tend to have arrived at more advanced ages, and Mexicans usually have been born here or come as children (Angel and Angel 1992). The current socioeconomic status of elderly Hispanics is also related to national origin: elderly Cubans are the most advantaged group in terms of education and income; Puerto Ricans, the least advantaged; and Mexicans, in the middle (Angel and Angel 1992, Krause and Goldenhar 1992). Once in the United States, Hispanic elderly move less frequently than do their non-Hispanic counterparts (Biafora and Longino 1990).

Most research on the Hispanic elderly focuses on their levels of acculturation, social isolation, and support and how these factors interact to affect physical and mental health. In general, elderly Hispanics are more likely to have difficulty adjusting than younger migrants are (Angel and Angel 1992), to have more traditional values regarding kinship, and to be more likely to live in extended family systems than are nonminority elderly (Biafora and Longino 1990). These tendencies are, however, mediated to some extent by their level of acculturation and the presence of supportive ethnic communities in the United States.

A study of 1,339 elderly Hispanic migrants to the United States found no differences in language acculturation between elderly Cubans and Mexican Americans (Krause and Goldenhar 1992). The tendency of Mexicans to need English more than did enclave-residing Cubans was offset by the Mexicans' lower level of education, which was associated with less proficiency in English. Puerto Ricans, though, usually had better English-language skills than Cubans did, despite their more modest educational backgrounds. Thus elderly Hispanics' level of acculturation would appear to depend less on socioeconomic factors than on the characteristics of the communities in which the elderly resided.

Zamanian and colleagues (1992) studied 159 Mexican Americans aged sixty years and older in Fresno, California. They found higher levels of depression among the less acculturated, whereas the bicultural and highly acculturated groups were virtually indistinguishable. Socioeconomic status had no effect on the relationships. They concluded that abandoning Mexican culture in favor of Anglo culture was beneficial to some degree. Similarly, Krause and Goldenhar (1992) found support for the argument that overall, acculturation appears to positively affect elderly well-being through the advantages of being better off economically and less socially isolated.

The ramifications of acculturation may be more complex, however. Wallace, Campbell, and Lew-Ting (1994) argued that acculturated families, like non-Hispanic families, may provide lower levels of informal support to the elderly. Likewise, Weeks and Cuellar (1983) provided evidence that native-born Hispanics are likely to be more similar to non-Hispanic elders in their levels of isolation, suggesting that the effect of acculturation across generations ultimately eroded the extended kinship ties characteristic of more traditional Latino families.

Apart from the process of acculturation itself, the effects of acculturation are also mediated by the level of integration into the community to which the elderly migrate. Angel and Angel (1992) found that Cubans' relatively lower level of assimilation into the dominant culture was not detrimental to their well-being because of the supportive nature of Cuban enclaves. The Cubans reported better health and more life satisfaction than did Mexican Americans. For Hispanics overall, those migrating in late adulthood reported poorer health and satisfaction than did those migrating earlier, likely due to the difficulty of establishing social contacts. Indeed, Zamanian et al. (1992) suggested that the depression they observed in their sample among less-acculturated persons resulted from lack of familiarity and comfort with the new culture, making them less likely to establish social ties and thus more isolated. These somewhat discrepant findings may be reconciled by examining the interaction between acculturation and social isolation or support.

From family members and friends to participation in churches and community events, social networks and activities are important to the emotional and physical health of Hispanic elderly (Angel and Angel 1992). In addition to the normal problems of aging, migrants are more dependent on their children for all kinds of support, such as translation, transportation, and assistance with adjustment to a new culture (Biafora and Longino 1990). Older Hispanic migrants from abroad are less likely to live independently and more likely to live with their children than are those Hispanics moving within the United States. Not surprisingly, therefore, in a study of elderly Latinas in psychotherapy, the most frequent single complaint was being ignored by their children, usually a son, giving rise to feelings of displacement in the family (Gonzalez del Valle and Usher 1982). Besides culture, part of the reason for this dependence on children is economic: the household income of elderly Hispanic immigrants is more likely to be below the poverty level. In this way, economics interacts with traditional kinship values in determining residency patterns.

Weeks and Cuellar (1983) reported that overall, Hispanic elders were the least isolated of a wide variety of ethnic groups studied, including Asians, blacks, and non-Hispanic whites. Recent Hispanic immigrants were more isolated in their homes and neighborhoods than were native-born Hispanics. Foreign-born Hispanics who had lived in the United States for a long time were the least isolated, though the differences between them and the native born were relatively minor. These findings indicate that with time, Hispanic immigrants usually become well integrated into their communities and social networks.

In regard to differences among Hispanic ethnic groups, whereas elderly

Cubans have half as many children as Mexicans and Puerto Ricans do, Angel and Angel (1992) found that these latter two groups, both of which were less economically secure, were more likely to be married or living with their children. Their study also revealed differences in social activities: elderly Mexicans went to church more often than the others; Cubans got together more frequently with friends; and Puerto Ricans were less likely to go to sporting events, movies, or meetings of any kind. Those who migrated later in life showed evidence of attenuated social networks, poorer health, and lower life satisfaction than did those who migrated earlier, likely due to the difficulty of establishing social contacts. They also reported that Cubans seemed to benefit from migration into ethnic enclaves by being able to recreate their social networks more easily.

As a consequence, Krause and Goldenhar (1992) discovered that Cubans were also the least socially isolated. Mexican Americans' greater isolation was due to financial problems and language barriers. In contrast, the greater isolation of Puerto Ricans was not due to either economics or language but, rather, to other factors not included in the study. As predicted by their relative isolation, Puerto Ricans evidenced higher levels of depression than did Cubans. But within the influences of education, income, and acculturation that accounted for higher levels of depression among elderly Mexicans, there appeared to be unexplained beneficial effects of being Mexican.

The tangible effects of social contact are evident in the fact that elderly Hispanics who had more contact with their children were also more aware of social services and used them more often as a result (Biafora and Longino 1990). The most frequently used service in one sample of Hispanic elders was senior centers, particularly the meals provided by the centers (Talamantes, Lawler, and Espino 1995). The authors' case studies led them to recommend that hospices reach out to elderly Hispanics and their caregivers to educate them about services, since this population may be unaware of available assistance. It is also important for service providers to realize that elderly Latino migrants may expect a friendly interest to prevail over a strictly businesslike relationship, feeling a sense of betrayal when caretakers do not maintain a consistent and personal relationship. Such disappointments can interfere with these migrants' future use of services (Gonzalez del Valle and Usher 1982). Those working with elderly Hispanics should also try to provide activities that encourage and help them become more conversant with Anglo culture while incorporating elements of Latino culture (Zamanian et al. 1992).

The impact of these culturally appropriate interventions is limited, however, to the extent that Hispanic elderly persons lack access to social services. Wallace,

Campbell, and Lew-Ting (1994) determined that in Latino families, and among Latino elderly in particular, the lack of insurance was more often experienced as a family financial problem during a serious illness than it was among non-Latino whites. They attributed this to the Latinos' concentration in occupations with few benefits and their residential concentration in states with more stringent Medicaid policies, such as Florida and Texas. Wallace et al.'s study of formal in-home services showed that Latinos faced disproportionate structural barriers to care, owing to lower income, less education, and less proficiency in English, coupled with high levels of disability, making this social problem especially serious.

Gender Relations and Immigration

Relationships between men and women are being shaped and reshaped by immigration and acculturation processes. Historically, male and female roles have been strictly divided, with an emphasis on responsible male authority and female devotion to home, children, and husband. These common stereotypes of *macho* men and domesticated women are today, however, an increasingly less accurate depiction of male-female relations in Latin America. Women of the lower classes have always been apt to work outside the home. As Mexico and other Latin American countries industrialize, however, educated women as well are moving into the workforce. This transition is helping produce more egalitarian gender ideals and is changing the nature of family life. The experience of moving to another country and the process of adaptation to it are also bringing important changes in the relative status of men and women in both the family and the larger society.

There has been relatively little research on the contemporary Latino family in the United States and especially on the changes in family life patterns resulting from immigration. Hondagneu-Sotelo (1994) studied a nonrandom sample of forty-four men and women in a Mexican migrant *barrio* in California, referred to by the pseudonym of "Oakview." Although the study was exploratory, it did help explain this important issue. Much of the following discussion is based on her results, but research on other Latino immigrant populations in other locales of the United States yielded similar findings.

Since the economic crises of the 1980s in Mexico, men and women of all socioeconomic strata have migrated. This means that more urban and educated women, influenced by feminist movements and used to being relatively independent of men, form a larger proportion of the migrant pool than in earlier decades (Hondagneu-Sotelo 1994). For them, migration to the United States has brought little change in their views of themselves or their relations with men. Couples and families of the middle and upper classes thus migrate together more frequently because they have the economic resources to do so and because women are more involved in the decision to migrate.

For many other women and men, however, gender plays a larger role in shaping the migration experience at every stage of the process. For example, the Bracero program exclusively recruited men, who often left their wives behind. Married men unaccompanied by their families still represent the largest group of male migrants, leaving them vulnerable to loneliness, depression, and ambivalence about separating their work life from their family life (Guendelman and Perez-Itriago 1987). Most wives also want to go with their husbands (Hondagneu-Sotelo 1994), and married women seeking reunification with their husbands continue to form a substantial portion of migrants (Wilson 1995). When unable to accompany their husbands, women left on their own in Mexico ultimately gained greater autonomy and independence. This process of gaining social power and resources often culminated in women's autonomous decisions to migrate, bringing their children along with them, sometimes even surprising their husbands upon their arrival.

Because of the risk and expense involved, not to mention the prospect of regular paychecks, migration for men often means an elevation of their own status in the eyes of their home communities where opportunities have disappeared and in their own self-estimation (Guendelman and Perez-Itriago 1987). Meanwhile, without women around to perform the traditional domestic chores in the United States, migrant men are forced to take care of these tasks themselves. Often by the time their wives and children arrive, family roles have noticeably changed.

The fact that women usually have to work for pay in the United States in order to make ends meet helps solidify their new status and roles in the family as well as their spatial mobility and autonomy outside the home (Guendelman 1987, Hondagneu-Sotelo 1994). In some cases, the burdens tilt disproportionately onto the shoulders of women, who may overloaded by the responsibility of performing too many roles even as their status rises (Vargas-Willis and Cervantes 1987). In addition, decision making can be a burden on the woman who is the less powerful partner; it does not always signify greater power (Chavira-Prado 1992). Furthermore, the discrepancy in appropriate gender behavior between the United States and the country of origin is usually greater for women than for men, causing resentment in men (Espín 1987b) and stress in women (Melville 1978). In general, even though their relationships still fall short of complete equality, women gain in migration through their greater share of power and autonomy relative to that of the men in their lives. In some instances, men continue to perform many domestic chores even after their wives arrive (Chavira-Prado 1992, Guendelman and Perez-Itriago 1987, Hondagneu-Sotelo 1994, Pessar 1984).

The undocumented status of some immigrant men also compounds this leveling effect. Men who are in the United States illegally find their spatial mobility more restricted, not only because of the longer shifts that undocumented men often must work (Guendelman and Perez-Itriago 1987), but also because of possible apprehension by the INS authorities, limited mobility and autonomy at work, and little disposable income (Hondagneu-Sotelo 1994). Even women of the "Oakview" *barrio* who had been secluded in their homes in Mexico and initially in the United States quickly became more independent and mobile by having to work outside the home; by having contact with their employers, public services, and other organizations; and by developing more informal social contacts outside the home. Thus, as a result of immigration, women's economic contributions become more crucial to the household.

Women who remain unemployed often feel even more dependent on their partners in the United States than they did in Mexico, for money, transportation, and other necessities for carrying out domestic responsibilities. Although staying at home is a symbol of middle-class respectability for some women (Pessar, 1994), unemployment is often not by choice: for example, Chavira-Prado (1992) presented evidence from a migrant labor camp in Illinois that women were barred from agricultural employment except when their reserve labor was needed. Cut off from social supports, these women were more vulnerable to relationship difficulties, abuse, loneliness, and low self-esteem (Chavira-Prado 1992, Melville 1978, Wilson 1995). Yet male partners were not always pleased by the woman's unemployment: the greater necessity in the United States of helping women perform domestic tasks on top of a highly routine work life sometimes caused men to feel overburdened as well (Guendelman and Perez-Itriago 1987).

Single or married women who migrate alone also constitute an increasing proportion of migrants (Wilson 1995). They migrate partly in response to an increase in low-wage domestic work and garment and electronics assembly jobs that recruit women. Women's solo migration is not always the result of being "sent" by their families. They may remit some money to their families initially, but their decision to migrate is not generally in response to family economic need (Hondagneu-Sotelo 1994), nor is it often undertaken with the assistance of male family members (Repak 1994). On the contrary, some leave to escape their families or simply to become more independent. Because young men often live in a peer culture of migration as a male rite of passage, a sign of independence against a father's authority, their independent actions are seen as legitimate. But young women must negotiate their way out of patriarchal family restrictions or sometimes violent or abusive relationships (Arguelles and Rivero 1993, Espín 1987b, Repak 1994). They do so by using the increasingly strong single-women's migration networks. The freedom from family control they gain allows them to acculturate more quickly, and in fact, rapid acculturation may be necessary for their survival, but the new behaviors required of them can also be a source of inner conflict and external criticism of their nontraditional activities (Espín 1987b).

Women's networks are also crucial to obtaining employment in the United States. New immigrants most frequently take on "job work": numerous separately negotiated employment contracts, often as domestic workers (Hondagneu-Sotelo 1994). They get their start in locating employment through other women. Working conditions are often exploitative because of their private nature, but there is usually upward mobility within the occupation, which can also serve as a foothold while pursuing more desirable employment. Newly arrived women are particularly vulnerable to exploitation, not only by employers, but also by the other women in their networks. Inexperienced domestic workers are usually faced with two options: live-in domestic work, at extremely poor wages, or a subcontract of their services through other women they know, often poorly remunerated as well. Subcontracting in this way, however, is more likely to lead to other, better opportunities and gives women a chance to learn to use the tools of the trade. Learning to drive and learning English also seem to be two key factors in achieving higher wages, by allowing women to take on more jobs and by enhancing communication with employers (Hondagneu-Sotelo 1994). Salgado de Snyder (1987) also found that a lack of fluency in English was strongly correlated with depression in Mexican immigrant women.

Women's kin and social networks are a significant resource in other aspects of settlement (Hondagneu-Sotelo 1994). These relationships contribute to permanent settlement through the creation of community social ties, stable employment, and connections to public and private forms of assistance. Latinas are often involved alongside the men in advocacy organizations aimed at improving their situations by obtaining community services, gaining literacy and skills, and seeking legal status. Women often have broader, denser, and more resilient networks from which to draw support and mobilize participants in activism. If men are the pioneers, women are the community builders through these connections. Women and families aid in the process of becoming more self-reliant. Women's social ties bind many of these organizations internally and to one another. Thus women's efforts at establishing permanent settlement also serve to elevate their own status.

Hondagneu-Sotelo (1994) also pointed out that these changes are neither the result of Anglo "modernizing" influences nor the blossoming of a feminist self-consciousness. Rather, they arise out of the changing bases of male and female structural power brought about by the experience of migration itself. Migration elevates the status of women in relation to men, whereas men's status drops from what they enjoyed in Mexico, both in the family and in the wider U.S. society (Espín 1987b). These changes explain in part why the men in the "Oakview" *barrio* study stated more often than the women did that they wished to return to Mexico, even though both men and women tended to settle in the United States. At the same time, we have seen how these rearrangements in roles and status can create stress for both men and women. The increasing prevalence of women's networks (in part due to occupational gender segregation), the continuing global economic changes, and the shift in gender relations in both the United States and Mexico all point to future increases in women's migration.

Lesbian and Gay Issues

Although Latino cultures have traditionally enforced heterosexual norms, many Latinos have gay or lesbian orientations. Gay and lesbian Latinos migrate to the United States for much the same reasons as others—to reunite with family members and to look for better economic opportunities. Not insignificantly, however, their motives are also bound up in issues of sexual identity. Many seek to avoid persecution in their home countries or simply to be able to have a more open gay life (Arguelles and Rivero 1993, Constable 1997, Tori 1989, Zamora-Hernández and Patterson 1996). For instance, thousands of mostly male homosexuals may have migrated in the Mariel boat exodus from Cuba to escape persecution (Arguelles and Rich 1989, Suarez 1990).

Although homosexuality is legal in most Latin American countries, the police sometimes use public morality laws to harass homosexuals, particularly those of the lower classes and those who are more flamboyant (Arboleda 1987, Tielman and Hammelburg 1993). As a result, the persecution and murder of known homosexuals are not uncommon (Constable 1997, Mott 1990, Murray and Taylor 1990, Tori 1989). Lesbians and gays who face persecution based on their homosexuality in their home countries can in some cases avail themselves of asylum provisions in the United States, although proving a case can be difficult if judges are not sympathetic to gay rights. Sexual orientation persecution has been a factor in granting asylum and suspension of deportation for immigrants from Nicaragua, Cuba, and Venezuela (Lesbian and Gay Immigration Rights Task Force 1996b, c; 1997).

Despite persecution, some factors actually make homosexual activity less risky in Latin America than in the United States: a legal tradition of indifference that minimizes interference in private lives (Arguelles and Rich 1989, Murray and Taylor 1990, Taylor 1986) and a system of gender and sexual ideology that offers opportunities for homosexual activity with relatively little threat to heterosexual identity, at least for men (Arboleda 1987, Lancaster 1988; Murray 1987, 1990). Likewise, Hispanic women are unlikely to be overtly rejected by their families for their lesbianism; rather, family members may attribute a woman's lack of interest in men and marriage to being highly dedicated to her work or to her family of origin (Espín 1987a, Hidalgo and Christensen 1976/77).

Once in the United States, gay and lesbian immigrants are likely to live initially in social networks or enclaves composed primarily of other Latinos. Within these networks, the norms are not much different from those of the communities they left behind. The more immersed a migrant becomes in urban gay and lesbian culture, however, the greater the clash will be between Latino and U.S. understandings of homosexual identity and practice. Latino conceptions of homosexuality, as opposed to those of U.S. gays, tend to be more fluid. A small literature has developed to describe Latino male sexual orientation, which is conceived more in terms of the role (active or passive) one plays in intercourse rather than the gender (same or opposite) one desires (Carrier 1976, Lancaster 1988, Magaña and Carrier 1991).

Comparatively little is known about the sexual orientation and behavior of Latinas. Close friendships between women (*amigas íntimas*), including being physically affectionate and even sleeping at each other's homes, may be viewed with little suspicion in Latino cultures compared with the dominant culture (Hidalgo and Christensen 1976/77). This feature of Latina friendships and the fact that being "out" is somewhat an economic privilege can combine to make Latina lesbians less visible than gay men. Interviews with lesbian émigrés from Cuba also reveal that the difficulty of being out of the closet in the Cuban enclave of Miami is further compounded for women by *machismo*: rejecting men for another woman is characterized as "the lowest of the low" (Rich and Arguelles 1985). This lack of acceptance of overt lesbianism was also demonstrated in a study of Puerto Rican lesbians in the United States and the communities they lived in: 80 percent of the local men indicated a desire to prove that they could change a lesbian's orientation to heterosexuality (Hidalgo and Christensen 1976/77).

For both gay men and lesbian women, migration to a Latino enclave in the United States may be only the first phase of the journey to a more open life. Rich and Arguelles (1985) argued, for example, that the "freedom" from persecution that the Marielito Cuban gays were expecting had instead a bitter taste, when, in the wake of antigay crusades sweeping Florida at the time, they encountered the strong antigay sentiment of the Cuban communities where they had hoped to find moral support. To the extent that lesbians and gays migrate in order to escape cultural and patriarchal constraints in the old country, these men and women will be more likely to travel farther afield than the Latino communities where the majority of immigrants settle.

This second phase of lesbian and gay migration comes at the cost of separation from family and culture, however. The conflict between a gay or lesbian identity, on the one hand, and a Latino or Latina identity, on the other, thus is manifested itself in feelings of not belonging fully in either community for both Latina lesbians (Espín 1987a, Hidalgo and Christensen 1976–77, Ramos 1987) and Latino gay men (Baez 1996, Zamora-Hernández and Patterson 1996).

Studies of violence also suggest that the United States is less than liberating for lesbian and gay Hispanics. Hispanic men and women face higher rates of harassment and victimization, even in predominantly gay and lesbian neighborhoods, than do white gays and lesbians (Comstock 1989). Forty percent of the youths coming to the New York City–based Hetrick Martin Institute for gay and lesbian youths, an agency whose clientele is predominantly Latino, reported suffering violent physical attacks (Hunter 1992). Almost half the assaults were gay related, and more than half occurred within their own families. One-third to one-half the young men and women who had been assaulted had thought about or attempted suicide. Often homeless and involved in prostitution or drugs, the subjects of this study were probably not typical of the majority of Latino gay and lesbian youth; nevertheless, it would be a mistake to assume that the difficulties these youths faced in establishing a positive gay or lesbian identity were not directly linked to their homelessness or any of the other problems for which they sought services.

Latino gays and lesbians immigrate not only to escape persecution or to live a more open life but also for love. But until gay and lesbian relationships are placed on an equal footing with heterosexual marriage, binational lesbian and gay couples face substantial emotional, financial, and legal obstacles and hardships: they are not granted spousal immigration rights. In some instances, Nicaraguan and Mexican immigrant partners have been allowed to remain in the United States based on the hardship that separation would cause for the U.S. citizen or permanent resident partner, but these cases are relatively rare and do not constitute standard policy; rather, each case is decided on its own merits (Constable 1997, Lesbian and Gay Immigration Rights Task Force 1996d, 1997).

Those couples who try to stay together in the United States must find a way to maintain legal residency or tourist status for the foreign partner or lapse into undocumented status (Constable 1997). This challenge often requires enormous cash outlays in the form of multiple entries and exits in order not to overstay one's tourist visa or to visit in each other's countries, or perpetual enrollment in school to maintain a student visa (Anjani Millet, Seattle chapter coordinator of the Lesbian and Gay Immigration Rights Task Force, personal communication, 1997). Latino immigrants, who tend to be poorer, are often unable to afford these options and are thus more likely to give up the relationship or to become undocumented in order to remain with a partner. Furthermore, when immigrants become undocumented or cannot afford repeated travel expenses, they sometimes must choose between their Latino background and family roots in the country of origin and their relationship in the United States.

Perhaps the most debilitating disadvantage of binational same-sex couples is that the secrecy they must maintain for fear of detection poses a crucial mobilization problem for social change activism. This predicament makes it essential for social workers with legal residency and a voice to advocate for couples for whom speaking out could mean losing their most cherished relationships through deportation of the foreign partner.

HEALTH NEEDS AND ISSUES

Hispanic Health Across the Life Cycle

The connection between Latino ethnicity and AIDS appears comparatively well researched when we consider that studies of the other health needs of Hispanics are quite limited. In 1992, the Government Accounting Office reported that "the health status of Hispanics, especially Hispanic subgroups is imprecisely known and thus far been insufficiently analyzed." The description of health needs presented here derives from this report (Delgado 1995). The knowledge we do have suggests some noticeable strengths as well as difficulties and also important and interdependent class and national-origin group differences of which health and mental health providers should be aware. In general, Puerto Rican and Mexican Americans show greater health needs and experience greater access problems than do Cuban and other relatively better off Latinos.

Latina mothers are far less likely to have late or no prenatal care compared with non-Hispanic white mothers. Nevertheless, their rates of infant mortality and low birth weight compare favorably with those of whites, with the exception of Puerto Ricans, who have a high infant mortality rate (9.0 versus 7.1 per 1000 births) and a high level of low-weight births (9.4 percent versus 5.7 percent). Immigrant women have even lower infant mortality rates and fewer low-weight births, and Puerto Rican women born on the island have lower rates than do those born on the continent. Hispanic mothers are also less likely to use alcohol or abuse illicit drugs than white mothers are. Furthermore, they report eating more fresh fruits and vegetables than their white counterparts do.

Despite these strengths, Hispanic children and adolescents are at risk of health-related problems. Hispanic children have the highest rate of school absences due to health reasons. A minority (43 percent) have received their immunization series by age two. A number of chronic illnesses are high among Hispanic children: asthma, bronchitis, and elevated blood-lead levels. Asthma is a particular problem for Puerto Ricans, with twice the rates of other Hispanic children. Hispanic children also report less exercise and more days restricted to bed than white children do.

Hispanic adolescents are the least likely to use family-planning services, and sexually active Hispanic males are more likely to report ineffective or no contraceptive use than their non-Hispanic white peers are. Hispanic adolescents are as likely as their non-Hispanic white peers are to use alcohol and are more likely to have used illicit drugs such as marijuana and cocaine/crack. Acculturation appears to be related to this pattern in that immigrant adolescents are less likely to report using alcohol and drugs than are Latino adolescents born in the United States. Studies indicate that although Hispanics are less likely than non-Hispanic whites to smoke, it is largely due to the lower rates among Hispanic women than among Hispanic men. Unfortunately, there is evidence that smoking is increasing among Hispanic women.

Diabetes rates are particularly high among Puerto Rican and Mexican American adults, though the rates for Cuban American adults are moderately higher than the rates reported for non-Latino adults. Although genetics are implicated in these findings, high-fat diets and low rates of exercise are also associated with the disease. Adult Hispanic men report higher levels of serum cholesterol, and both Hispanic men and women are more likely to be overweight than non-Hispanic whites.

Patterns of Sexual Behavior, Substance Use, and AIDS

The disturbing level of HIV infection among all Latinos, regardless of sexual orientation, warrants special concern: by 1990, Latinos and African-Americans accounted for 70 percent of all the AIDS cases among heterosexual adults and 75 percent of infant cases in the United States (Lesnick and Pace 1990). In 1989, the number of AIDS cases among Latinos was three times that of non-Latino whites, and the rate of HIV infection for the Latino proportion of the population was double that of the non-Latino population (Castro and Manoff 1988, Marin 1989).

Most researchers have found higher rates of bisexuality among Latino men, thereby spreading HIV through unprotected sex with both men and women and accounting in part for these high figures (Amaro 1991, Chu et al. 1992, Diaz et al. 1993, Singer et al. 1990), although Ryan, Longres, and Roffman (1996) found no differences in the prevalence of bisexuality among non-Hispanic whites, blacks, and Latinos. Homosexually transmitted AIDS is more common among Cubans than among "other" Latin Americans and Puerto Ricans and least common in Mexicans (Singer et al. 1990). One study found that Latino men who had sexual contact with other men were more likely than either black or non-Latino white men, with similar levels of same-sex involvement, to identify as heterosexual (Doll et al. 1992). This phenomenon suggests either cultural variations in the understanding of sexual identity or a significant conflict between conduct and identity for some Latinos. In any case, non-gay-identified men who have sex with men are likely to disregard the prevention messages targeted at the gay community and the peer support of safer sex practices, leaving them at higher risk for HIV infection (Singer et al. 1990). Singer et al. (1990) also noted that young Latino male prostitutes, who are a disproportionate percentage of all male prostitutes and also likely to be using drugs, are a population at extremely high risk for contracting HIV.

In contrast, Latina women were more likely than Latino men to contract HIV through intravenous drug (IV) use (Singer et al. 1990). Higher rates of IV-drug use among Latinos accounted for much of the difference in HIV infection rates between Latina and non-Hispanic white women and children. Women's involvement with IV-drug users or homosexually active men put them at serious risk of contracting HIV because of gender norms making it difficult for Latina woman to insist on condom usage or to refuse sexual advances (Singer et al. 1990).

Risk factors and modes of HIV transmission showed substantial geographic variations, in terms of both the country of origin and the place of residence in the United States of those most affected. Homosexual behavior accounted for almost 50 percent of the AIDS cases among Latino males born in the United States and the Dominican Republic, as well as 65 percent of cases reported among males born in Cuba, Mexico, and Central and South America (Castro and Manoff 1988, Diaz et al. 1993, Marin 1989, Singer et al. 1990). Homosexual transmission, as opposed to transmission through needle sharing, tends to be a western and southern U.S. phenomenon among Latinos, more prevalent in Florida, Texas, and California. Latinos in the northeastern United States, where more Puerto Ricans reside, usually were infected more often through needle sharing, particularly for drug use but also for therapeutic reasons (Lafferty, Foulk, and Ryan 1990; Marin 1989). When comparing Latino groups, Latinos born in Puerto Rico had the highest incidence of AIDS and were the group most commonly contracting HIV through needle sharing (Singer et al., 1990). Next in prevalence were Cuban-born Latinos, most of whom contracted HIV through homosexual contact, and last were Mexican-born Latinos, whose disease patterns mirrored those of non-Latino non-Hispanic whites.

In comparison with the general population, Latinos more often held mistaken notions about how HIV was transmitted, and these misconceptions were more prevalent among the less acculturated (Singer et al. 1990). A study of northeastern and Puerto Rican Hispanics provided evidence of substantial misconceptions about HIV transmission, even among gay men, who were disproportionately affected by the virus, and among infected persons capable of transmitting HIV (Amaro 1991). The biggest gaps in knowledge were among younger adolescents, those who spoke Spanish, men, and the less educated. Some of the misconceptions included believing that AIDS could be cured or that an infected person could be identified by simply looking at him or her. Men were more likely than women to engage in high-risk drug use and sexual behaviors. Less-educated gay men and intravenous drug users were more likely to engage in unprotected sex with women. More than one-quarter of Hispanic men identifying as gay in the study reported having unprotected sex with a woman in the past year, again showing evidence that bisexual behavior was fairly common, especially among less-educated men.

Some differences in the experience of living with HIV and AIDS are unique to Hispanics. Latinos with AIDS tend to live a shorter length of time than do whites with AIDS, partly because of inadequate access to health care, poor nutrition, and more stressful lives (Singer et al. 1990). Some Latinos believe that contracting HIV is a just punishment for their homosexual activity, a belief that makes them more reluctant to use conventional medical treatments (Baez 1996). HIV-positive Latino gay men also experienced higher levels of stress and anger related to their homosexuality than did non-Latino whites (Ceballos-Capitaine et al. 1990).

HIV-infected Hispanic men were very careful about disclosing their HIV status, and less acculturated Hispanic men were less likely than non-Hispanic white men to tell family, friends, and lovers (Marks et al. 1992, Mason et al. 1995;

see Ryan et al. 1996 for contradictory evidence). Family members who were close and aware of gay Hispanics' sexual orientation were more likely to be told. Latinos were more likely than whites to cite the reason for nondisclosure as protecting others (e.g., not worrying a loved one about the implications of HIV disease), perhaps because of cultural values of familism and *simpatía*, as a way to camouflage their fears of rejection, or to prevent the addition of yet one more stigmatized status on top of being poorer or undocumented (Mason et al. 1995).

By utilizing preexisting social networks and supports, members of Latino families have been effectively mobilized to support Latino gay men with HIV (Kaminsky et al. 1990). This kind of social support acts as a safety net with positive effects on overall health and the immune system of HIV-infected Latino gay men, who are more likely than non-Latino white HIV-positive men to report being hassled because of their gayness (Siegel and Epstein 1996). These findings show that Latino families have the potential to be more supportive of their homosexual members than is often perceived. The same may be true for Latino (mostly Puerto Rican) IV-drug users, who are less likely than other ethnic groups to be rejected by their families (Singer et al. 1990). Those who work with Latino populations affected by HIV and AIDS, regardless of sexual or drug use practices, may therefore find untapped strengths and resources unique to Latino family support systems in providing treatment services.

The Responses of Latino Immigrants

In attempting to serve the needs of the Latino population, social workers can be more effective by getting acquainted with the ways in which Latino immigrants themselves have responded to their social welfare needs in U.S. society. Latinos have organized grassroots service organizations, self-help groups, and a host of other resources to help ensure the well-being of their constituencies (Campos 1995, Curiel 1995). Many of these can be used by social workers to provide services to Latinos.

Early in the twentieth century, for instance, Mexican Americans established mutual aid and voluntary associations that provided funeral and insurance benefits, low-interest loans, and other forms of economic assistance (Curiel 1995). These associations also served a social function, as an arena for discussing community concerns and as a base of operation for community development projects. After World War II, returning Mexican American veterans established the American GI Forum in the hope of ensuring for themselves the same economic and political opportunities available to Anglo veterans (Curiel 1995). In that same period, community service organizations were organized to mobilize

Mexican Americans, inform them of political issues, and encourage them to exercise their right to vote (Curiel 1995). More recently, a number of Mexican American national organizations have been established. The Southwest Council of La Raza, or La Raza, began as a small coalition of interest groups funded by the Ford Foundation. When the funds ran out in 1970, they moved to Washington, D.C., where they continue to operate as a national coordinating advocacy agency for more than 150 community-based affiliates in thirty-seven states, Puerto Rico, and the District of Columbia (Curiel 1995). La Raza supports research, policy analysis, technical assistance, and capacity-building training for community groups. In 1973, the Coalition of Spanish-Speaking Mental Health Organizations was incorporated in the District of Columbia (Curiel, 1995). This organization advocates on behalf of the physical and mental health needs of Cubans, Mexicans, Puerto Ricans, and other Latinos. It supplies research and technical support for community-based agencies in the development of model mental health programs.

In addition to formal service organizations, Latino *barrios*, or neighborhoods, are rich in natural support networks, many of which are open to social workers seeking resources for clients. Delgado and Humm-Delgado (1982) identified three kinds of support systems in addition to the extended family networks already described. All these systems provide Spanish-language services and are accessible to community members. They provide emotional support, friendship and companionship, and role models for immigrants and their children, and they all help sustain Latino customs and traditions.

Merchants and social clubs can be found in most Latino *barrios* or neighborhoods (Delgado and Humm-Delgado 1982). Latino-owned grocery, beauty, and other businesses fulfill both formal and informal roles. They meet the commercial needs of Latinos while also serving as meeting places where information and referrals may be exchanged. Certain businesses, such as *botanicas, bodegas, or mercados*, specialize in traditional herbs and native food products that are often hard to find in the United States. Social clubs, especially in Puerto Rican neighborhoods, provide recreation and leisure-time activities.

Religious organizations are extremely important to the Latino community and often provide services in time of crisis (Delgado and Humm-Delgado 1982). Although Latinos are readily identified with the Catholic Church, alternative churches—Pentecostal, Seventh Day Adventist, and Jehovah's Witness—are increasingly popular.

A long tradition of folk medicine has given rise to many kinds of folk healers that serve as alternative sources of medical and mental health services (Delgado and Humm-Delgado 1982). Any one of five kinds of folk healers are visible in

Hispanic *barrios*: *curanderos*, *espiritistas*, herbalists, *santeros*, and *santiguadores*. Each of these serves a particular culturally defined function. *Espiritistas* and *santeros* focus primarily on emotional and interpersonal problems. Spiritism (*espiritismo*) is the belief that good and bad spirits permeate the world and influence human behavior. *Espiritistas* try to manipulate these spirits to both cause and prevent illness. *Santerismo* combines elements of African and Roman Catholic beliefs and rituals in an effort to diagnose and cure illness. Herbalists and *santiguadores* concentrate mainly on physical ailments. Herbalists use "naturalistic" remedies, usually plants, to cure illnesses. *Santiguadores* specialize in treating chronic and intestinal diseases. The *curandero*, visible largely in Mexican American neighborhoods, maintains a balance between the physical and mental spheres. *Curanderos* reinforce Roman Catholicism and Mexican family and cultural traditions, for illness and bad fortune are considered the result of weakening ties with church, family, and culturally determined lifestyles. *Curanderos* who do not see themselves in conflict with the church because they use folk methods to return individuals to harmony are especially popular in Mexican American communities.

Barriers to Service and the Role of the Social Worker

It is clear that Latinos have a multitude of social service needs, some of which are exacerbated by the acculturation processes. What is less clear is whether needy Latinos voluntarily seek services. A number of cultural and noncultural barriers are associated with service use. Culturally, the ways in which Latinos define their needs and seek and accept help determine their use of formal social and health services. Since native-born Latinos tend to use voluntary services at higher rates than do immigrants, acculturation appears to mitigate the effects of many of these cultural barriers (Hough et al. 1987; Wells et al. 1987). Other barriers are imposed by social service systems themselves and include physical, economic, and language inaccessibility as well as inaccessibility brought on by the behaviors of agency personnel that can generate misunderstanding, prejudice, and discrimination. The emergence of ethnic sensitivity has helped increase the likelihood that Latinos will voluntarily use social services. Services that are accessible, well advertised, and perceived to be credible will be used. Since language accessibility is a central determinant of voluntary service use, the availability of Spanish-speaking service providers is crucial (Delgado et al. 1995). O'Sullivan and Lasso (1992), for instance, found that when community mental health services were provided by ethnic agencies or by therapists of the same ethnic background, Latinos were more likely to use the service.

The true test of a service is its effectiveness. In this regard, culturally competent services must be judged on outcomes besides simply their ability to attract and maintain clients. Social work researchers continue to doubt that human and social services help individuals and families, let alone whole populations of people (Lindsey and Kirk 1992), and they still fear that using human and social services will stigmatize and control those who use them. When personal, interpersonal, family, and community problems have been significantly improved, the social services will have helped Latinos. To date, there have been very few studies on the effectiveness of services to minorities, including Hispanics. Videka-Sherman (1985) observed that most effectiveness studies have not controlled for client ethnic background. Likewise, save for consumer satisfaction (Gomez et al. 1985), we have no test of whether culturally sensitive services fare any better than culturally insensitive services at resolving the individual and social problems experienced by Latinos.

Beyond language, issues of accessibility, and respect for differences, definitions of cultural competence become vague. In a recent statement, the Committee on Latino Affairs (n.d.) defined cultural competence as "a set of congruent behaviors, attitudes, and policies that come together in a system, or among professionals and enable that system, agency or those professionals to work effectively in a cross-cultural situation." But this definition does not explain what the congruent behaviors, attitudes, and policies are nor does it list the criteria for measuring effectiveness. Instead, the committee encourages the development of standards and models that define cultural competence.

With this encouragement in mind, we close by identifying three tasks that any model of culturally competent practice should include. These tasks cannot easily be carried out by generalists and will therefore require coordination among specialized social workers working at different levels of intervention. The tasks nevertheless form a single entity because each derives from the realization that ethnic conflict—conflict between Latino and non-Latino Americans over scarce resources and cultural prominence—is fundamental to the continued subordination of Latinos in U.S. society. The role of all social workers, then, is to help ameliorate ethnic conflict and develop a unified multicultural society.

1. Social workers must work to change the circumstances that hinder the advancement of Latinos. We must assume the task of ensuring that Latinos living in the United States receive the opportunities necessary to achieve social and economic parity with non-Latinos. This means assuming political roles, including those of legislator, policy advocate, program developer, program administrator, community organizer, developer, and activist. The function of such roles

is to break down barriers to education and employment, enforce civil rights leg-islation, and develop equitable social welfare and agency policies for those re-quiring services. For the social workers in these roles, it also means enlisting the full participation of Latinos by connecting with and building from the informal and formal resources found in Latino communities.

2. Social workers must work to improve intergroup relations. Only through increased contact and communication will Latinos and non-Latinos be able to overcome the stereotypes and prejudices that separate them. Only when Latinos and non-Latinos learn to work and live together, in the same neighborhoods and in the same households, can the friendships necessary for overcoming eth-nic conflict be created. Relatively few social workers and even fewer social ser-vice agencies are dedicated to the intergroup practice suggested here. This is a promising area that has been overlooked in discussions of cultural competence.

Intergroup contact alone is not sufficient and indeed can be polarizing: working at the intergroup level requires reaching out to Latinos and non-Lati-nos and making opportunities available for interaction and the development of common interests. Such work can focus on political, social, economic, or reli-gious needs; and can take place in neighborhoods, schools, and universities, in parish halls and churches, and in service systems and institutions; anyplace where Latinos and non-Latinos inhabit the same or adjoining spaces. Working in this arena requires group facilitation skills as well as negotiation and media-tion skills.

3. Social workers must work to reduce the physical and emotional stress as-sociated with acculturation. This is the principal role of the direct-service social worker: to be sensitive to the way that problems presented by Latino individuals and families may be exacerbated by difficulties associated with integration into U.S. life. Coming to the United States is only the beginning of the journey to the enhanced life chances that are possible in the "land of opportunity," a journey that presents a multitude of stresses for immigrants. Acculturation, as suggest-ed in this chapter, does not stop with the first generation. Second- and even third-generation Latinos are often have acculturation-related problems, rang-ing from issues of ethnic identity and phenotype to issues concerning family and intergeneration relations.

Intervening in acculturation-related issues requires enormous sensitivity. Latino clients are often caught between the familiar and the new, struggling to find the right fit between them. Social workers must allow Latinos to reach their own solutions. They can act neither as agents of cultural conformity—keeping Latinos hooked into the past—nor as agents of cultural imperialism—promot-ing non-Latino ways. In supporting Latinos, social workers must always show respect for past traditions even as individuals and families participate in the creation of new ones that touch not only Latinos but also the larger society.

NOTES

1. We use the terms *Hispanic* and *Latino* interchangeably.

2. Latinos who consider themselves to be "American" may be sensitive about the use of the term; so for this reason, we generally attempt to avoid the common usage of "American" to refer exclusively to persons from the United States.

3. This information derives from a talk given by F. Torres-Gil, entitled "Demographics, Diversity, and Politics: Challenges to Social Policy and Aging." Northwest Geriatric Education Center, Seattle, January 24, 1992.

REFERENCES

Amaro, H. (1991). AIDS/HIV among Hispanics in the northeast and Puerto Rico: Report of findings and recommendations. *Migration World Magazine* 19 (4): 23–29.

Angel, J. L., and Angel, R. J. (1992). Age at migration, social connections, and well-being among elderly Hispanics. *Journal of Aging and Health* 4: 480–499.

Arboleda, M. (1987). Social attitudes and sexual variance in Lima. In S. O. Murray (ed.), *Male Homosexuality in Central and South America*. New York: Gay Academic Union.

Arguelles, L., and Rich, B. R. (1989). Homosexuality, homophobia, and revolution: Notes toward an understanding of the Cuban lesbian and gay male experience. In M. B. Duberman, M. Vicinus, and G. Chauncey (eds.), *Hidden from History: Reclaiming the Gay and Lesbian Past*. New York: Meridian Books.

Arguelles, L., and Rivero, A. M. (1993). Gender/sexual orientation violence and transnational migration: Conversations with some Latinas we think we know. *Urban Anthropology* 22: 259–275.

Baez, E. J. (1996). Spirituality and the gay Latino client. *Journal of Gay and Lesbian Social Services* 4 (2): 69–81.

Bean, D. D., Edmonston, B., and Passel, J. S. (eds.). (1990). *Undocumented Migration to the United States: IRCA and the Experience of the 1980s*. Washington, DC: Urban Institute.

Bean, F. D., Van Hook, J. V., and Glick. J. (1994/95). Mode of entry, type of public assistance and patterns of welfare recipiency among U.S. immigrants and natives. Paper no. 94-95-17. Austin: University of Texas, Population Research Center.

Becerra, R. (1988). The Mexican American family. In C. H. Mindel, R. W. Habenstein, and R. Wright Jr. (eds.), *Ethnic Families in America*. 3rd ed. New York: Elsevier.

Betances, S. (1972). The prejudice of having no prejudice in Puerto Rico, part I. *The Rican* 2: 41–54.

Betances, S. (1973). The prejudice of having no prejudice in Puerto Rico, part. II. *The Rican* 3: 22–37.

Biafora, F. A., and Longino, C. F. (1990). Elderly Hispanic migration in the United States. *Journal of Gerontology* 45: S212–S219.

Borjas, G. J. (1994). The economics of immigration. *Journal of Economic Literature* 22 (December): 1667–1717.

Borjas, G. J. (1996), The new economics of immigration. *Atlantic Monthly* 278 (3): 72–80.

Caetano, R. (1987). Acculturation and attitudes toward appropriate drinking among U.S. Hispanics. *Alcohol and Alcoholism* 22 (4): 427–433.

Campos, A. (1995). Hispanics: Puerto Ricans. In *Encyclopedia of Social Work*. 19th ed., vol. 2. Washington, DC: National Association of Social Workers Press.

Carrier, J. M. (1976). Cultural factors affecting urban Mexican male homosexual behavior. *Archives of Sexual Behavior* 5: 103–124.

Castrex, G. H. (1994). Providing services to Hispanic/Latino populations: Profiles in diversity. *Social Work* 39 (3): 288–296.

Castro, K. G., and Manoff, S. B. (1988). The epidemiology of AIDS in Hispanic adolescents. In M. Quackenbush and M. Nelson (eds.), *The AIDS Challenge: Prevention Education for Young People*. Santa Cruz, CA: Network Publications.

Ceballos-Capitaine, A., Szapocznik, J., Blaney, N. T., Morgan, R. O., Millon, C., and Eisdorfer, C. (1990). Ethnicity, emotional distress, stress-related disruption, and coping among HIV seropositive gay males. *Hispanic Journal of Behavioral Sciences* 12 (2): 135–152.

Cervantes, R. C., Padilla, A. M., and Salgado de Snyder, N. (1990). Reliability and validity of the Hispanic stress inventory. *Hispanic Journal of Behavioral Sciences* 12 (1): 76–82.

Chavez, L. R. (1985). Households, migration, and labor market participation: The adaptation of Mexicans to life in the U.S. *Urban Anthropology* 14: 301–346.

Chavez, L. R. (1989) Coresidence and resistance: Strategies for survival among undocumented Mexicans and Central Americans in the United States. *Urban Anthropology* 19 (1–2): 31–61.

Chavez, L. R. (1991). *Out of the barrio: Toward a new politics of Hispanic assimilation.* New York: Basic Books.

Chavira-Prado, A. (1992). Work, health, and the family: Gender structure and women's status in an undocumented migrant population. *Human Organization* 51: 53–64.

Chu, S. Y., Peterman, T. A., Doll, L. S., Buehler, J. W., and Curran, J. W. (1992). AIDS in bisexual men in the United States: Epidemiology and transmission to women. *American Journal of Public Health* 82 (2): 220–224.

Codina, G. E., and Montalvo, F. F. (1993). Chicano phenotype and depression. Unpublished manuscript. Worden School of Social Work, Our Lady of the Lake University, San Antonio, TX.

Committee on Latino Affairs. (n.d.). Cultural competence within the social work profession. New York: National Association of Social Workers Press, New York State chapter.

Comstock, G. D. (1989). *Violence Against Lesbians and Gay Men*. New York: Columbia University Press.

Constable, P. (1997). Fighting for their U.S. lives: New law gives gay illegal immigrants fewer ways to stop deportation. *Washington Post* (April 23): B3.

Cortes, C. C. (1980). Mexicans. In S. Theruston (ed.), *Harvard Encyclopedia of American Ethnic Groups*. Cambridge, MA: Harvard University Press.

Cubillos, H. L., with Prieto, M. M. (1987). *The Hispanic Elderly: A Demographic Profile*. National Council of La Raza. Washington, DC: Policy Analysis Center, Office of Research, Advocacy, and Legislation.

Curiel, H. (1995). Hispanics: Mexican Americans. In *Encyclopedia of Social Work*. 19th ed., vol. 2. Washington, DC: National Association of Social Workers Press.

de la Garza, R. O., Falcon, A., Garcia, F. C., and Garcia, J. A. (1992). *Latino Nation Political Survey: Summary of Findings*. Boulder, CO: Westview Press.

Delgado, J. (1995). Meeting the health promotion needs of Hispanic communities. *American Journal of Health Promotion* 9 (4): 300–311.

Delgado, M., and Humm-Delgado, D. (1982) Natural support systems: Source of strength in Hispanic communities. *Social Work*: 83–89.

Denton, N. A., and Massey, D. S. (1989). Racial identity among Caribbean Hispanics: The effect of double minority status on residential segregation. *American Sociological Review* 54: 790–808.

Diaz, T., Buehler, J. W., Castro, K. G., and Ward, J. W. (1993). AIDS trends among Hispanics in the United States. *American Journal of Public Health* 83 (4): 504.

Diaz, T., Chu, S. Y., Frederick, M., Hermann, P., Levy, A., Mokotoff, E., Whyte, B., Conti, L., Herr, M., Checko, P. J., Rietmeijer, C. A., Sorvillo, F., and Mukhtar, Q. (1993). Sociodemographics and HIV risk behaviors of bisexual men with AIDS: Results from a multistate interview project. *AIDS* 7 (9): 1227–1232.

Doll, L. S., Byers, R. H., Bolan, G., Douglas, J. M. Jr., Moss, P. M., Weller, P. D., Joy, D., Barthjolow, B. N., and Harrison, J. S. (1991). Homosexual men who engage in high-risk sexual behavior: A multicenter comparison. *Sexually Transmitted Diseases* 18 (3): 170–175.

Doll, L. S., Petersen, L. R., White, C. R., Johnson, E. S., and Ward, J. W., and the Blood Donor Study Group. (1992). Homosexually and nonhomosexually identified men who have sex with men: A behavioral comparison. *Journal of Sex Research* 29 (1): 1–14.

Edmonston, B., and Passel, J. S. (1994). Ethnic demography: U.S. immigration and ethnic variations. In B. Edmonston and J. S. Passel (eds.), *Immigration and Ethnicity*. Washington, DC: Urban Institute Press.

Eribes, R. A., and Bradley-Rawls, M. (1978). The underutilization of nursing home facilities by Mexican American elderly in the southwest. *The Gerontologist* 18 (4): 363–371.

Espenshade, T. J, Fix, M., Zimmerman, W., and Corbett, T. (1996/97). Immigration and social policy: New interest in an old issue. *Focus* 18 (2): 1–10.

Espín, O. M. (1987a). Issues of identity in the psychology of Latina lesbians. In Boston Lesbian Psychologies Collective (ed.), *Lesbian Psychologies: Exploration and Challenges.* Chicago: University of Illinois Press.

Espín, O. M. (1987b). Psychological impact of migration on Latinas: Implications for therapeutic practice. *Psychology of Women Quarterly* 11: 489–503.

Falcon, A., and Santiago, J. (eds.) (1992). *The Puerto Rican Exception: Persistent Poverty and the Conservative social policy of Linda Chavez.* New York: Institute for Puerto Rican Policy.

Fernandez, E., and Cresce, A. (1986). Who are the other Spanish? Paper presented at the Population Association of America Annual Conference, San Francisco. Cited in U.S. Bureau of Census. CPR, series P-23 (172), *The Hispanic Population of the U.S. Southwest Borderland.* (1991). Washington, DC: U.S. Government Printing Office.

Fitzpatrick, J. P. (1982). Puerto Rican. In S. Thernstrom (ed.), *Harvard Encyclopedia of American Ethnic Groups.* Cambridge, MA: Harvard University Press.

Fix, M., and Passel, J. S. (1994) *Immigration and Immigrants.* Washington, DC: Urban Institute.

Frisbie, W. P., Ortiz, W., and Kelly, W. R. (1985). Marital instability trends among Mexican Americans as compared to blacks and Anglos: New evidence. *Social Science Quarterly* 66: 587–601.

Gil, A. G., and Vega, W. A. (1996). Two different worlds: Acculturation stress and adaptation among Cuban and Nicaraguan families. *Journal of Social and Personal Relationships* 13 (3): 435–456.

Gil, A. G., Vega, W. A., and Dimas, J. M. (1994). Acculturative stress and personal adjustment among Hispanic adolescent boys. *Journal of Community Psychology* 22: 43–54.

Gomez, E, Zurcher, L. A., Farris, B. E., and Becker, R. E. (1985). A study of psychosocial casework with Chicanos. *Social Work* 30 (6): 477–482.

Gonzalez del Valle, A., and Usher, M. (1982) Group therapy with aged Latino women: A pilot project and study. *Clinical Gerontologist* 1 (1): 51–58.

Graebler, L., Moore, J. W., and Guzman, R. C. (1970). *The Mexican American People: The Nation's Second Largest Minority.* New York: Free Press.

Griswold, R. del Castillo. (1984). *La Familia: Chicano Families in the Urban Southwest; 1848 to the Present.* Notre Dame, IN: Notre Dame University Press.

Guendelman, S. (1987). The incorporation of Mexican women in seasonal migration: A study of gender differences. *Hispanic Journal of Behavioral Sciences* 9: 245–264.

Guendelman, S., and Perez-Itriago, A. (1987). Migration tradeoffs: Men's experiences with seasonal lifestyles. *International Migration Review* 21: 709–727.

Hidalgo, H. A., and Christensen, E. H. (1976/77). The Puerto Rican lesbian and the Puerto Rican community. *Journal of Homosexuality* 2 (2): 109–121.

Hondagneu-Sotelo, P. (1994). *Gendered Transitions: Mexican Experiences of Immigration*. Berkeley and Los Angeles: University of California Press.

Hough, R. L., Landsverk, J. S., Karno, M., Burnam, M. A., Bimbers, D. M., Escobar, J. I., and Regier, D. A. (1987). Utilization of health and mental health services by Los Angeles Mexican Americans and non-Hispanic whites. *Archives of General Psychiatry* 44: 702–709.

Hunter, J. (1992). Violence against lesbian and gay male youths. In G. M. Herek and K. T. Berrill (eds.), *Hate Crimes: Confronting Violence Against Lesbians and Gay Men*. Newbury Park, CA: Sage.

Kaminsky, S., Kurtines, W., Hervis, O. O., Blaney, N. T., Millon, C., and Szapocznik, J. (1990). Life enhancement counseling with HIV infected Hispanic gay males. *Hispanic Journal of Behavioral Sciences* 12 (2): 177–195.

Keefe, S. M., and Padilla, A. M. (1987). *Chicano Ethnicity*. Albuquerque: University of New Mexico Press.

Keefe, S. M., Padilla, A. M., and Carlos, M. L. (1979). The Mexican-American extended family as an emotional support system. *Human Organization* 38 (2): 144–154.

Kennedy, David M. (1996) Can we still afford to be a nation of immigrants? *Atlantic Monthly* 278 (5): 52–68.

Krause, N., and Goldenhar, L. M. (1992). Acculturation and psychological distress in three groups of elderly Hispanics. *Journal of Gerontology* 47: S279–S288.

Lafferty, J., Foulk, D., and Ryan, R. (1990). Needle sharing for the use of therapeutic drugs as a potential AIDS risk behavior among migrant Hispanic farmworkers in the Eastern stream. *International Quarterly of Community Health Education* 11 (2): 135–143.

Lancaster, R. N. (1988). Subject honor and object shame: The construction of male homosexuality and stigma in Nicaragua. *Ethnology* 27 (2): 111–125.

Lesbian and Gay Immigration Rights Task Force. (1996a). Anti-marriage bill in Congress passes House, would exclude gay spouses from immigration. *Lesbian and Gay Immigration Rights Task Force Update*. Retrieved from World Wide Web: http://www.lgirtf.org/newsletter/Summer1996/SU1.html.

Lesbian and Gay Immigration Rights Task Force. (1996b). Gay Venezuelan wins asylum: Threatened with violence after coming out on Caracas radio, stylist to the elite flees to the U.S.; HIV+ gay Brazilian wins asylum. *Lesbian and Gay Immigration Rights Task Force Update*. Retrieved from World Wide Web: http://www.lgirtf.org/newsletter/Fall1996/FA96-17.html.

Lesbian and Gay Immigration Rights Task Force. (1996c). In response to Rep. Barney Frank, INS General Counsel issues memorandum, detailing guidelines for asylum and sexual orientation. *Lesbian and Gay Immigration Rights Task Force Update.* Retrieved from World Wide Web: http://www.lgirtf.org/newsletter/Fall1996/FA96-14.html.

Lesbian and Gay Immigration Rights Task Force. (1996d). Judge grants suspension of deportation to Mexican lesbian. *Lesbian and Gay Immigration Rights Task Force Update.* Retrieved from World Wide Web: http://www.lgirtf.org/newsletter/Summer1996/SU2.html.

Lesbian and Gay Immigration Rights Task Force. (1997). Gay Nicaraguan granted suspension of deportation. *Lesbian and Gay Immigration Rights Task Force Update.* Retrieved from World Wide Web: http://www.lgirtf.org/newsletter/Winter97/W4.html.

Lesnick, H., and Pace, B. (1990). Knowledge of AIDS risk factors in South Bronx minority college students. *Journal of Acquired Immune Deficiency Syndrome* 3 (2): 173–176.

Lindsey, D., and Kirk, S. A. (1992). The continuing crisis in social work research: Conundrum or social problem? *Journal of Social Work Education* 28 (3): 370–382.

Magaña, J. R., and Carrier, J. M. (1991). Mexican and Mexican American male sexual behavior and the spread of AIDS in California. *Journal of Sex Research* 28 (3): 425–441.

Maldonado, L. A. (1989). The social world of Florida's Mariel Cubans. Footnotes: *American Sociological Association* 16 (2): 7–8.

Maldanado-Denis, M. (1972). *Puerto Rico: A Socio-Historic Interpretation.* New York: Vintage Books.

Marin, G. (1989). AIDS prevention among Hispanics: Needs, risk behaviors, and cultural values. *Public Health Report* 104 (5): 411–415.

Marks, G., Bundek, N. I., Richardson, J. L., Ruiz, M. S., Maldonado, N., and Mason, H. R. (1992). Self-disclosure of HIV infection: Preliminary results from a sample of Hispanic men. *Health Psychology* 11 (5): 300–306.

Mason, H. R. C., Marks, G., Simoni, J. M., Ruiz, M. S., and Richardson, J. L. (1995). Culturally sanctioned secrets? Latino men's nondisclosure of HIV infection to family, friends, and lovers. *Health Psychology* 14 (1): 6–12.

Massey, D. S. (1995). The new immigration and ethnicity in the United States. *Population and Development Review* 21 (3): 631–652.

Massey, D. S., Arango, J., Graeme, H., Kouaquci, A., Pellegrino, A., and Taylor, J. E. (1994). An evaluation of international migration theory: The North American case. *Population and Development Review* 20 (4): 699–751.

Massey, D. S., and Denton, N. A. (1992). Racial identity and the spatial assimilation of Mexicans in the United States. *Social Science Research* 21: 235–260.

Massey, D. S., and Espinosa, K. E. (1997). What's driving Mexico-U.S. migration? A theoretical, empirical and policy analysis. *American Journal of Sociology* 102 (4): 939–999.

Melville, M. B. (1978). Mexican women adapt to migration. *International Migration Review* 12: 225–235.

Montalvo, F. F. (1991). Phenotyping, acculturation, and biracial assimilation of Mexican Americans. In M. Sotomayor (ed.), *Empowering Hispanic Families: A Critical Issue for the '90s.* Milwaukee: Family Service of America.

Mott, L. (1990). Brazil. In W. R. Dynes (ed.), *Encyclopedia of Homosexuality.* Vol. 1. New York: Garland.

Moyerman, D. R., and Forman, B. D. (1992). Acculturation and adjustment: A meta-analytic study. *Hispanic Journal of Behavioral Sciences* 14 (2): 163–200.

Murray, S. O. (1987). The family as an obstacle to the growth of a gay subculture in Latin America. In S. O. Murray (ed.), *Male Homosexuality in Central and South America.* New York: Gay Academic Union.

Murray, S. O. (1990). Latin America. In W. R. Dynes (ed.), *Encyclopedia of Homosexuality.* Vol. 1. New York: Garland.

Murray, S. O., and Taylor, C. L. (1990). Mexico. In W. R. Dynes (ed.), *Encyclopedia of Homosexuality.* Vol. 2. New York: Garland.

Negy, C., and Woods, D. J. (1992). The importance of acculturation in understanding research with Hispanic-Americans. *Hispanic Journal of Behavioral Sciences* 14 (2): 224–247.

Neidart, L. J., and Farley, R. (1985). Assimilation in the U.S.: An analysis of ethnic and generation differences in status and achievement. *American Journal of Sociology* 50: 840–850.

Nelson, C., and Tienda, M. (1985). The structuring of Hispanic ethnicity: Historical and contemporary perspectives. *Ethnic and Racial Studies* 8 (1): 49–74.

O'Sullivan, M. J., and Lasso, B. (1992). Community mental health services for Hispanics: A test of the culture compatibility hypotheses. *Hispanic Journal of Behavioral Sciences* 14 (4): 455–468.

O'Sullivan, M. J., and Peterson, P. D. (1989). Ethnic populations: Community mental health services ten years later. *Journal of Community Psychology* 17: 17–30.

Pachon, H., and Wilhelm, T. (1996). The Latino vote at mid-decade. Claremont, CA: Tomas Rivera Center.

Padilla, F. M. (1985). *Latino Ethnic Consciousness: The Case of Mexican Americans and Puerto Ricans in Chicago.* Notre Dame, IN: University of Notre Dame Press.

Paulino, A. (1994). Dominicans in the United States: Implications for practice and policies in the human services. *Journal of Multicultural Social Work* 3 (2): 53–65.

Pedraza-Bailey, S. (1985). Cuba's exiles: Portrait of refugee migration. *International Migration Review* 19 (1): 5–34.

Pessar, P. R. (1984). The linkage between the household and workplace of Dominican women in the U.S. *International Migration Review* 18: 1188–1211.

Pessar, P. R. (1994). Sweatshop workers and domestic ideologies: Dominican women in New York's apparel industry. *International Journal of Urban and Regional Research* 18 (1): 127–142.

Primus, W. (1996/97). Immigration provisions in the new welfare law. *Focus* 18 (2): 1–10.

Ramos, J. (ed.). (1987). *Compañeras: Latina Lesbians*. New York: Latina Lesbian History Project.

Raymond, J. S., Rhoads, D. L., and Raymond, R. E. (1980). The relative impact of family and social involvement on Chicano mental health. *American Journal of Community Psychology* 8 (5): 557–569.

Repak, T. (1994). Labor recruitment and the lure of capital: Central American migrants in Washington, DC. *Gender and Society* 8: 507–524.

Rich, B. R., and Arguelles, L. (1985). Homosexuality, homophobia, and revolution: Notes toward an understanding of the Cuban lesbian and gay male experience, part II. *Signs* 11: 120–136.

Rodriguez, C. (1989). *Puerto Ricans: Born in the United States*. Boston: Unwin Hyman.

Rogler, L. H., Cortes, D. E., and Malgady, R. G. (1991) Acculturation and mental health status among Hispanics: Convergence and new directions for research. *American Psychologist* 46 (6): 585–597.

Rolph, E. S. (1992). *Immigration Policies: Legacy from the 1980s and Issues for the 1990s*. Santa Monica, CA: Rand Corporation.

Ryan, R., Longres, J. F., and Roffman, R. A. (1996). Sexual identity, social support and social networks among African-, Latino-, and European-American men in an HIV prevention program. *Journal of Gay and Lesbian Social Services* 5 (2–3): 1–24.

Salgado de Snyder, V. N. (1987). Factors associated with acculturative stress and depressive symptomology among married Mexican immigrant women. *Psychology of Women Quarterly* 11: 475–488.

Sanchez-Ayendez, M. (1988). The Puerto Rican family. In C. H. Mindel, R. W. Habenstein, and R. Wright Jr. (eds.), *Ethnic Families in America*. 3rd ed. New York: Elsevier.

Shorris, E. (1992). *Latinos: A Biography of the People*. New York: Norton.

Siegel, K., and Epstein, J. A. (1996). Ethnic-racial differences in psychological stress related to gay lifestyle among HIV-positive men. *Psychological Reports* 79: 303–312.

Singer, M., Flores, C., Davison, L., Burke, G., Castillo, Z., Scanlon, K., and Rivera, M. (1990). The economic, social, and cultural context of AIDS among Latinos. *Medical Anthropology Quarterly* 4 (1): 72–114.

Soriano, F. I. (1991). AIDS: A challenge to Hispanics and their families. In M. Sotomayor (ed.), *Empowering Hispanic Families: A Critical Issue for the '90s*. Milwaukee: Family Service of America.

Stolzenberg, R. M. (1990). Ethnicity, geography, and occupational achievement of Hispanic men in the United States. *American Sociological Review* 55 (1): 143–154.

Suarez, P. J. (1990). Cuba. In W. R. Dynes (ed.), *Encyclopedia of Homosexuality*. Vol. 1. New York: Garland.

Szapocznik, J., and Hernandez, R. (1988). The Cuban American family. In C. H.

Mindel, R. W. Habenstein, and R. Wright Jr. (eds.), *Ethnic Families in America*. 3rd ed. New York: Elsevier.

Talamantes, M. A., Lawler, W. R., and Espino, D. V. (1995). Hispanic American elders: Caregiving norms surrounding dying and the use of hospice services. *Hospice Journal* 10 (2): 35–49.

Taylor, C. L. (1986). Mexican male homosexual interaction in public contexts. *Journal of Homosexuality* 11 (3–4): 117–136.

Tielman, R., and Hammelburg, H. (1993). World survey on the social and legal position of gays and lesbians. In A. Hendriks, R. Tielman, and E. van der Veen (eds.), *The Third Pink Book: A Global View of Lesbian and Gay Liberation and Oppression*. Buffalo, NY: Prometheus Books.

Tienda, M. (1989). Puerto Ricans and the Underclass Debate. *Annals of the American Academy* 501: 105–111.

Tori, C. D. (1989). Homosexuality and illegal residency status in relation to substance abuse and personality traits among Mexican nationals. *Journal of Clinical Psychology* 45: 814–821.

U.S. Bureau of the Census. (1932). *Fifteenth Census of the United States: 1930*. Characteristics of the Population. Vol. 3, part 1. Washington, DC: U.S. Government Printing Office.

U.S. Bureau of the Census. (1943). *Sixteenth Census of the United States: 1940*. Characteristics of the Population. Vol. 2. Washington, DC: U.S. Government Printing Office.

U.S. Bureau of the Census. (1955). *The 1950 Census: How They Were Taken*. Washington, DC: U.S. Government Printing Office.

U.S. Bureau of the Census (1990). *The Hispanic Population of the United States: March 1990*. CPR, series P-20, no. 475. Washington DC: U.S. Government Printing Office.

U.S. Bureau of the Census. (1991). *The Hispanic Population of the United States Southwest Borderland*. CPR, series P-23, no. 172. Washington, DC: U.S. Government Printing Office.

U.S. Bureau of the Census (1996). *Population Projections of the United States by Age, Sex, Race, and Hispanic Origin: 1993 to 2050*. CPR, series P-25-1104. www.census.gov/population/socdemo/language/table1.dat.

U.S. Bureau of the Census (1997). *The Hispanic Population of the United States*. CPR, series P-20, no. 511. Washington, DC: U.S. Government Printing Office.

Vargas-Willis, G., and Cervantes, R. C. (1987). Consideration of psychosocial stress in the treatment of the Latina immigrant. *Hispanic Journal of Behavioral Sciences* 9: 315–329.

Vazquez-Jimenez, R. (1995). Cuban Hispanics. In *Encyclopedia of Social Work*. 19th ed., vol. 2. Washington DC: National Association of Social Workers Press.

Vega, W. A., and Kolody, B. (1985). The meaning of social support and the mediation of stress across cultures. In U.S. Department of Health and Human Services, National Institute of Mental Health (ed.), *Stress and Hispanic Mental Health: Relating Research to Service Delivery*. Washington, DC: U.S. Government Printing Office.

Videka-Sherman, L (1985). *Harriett M. Bartlett Practice Effectiveness Project: Report to National Association of Social Workers Board of Directors*. Silver Spring, MD: National Association of Social Workers Press.

Wagner-Echeagaray, F. A., Schultz, C. G., Chilcoat, H. D., and Anthony, J. C. (1994). Degree of acculturation and the risk of crack cocaine smoking among Hispanic Americans. *American Journal of Public Health* 84 (11): 1825–1827.

Wallace, S. P., Campbell, K., and Lew-Ting, C. (1994). Structural barriers to the use of formal in-home services by elderly Latinos. *Journal of Gerontology* 49: S253–S263.

Wallerstein, I. (1974). *The Modern World System: Capitalist Agriculture, and the Origins of the European World Economy in the Sixteenth Century*. New York: Academic Press.

Weeks, J. R., and Cuellar, J. B. (1983). Isolation of older persons: The influence of immigration and length of residence. *Research on Aging* 5: 369–388.

Wells, K. B., Hough, R. L., Golding, J. M., Burnam, M. A., and Karno, M. (1987). Which Mexican-Americans underutilize health services? *American Journal of Psychiatry* 144: 918–922.

Wilson, D. (1995). Women's roles and women's health: The effect of immigration on Latina women. *Women's Health Issues* 5: 8–14.

Wilson, F. D., and Jaynes, G. (1996/97). Immigration and labor market outcomes for native workers. *Focus* 18 (2): 1–10.

Zamanian, K., Thackrey, M., Starrett, R. A., Brown, L., Lassman, D. K., and Blanchard, A. (1992). Acculturation and depression in Mexican-American elderly. *Clinical Gerontologist* 11 (3–4): 109–121.

Zamora-Hernández, C. E., and Patterson, D. G. (1996). Homosexually active Latino men: Issues for social work practice. *Journal of Gay and Lesbian Social Services* 5 (2–3): 69–91.

CHAPTER 4

SOCIAL WORK PRACTICE WITH AFRICAN-DESCENT IMMIGRANTS

E. Aracelis Francis

AFRICAN-DESCENT IMMIGRATION

The 1965 Immigration and Nationality Act has had a major impact on the size and nature of the immigrant population in the United States. Projections are that by the year 2050, the majority of the U.S. population will be people of color. This chapter discusses immigrants who have come to the United States from Africa and other areas with large numbers of African descendents, including people from the English-, French-, and Dutch-speaking Caribbean islands and the African-descended populations of South America, such as Guyana. This discussion excludes people from the Spanish-speaking Caribbean because they are classified as Hispanics.

In 1939, Reid stated in *Negro Immigrants* that the effects of the immigration of the 100,000 foreign-born Negroes to the United States were scarcely known. When he had first become interested in the subject ten years earlier, he had been concerned by the paucity of specific documentary materials on this group. His first task, therefore, was to find out what was known about Negro immigrants and Negro foreign-born peoples (Reid 1939). Today's challenge is just as difficult. Although the number of books, articles, and studies on West Indian populations in the large cities of the United States has increased, many issues still have not been addressed. Even as the extent of the African presence in the United States is acknowledged, there is still little information about some of the same issues that Reid cited in 1939.

African-descent immigrants are automatically included in the United States' definition of black persons, even though each immigrant country's definition of its racially mixed populations may be quite different. For example, people from the Caribbean, Latin America, or Africa (the Coloreds of South Africa would be included) are often a polyglot of nationalities and ethnicities, as seen in General Colin Powell's and Tiger Woods's own descriptions of their mixed racial and ethnic background. All immigrants to the United States whose African heritage is clearly visible are considered black and are subjected to the same racism and discrimination experienced by African Americans. This consideration also means that they are less visible as distinct ethnic groups and that the size of these immigrant groups is disregarded by both black and white Americans. Ostine (1998) suggested that because of the recent increase in the foreign-born black population, sociologists cannot continue to think of race as the most salient characteristic, because black does not necessarily mean African American. For example, immigrants from Santo Domingo and Panama are considered Hispanic even if their skin color is black. The baseball player Sammy Sosa is Hispanic, although he looks black. On federal government forms asking for racial/ethnic status, the description black (not of Hispanic origin) is used to differentiate the Spanish-speaking population, which includes people of black skin color.

These changes in immigration patterns and definitions of ethnicity and race are challenging this country's history of assimilation and its notion of a melting pot. Nevertheless, all black immigrants face some challenges given this country's history of racial discrimination against its African American population and its failure to fully integrate them into the American dream. In his *We Are All Multiculturalists Now,* Glazer writes that "the change that has shaken our expectations for the future of American society . . . is rather the change in our expectations as to how and when the full incorporation of African Americans into American life will take place." He goes on to say that only twenty years ago, he believed that African Americans would become "simply Americans of darker skin." Although he still believes African Americans will be fully integrated, he concedes that there has been serious backsliding and an institutionalization of differences that may not be overcome in the near future (Glazer 1997:149).

Glazer's term *serious backsliding* merits discussion in regard to the apartness of blacks. He looks at three phenomena to describe the differences between American blacks and other immigrants. The first phenomenon is intermarriage, which provides key evidence for powerful assimilatory forces. The evidence shows that blacks are not subject to these forces to the same degree as others because blacks still have the lowest rate of intermarriage. Ninety-nine percent of black native-born women marry other blacks, and only 10 percent of black men outside the South are involved in intermarriage. Conversely, despite the recency of Hispanic and Asian groups' immigration, their rates of intermarriage are approaching the levels of European groups. The second phenomenon is residential segregation. Thirty years of public and private effort, assisted by antidiscrimination law and a substantial rise in black earnings, have made little impact on the degree of blacks' residential segregation. The high level of segregation experienced by blacks today is unique compared with the experience of other large minority groups, such as Hispanics and Asians. Where suburbanization has increased, it has been into suburban areas that are in effect extensions of central-city black areas or into suburbs that have become predominantly black. This has also had consequences for school integration. The third phenomenon is the effect of this separation on language and the capacity to communicate. Despite the impact of television and the other mass media, speech variants are now even further apart. Glazer sees multiculturalism as the price that America is paying for its inability or unwillingness to incorporate African Americans into its society in the same way and to the same degree it has incorporated so many other groups.

America's racial stratification requires a major adjustment by black immigrants as they move from being part of a racial majority into being part of a racial minority (Reid 1939). Bryce-Laporte (1972) stated that immigrants of African ancestry suffer a "double invisibility" because of their race and origin. Although immigrants of African ancestry have contributed greatly to American society, their cultural impact has been ignored. In 1998, Ostine reported that black immigrants lose status if they lose their cultural distinctiveness, because unlike white immigrants, becoming African American lowers their status in the dominant society. Gladwell (1996) supported Ostine's position in his description of studies on employment by Neuman and Waters, in which employers issue blanket condemnations of American blacks and hold up West Indian blacks as a cultural ideal because of their work ethic. Gladwell defined this as *multiculturalism racism*, in which one racial/ethnic group is played off against the other. Immigrants in American history have always profited from adopting the country's language, customs, and culture. For the West Indians, however, their advantage is in remaining outsiders, remaining unfamiliar, and having customs, a culture, and a language distinct from those of the American blacks that they resemble. "There is already some evidence that the considerable economic and social advantages that West Indians hold over American blacks begins to dissipate by the second generation when the accent has faded" (Gladwell 1996:79). By then, those in positions of power who distinguish between good and bad blacks include West Indians with everyone else. Thus for West Indians, assimilation is tantamount to suicide. As Ostine concluded in regard to white immigrants, becoming citizens adds to their status because they become part of the dominant majority. But for African or Caribbean immigrants, becoming a citizen makes them members of the group of despised black Americans. As a result, they retain their cultural distinctiveness to distinguish themselves from other black Americans. This desire for cultural distinction was evident to the Census Bureau in 1994 when it held hearings to consider adding new categories to the current census choices for race. Blacks from the Caribbean expressed a preference for being labeled according to their country of origin, such as Jamaican or Haitian American, and "Africans who are not Americans" found the term African American inaccurate. However, one in three black Americans wanted the Census Bureau to adopt the term African American (Lander, Foster, and Jacobs 1994:4).

DEMOGRAPHICS

In 1992, the black civilian population (i.e., not including those in the armed forces, prisons, or asylums) numbered 31.4 million and made up 12.5 percent of the total U.S. population, up from 11.7 percent in 1980.

> Since 1980 the Black population has grown faster than the white population and the population as a whole, increasing an average of 1.4 percent a year. Eighty-four percent of Black population growth was due to natural increase. Immigration, which has increased substantially since 1980 for the Black population, made up the remaining 16 percent (Jones, Jacobs, and Siegel 1995:7).

This chapter discusses this 16 percent population group.

African Immigrants

According to Ungar (1995), the number of Africans voluntarily coming to the United States to live has always been very small. Except for students who have been accepted at educational institutions and a few political exiles from places like South Africa, Africans have usually had difficulty obtaining immigrant visas, and the long and expensive journey has been beyond the reach of most African families. Dinnerstein and Reimers (1975) reported that the percentage of migrants of African origin from Africa was never higher than 0.71 percent between 1901 and 1965. Fariyal Ross-Sheriff (1995) limited her discussion of

African immigrants to those who emigrated directly from the continent of Africa, whose ancestry was African, and who came to the United States after the 1965 Immigration Act, when preference categories were established. This group excludes Asian refugees, white South Africans, and others. Her data show that only a small number of people from Africa qualified for entry to the United States under the rules of the 1965 Immigration Act. A very small number of Africans were eligible for immigration under the terms of the preference system. There was, however, an increase in the emigration in the 1980s of well-educated persons from sub-Saharan Africa. As a result, the percentage of immigrants from Africa doubled after 1965. Between 1964 and 1965, the number of immigrants from Africa was 0.7 percent of the total number of immigrants to the United States, and between 1965 and 1974, this percentage increased to 1.5. Data from 1983 to 1992 indicate that the number of immigrants rose again to 2.7 percent (or 15,084) in 1983 and continues to be above the 2 percent range. For example in 1988, 18,882 Africans, or 2.9 percent, immigrated: in 1991, the number had increased to 36,179, or 2.0 percent; and in 1992, 27,086 Africans, or 2.8 percent, had immigrated to the United States.

In 1995, the percentage of alien immigrants born in Africa climbed to 59.8. The 1995 total of 42,456 immigrants, compared with 26,712 for 1994, was the highest ever recorded for that continent (see table 4.1). This increase was due primarily to the new diversity program that was established in 1995 under the 1990 Immigration Act. In 1990, Congress sought to make visas available to countries adversely affected by the Immigration and Nationality Act Amendments of 1965. IMPACT 90 allowed for 40,000 immigrants to enter as Diversity Immigrants each year during the transition period. Natives of thirty-four countries were eligible for the program in 1992, based on a decrease in total immigration after the 1965 amendments went into effect. Africa was allocated 20,200 visas in 1995. Africa was one of six geographic regions, and the leading African countries of admission in 1995 were Ethiopia (3,088) and Nigeria (2,407) (1995 Statistical Yearbook of the INS).

Apraku (1991) attributed the poor economic and political conditions in Africa for the increase in emigration from Africa of well-educated persons. During this period, sub-Saharan Africa fared worst among the developing countries, contributing to immigration from that region that exceeded Africa as a whole. He noted that a 9 percent increase in emigration for the whole of Africa in 1980 was matched by a 28 percent increase for sub-Saharan Africa. His analysis of the 1992 data indicated that the African immigrant population is highly skilled and well educated. Of the 8,716 immigrants who were subject to numerical limitations—that is, family-sponsored and employment-based preferences—

TABLE 4.1
Immigrants Admitted by Region and Selected Country of Birth, Fiscal Years 1985–1995

	Year					
Country	1985	1987	1989	1991	1993	1995
Africa	17,117	17,724	25,166	36,179	27,783	42,456
Caribbean[a]	39,160	49,125	42,117	88,385	40,352	40,339
Guyana	8,531	11,384	10,789	11,666	8,384	7,362

[a] The Caribbean figures exclude Cuba and Santo Domingo.

Source: U.S. Immigration and Naturalization Service, Statistical Yearbook of the Immigration and Naturalization Service, 1995 (Washington, DC: U.S. Government Printing Office, 1996).

more than half (4,967) were admitted for their professional expertise and technical skills. Only 166 fell into the category of unskilled workers and their families. The percentage of African immigrants in the employment-based preference category was relatively high (18 percent), compared with the total percentage of immigrants in this category (12 percent). But the percentage of immigrants in the family reunification/sponsorship category was relatively low (14 percent), compared with the total percentage in this category of 22 percent (Ross-Sheriff 1995:131).

The passage of the Refugee Act in 1980 also offered new opportunities for African immigration, and Ethiopians and Eritreans were among the first in Africa to take advantage of them. In 1980, about nine hundred Ethiopian refugees came to America, and for the rest of the 1980s, a substantial majority of the African refugees admitted to the United States were from Ethiopia or Eritrea. In addition to Ethiopians, refugees continue to come from all over the African continent and include Liberians, Mozambicans, Somalis, Sudanese, and Zairian refugees who were also designated for special consideration in fiscal year 1992. Nevertheless, Africans constitute less than 3 percent of all refugees resettled in the United States, and the funding for refugees from Africa was lower than that for refugees from other parts of the world (Ross-Sheriff 1995).

As late as 1992, the United States planned to admit only 6,000, or 5 percent, of the total 120,000 refugees wanting to be admitted. In the late 1980s and 1990s, refugees tended to migrate because of economic deprivation. Most were from rural areas where they had spent their entire lives working in subsistence agriculture. Although they came to join established communities of émigrés in the United States, many were illiterate in English as well as their own language and ended up as laborers who were easily exploited. Ungar (1995) reported that the most reliable, but unofficial, estimates indicate that all together there are probably 75,000 Ethiopian immigrants in the United States and that about 15,000 may be Eritreans.

Unlike the refugees, skilled African immigrants represent a very different population. Apraku (1991) found that the average African immigrant is a highly trained and experienced male of an economically productive age, who is well paid and highly satisfied with his current job. These immigrants maintain close ties with their country, family, and friends through annual remittances for family support and personal investment projects and frequent visits home. They all planned to resettle in their home countries in the future.

Haitian Immigrants

Bastien (1995) described the Haitian migration of the twentieth century as consisting of four waves. The first wave predated the 1964 changes in the Immigration Act, and immigrants came because of political oppression during the first decade of the Duvalier regime. The second wave consisted of skilled craftsmen coming to better their living conditions brought down by economic hardships in Haiti. The third wave, around 1980, were peasants who had been dispossessed of their land or were unable to make a living on the deteriorated soil. Portes and Stepick (1993) defined this group as "boat people." Between 1977 and 1981, approximately sixty thousand Haitians arrived by boat in South Florida. Because their arrival peaked at the time of the Cuban flotilla, in the public's mind the two became one, even though they were very different. The Cuban exodus had been sponsored by the Cuban American community, and many of the arrivals had relatives in Miami. The Haitians, however, had no solid ethnic networks in Miami on which to rely. The reaction of the native whites in Florida was to reject the new arrivals and try to stop their entry. In response to the representations by Miami leaders and the local staff of the Immigration and Naturalization Service (INS), federal officials initiated a Haitian Program in 1979. The program's objective was to accelerate deportation proceedings and make a concerted effort to discourage Haitian boat people from applying for political asylum. But this program failed owing to the efforts of churches, philanthropic organizations, the creation of the Haitian Refugee Center, legal representation, and the efforts of the African American community, the Congressional Black Caucus, and Senator Edward Kennedy, who attacked U.S. policy as racially biased and demanded to know whether Haitians would be treated the same as Cubans. The Carter administration responded to these attacks, and from then on, any government action toward the "entrants" (the term used to describe both the Mariel Cubans and the Haitians) had to be equitable.

These efforts resulted in the consolidation of a Haitian community in Miami. At the beginning of the Reagan administration, U.S. Coast Guard cutters were ordered to patrol Haitian waters around the clock so that Miami-bound boats could be intercepted at sea before reaching U.S. jurisdiction. Bastien described the fourth wave as coming after the 1991 coup d'état that overthrew Jean-Bertrand Aristide. Bastien saw this latest group as made up of mainly young students; members of grassroots organizations of peasants, women, or merchants; and human rights activists. She pointed out that since the Haitian boat people had begun arriving, the United States had tried to return as many of them as possible. Haitian advocates claim that the U.S. government's treatment of Haitians is racist, ideologically based, and illegal under both international and U.S. law because the United States is committed to protect refugees. Nevertheless, the United States has maintained that the Haitians are economic and not political refugees. Haiti is a poor country and people do leave for economic reasons, but the extent of the political oppression and corruption suffered by the Haitian people and by many of the boat people makes these distinctions almost moot. Rather, America's racial history and its support of the corrupt Duvalier regime cloak the underlying reasons for describing the Haitians as economic refugees.

It is estimated that one million Haitians reside in the United States, with the largest number living in the New York metropolitan area. Other states with substantial numbers of Haitian immigrants are California, Connecticut, Florida, Georgia, Illinois, Massachusetts, and New Jersey. Within this group are legal residents, naturalized citizens, and illegal residents who live in limbo because their claim of political asylum has been denied.

Illegal Immigrants

According to Ahearn (1995), there is no accurate count of the number of illegal aliens in the United States, but estimates range from 1 million to 12 million. Illegal immigrants come into the United States from around the world and in a variety of ways. Some cross the border and "enter without inspection" or enter the country with fraudulent documents. Others enter legally as tourists, students, or temporary workers and stay beyond their authorized stay, and others are asylum applicants who have not submitted their applications. The number of new illegal aliens joining the long-term population is estimated to be about 420,000 annually. According to the Immigration and Naturalization Service (INS), the illegal population in October 1996 was 5 million people, or 20 percent of the United States' foreign-born population (Center for Immigration Studies 1997:18). Since the passage of the Immigration Reform and Control Act of 1986 (IRCA), more than 3 million illegal aliens have become permanent residents, of which 2 million were from Mexico; 123,00 were from Caribbean nations; 16,000 from Africa, mostly from Nigeria; 286,00 were from Central America; 40,360 were from Europe, mostly from Poland; and 73,000 were from Asia (Ahearn 1995).

One of the public perceptions of illegal immigrants, such as the pariah status of the Haitian boat people, is described by Portes and Stepick as "a consequence of both their race and the highly visible manner of their arrival" (1993:58). California's Proposition 187 against illegal immigration is another example of the public's negative attitude toward illegal aliens. Matthews (1997), writing about the labeling of immigrants, argued that this attitude allows this group to be publicly alienated from the rest of society and sets them up for various forms of discrimination. He recommended the term *undocumented immigrant* as more appropriate and less manipulative than the term *illegal alien*.

WHERE THE POPULATIONS SETTLED

Census Bureau figures show that since the 1965 changes in the Immigration Act, the number of immigrants in America's cities has risen substantially. In fiscal year 1995, the largest number of new arrivals from the English-speaking Caribbean came from the islands of Jamaica (12,212), Trinidad, and Tobago (3,095). Fifty-three percent of the Jamaicans and 56 percent of the Trinidadians went to New York City, and 32 percent of the Jamaicans and 36 percent of the Trinidadians went to Miami, both cities already housing large West Indian populations. Many of the 6,383 new immigrants from Guyana were people of East Indian descent, and approximately 89 percent settled in New York. (Guyana's population is approximately 50 percent East Indian and 50 percent African descent.) Of the new arrivals from Africa, 4,015 were from Ethiopia, 3,958 from Nigeria, and 1,913 from Ghana, of whom 39 percent of the Ghanaians and 39 percent of the Nigerians went to live in New York. Of the 8,395 new arrivals from Haiti, 51 percent went to Miami and 46 percent went to New York (*1995* Statistical Yearbook of the INS).

Of the Ethiopian and Eritrean population, one-third lives in the Washington, D.C., area, and the rest are divided among Los Angeles, the San Francisco Bay area, Dallas, Houston, and Atlanta. When the Ethiopians congregated in Washington, they stimulated the growth of an Ethiopian cultural environment. Washington now has many Ethiopian restaurants, nightclubs, and grocery stores. A half-dozen churches cater to the community and offer alternative services in their native languages. Many Ethiopians are the owners of parking garages, taxi companies, and travel agencies, and the Washington-Baltimore area now has an estimated twenty-five Ethiopian and Eritrean physicians. Besides the newspapers published in their various languages, the *Ethiopian Yellow Pages*, published in Alexandria, Virginia, is designed to promote Ethiopian businesses and inter-Ethiopian business networking and is evidence of the strength and growth of this community (*Ethiopian Yellow Pages* 1997/98). Notwithstanding the vitality of the Ethiopian and Eritrean communities in Washington, D.C., they are virtually unnoticed by the media and the larger community. In addition, political differences between the Ethiopians and Eritreans remain. Although Eritreans in Washington tend to have a lower socioeconomic status than many of the Ethiopians, they now feel triumphant because their country and culture have achieved official international recognition after years of repression and subjugation by the Ethiopian Amhara establishment. Eritreans in Washington increasingly spend their time apart from the Ethiopians at their own cultural center or in the few Eritrean restaurants that have opened to serve their own distinct cuisine (Ungar 1995).

Millman (1997) described the past two decades as the period of the first mass migration of Africans to this continent in more than two centuries, with more Africans coming annually at the end of the twentieth century than at any time during the height of the slave trade. These Africans are from two places, English-speaking Africa—mainly Liberia, Ghana, and Nigeria—and French West Africa. The English speakers compose the vast majority, of which at least a quarter million are Nigerians. Immigrant enclaves have been established for at least a decade. For example, the Ghanaians live in East Orange, New Jersey, and the Liberians, in Staten Island, New York. Georgia Avenue in Washington, D.C., is another stronghold of Nigerian businesses, extending from Howard University into Silver Spring and Takoma Park, Maryland. The Washington metropolitan area has one of the biggest African communities in the United States, followed by Houston, Texas, where perhaps 100,000 immigrants are spread over several westside wards. Like the West Indians, they are in the service industries— Ghanaians in taxi driving, Nigerians in health care, and Ethiopians in the hotel industry. The English-speaking Africans mirror other groups with their chain migration, built by families carving out niches in specific industries. Many came as university students and remained to pursue opportunities not available at home, part of the "brain drain" that Apraku described. The French speakers, numbering fewer than 100,000, arrive as peddlers and come intent on establishing a piece of Africa in the heart of black America. They have defied distance, poverty, and language barriers to establish themselves in U.S. cities. A few come as students, usually arriving through legal channels, but most are self-employed so they do not compete with the native-born Americans (Millman 1997).

Each group is different. For example, some twenty thousand Senegalese live in New York and are involved in commerce in America's most impoverished black neighborhoods. After coming to the United States, many of them become peddlers, either bartering African souvenirs for start-up cash or relying on relatives who bartered. The Senegalese have set up marketplaces in cities like New York and are very skillful at staying above the law by using a series of commercial connections and portable merchandise. The Senegalese are barterers by history and tradition, to them, "doing business" is selling, bartering, or transporting or searching for goods and the consumers to whom they sell. Business can also be street vending, owning a restaurant, owning a snack stand, or being a middleman, a wholesaler, a moneylender, or a money changer. *Baol-baol* means "making it in your own way" and being responsible for your own livelihood and that of any extended family that you can support (Millman 1997).

The largest numbers of sub-Saharan Africa have been Nigerians, and they have been generally highly trained and skilled workers. According to a 1967 United Nations study of 417 Nigerian immigrants admitted to the United States between June 30, 1963, and June 30, 1967, 255 were highly trained professionals such as physicians, nurses, and engineers. Nigerians represent the single largest immigrant group from Africa—a total of 1.62 million in 1995. In the 1980s, although the immigrants were younger and less well educated and had less work experience (Tukali-Williams 1997), the large Nigerian community supported them. Despite the presence of large Nigerian communities in all the large cities in the United States, they, like other black immigrants, are invisible to the larger society.

SALIENT CULTURAL FACTORS

Certain cultural factors, customs, traditions, and value systems of West Indian and African immigrants distinguish the immigrant communities and affect their experiences in the United States.

West Indian Immigrants

West Indians are a diverse people from a number of islands identified as the Anglophone Caribbean. In addition, immigrants from this area have included African-descent immigrants from Guyana in South America and French-speaking Haitians. The distinctiveness of each of these islands is reflected in the development of various island organizations by, for example, immigrants from Jamaica, Trinidad and Tobago, Grenada, St. Kitts, Antigua, Guyana, and other islands. Although the British ruled all these islands, each has a unique history and culture, with differences in celebrations, food preferences, ethnic composition, and ways of perceiving those from the other islands. The large West Indian settlements in the cities, for instance, identify themselves as either West Indian or Caribbean.

West Indians have lived in New York City since the turn of the century. Reid's initial interest in the "Negro Immigrant" and Cruse's discussion of the West Indians' role in Negro intellectual life acknowledge the impact of this group's cultural distinctiveness (Cruse 1967; Reid 1939). Kasinitz (1992) observed that race, not ethnicity, dominated the public activities of the first West Indian immigrants. They identified with the native-born African Americans, and they and their descendants have been disproportionately well represented among the political and economic leaders of New York's black community.

Beginning in the 1980s, however, ethnicity played an increasingly public role in the lives of West Indians in New York. Kasinitz (1992) asked why an immigrant group would play down its separate identity and integrate itself into a larger category at one point in its experience in America and then choose to emphasize this identity during another. He reflected that this could be related to the dramatic increase in the size of the group since the 1965 changes in the immigration laws. It could also be attributed to the fact that the post-1965 immigrants left independent or soon-to-be independent microstates. He concluded that this reasserted identity was related to changes in the role of race in American culture. Although race continues to be important, it is not as monolithic as it once was. Changes in New York's African American political structure saw the emergence of new leaders that displaced the older political leaders, many of whom were of West Indian heritage. Also in the 1980s, politicians such as Mayor Ed Koch and Brooklyn borough President Howard Golden publicly courted Caribbean leaders and would-be leaders. In the 1990s, the Republican Party courted General Colin Powell as a presidential or vice-presidential candidate for the United States, but polls showed that he would not attract a large number of African Americans to join the party. (Heilemann 1996:47). There were also rumblings in the larger African American community that he was a West Indi-

an and an outsider. Kasinitz argued "that the state's willingness at certain historical junctures to respond to 'ethnic' demands and perhaps even create ethnic
constituencies, accounts for a significant part of the growth of such demands
and constituencies" (1992:11). Race continues to assert itself in various issues,
and ethnicity continues to be a constant factor.

The focus on ethnicity differentiates West Indians from Africans Americans
and white Americans, but it also unites people of various national origins. It
brings together immigrants from the Anglophone Caribbean, including dozens
of similar but distinct strains of Afro-Creole culture within contemporary New
York's West Indian community. Indeed, this sense of pan–West Indian identity
is becoming a cultural political force in New York and the Caribbean and is a
conscious strategy of adaptation. By joining together the various island communities, these immigrants have gained strength in numbers and political clout
and have been able to assert their ethnic identity and distinguish themselves
from African Americans (Kasinitz 1992).

As an example, although Carnival is not celebrated in all the West Indian islands, the Labor Day Carnival held in Brooklyn has come to be a major cultural
event in the West Indian community, a chance to duplicate in New York City an
island festival that includes music, dance, food, and costumes. Although Carnival is primarily a Trinidadian custom, all of New York's island communities participate. Over the years, accommodations have been made for the differences in
the various island groups; for example, calypso is native to Trinidad and reggae
to Jamaica, and as the Haitian community becomes more involved in Carnival,
a special night has been designated for Haitian cultural events (Kasinitz 1992).
Other American cities with large West Indian populations, such as Atlanta,
Washington, and Baltimore, now hold their own Carnival activities.

Religion is another important cultural factor for immigrants, particularly
Haitians. Catholicism was for centuries the predominant Christian faith in
Haiti, but in the last four decades, other religions have made inroads. Now 80
percent of Haitians identify themselves as Catholics and 20 percent as Protestants. Voodoo, an important part of many Haitians' belief system, integrates elements of Christian theology in its rituals. Although all social classes practice
voodoo, members of the lower classes embrace it more openly. Haitians' belief
in God or voodoo gods explains their jobs and sufferings, poverty and wealth,
health and illness, hopes and fears. The "rituals performed to please or appease
supernatural forces emphasize the importance of external forces and minimizes
the ability of Haitians to self-determine their existence. This emphasis places
the responsibility for change on the external world rather than on the individual Haitian" (Bibb and Casimir 1997:102).

Hard work and education are valued by all the Caribbean groups, who believe that the path to success is higher education. With education, both job security and social mobility are possible, and so children are expected to take advantage of the opportunities available to them in the United States. Toward this end, families make many sacrifices to purchase homes or a better education for their children, efforts that are supported by various social and kinship networks.

African Immigrants

In addition to differences in religion, dress, food, and language, other African customs, traditions, and values may conflict with the dominant society in the United States. One is the issue of female circumcision or female genital mutilation.

The following discussion of female genital mutilation illustrates how cultural factors separate populations and cause conflicts with accepted norms in America. Black and Debelle (1995) use the term *female genital mutilation* instead of *female circumcision,* because female circumcision implies that it is a minor operation equivalent to male circumcision; whereas in many cultures, the female genitals are extensively mutilated. The consequences and practice of female genital mutilation are a relatively unexplored area in social service delivery. It is practiced in twenty-six African countries, with prevalence rates ranging from 5 percent to 99 percent. An estimated 100 million women have been circumcised, across socioeconomic classes and among different ethnic and cultural groups, including Christians, Muslims, Jews, and followers of indigenous African religions. According to Toubia, it has a particularly strong cultural meaning because it is closely linked to women's sexuality and their reproductive role in society (Toubia 1994). It is also deeply ingrained in the cultural traditions of these women and, like many other female problems, is not openly discussed or acknowledged.

European countries like Great Britain and France, with older African immigrant communities, have had to address the issue of female genital mutilation. In 1985, the British Parliament passed the Prohibition of Female Circumcision Act (MS 4:1, J/A 1993), and since 1990, social workers in the United Kingdom have had the power to monitor and counsel families with girls considered to be at risk (MS 4:1). France has also made the practice illegal and in 1993 sentenced a Gambian woman to five years in prison after she paid to have her two daughters circumcised.

Female genital mutilation is also practiced in the United States among the more than 100,000 people who immigrate here each year from the countries in which it is practiced, but little is known about the prevalence and circumstances of its occurrence in this country. Female genital mutilation is typically performed on girls at the age of seven and is regarded in home cultures as a rite of passage and a crucial way to ensure that women are chaste and desirable marriage partners (Kent 1986). The request for political asylum by Fauziya Kasinga, who fled Togo when she was forced to become the fourth wife of a man who insisted that she undergo genital mutilation, focused attention on both U.S. refugee policy and the practice of female genital mutilation. The case received extensive newspaper and television coverage. Kasinga was granted asylum in 1996 and has now written a book on her experience (Kassindja and Bashir 1998; *Network News* July 8, 1996).

Several women's rights groups have formed a loose information and activist network working to eliminate female genital mutilation. There have been several unsuccessful attempts to pass legislation, drafted by the Congressional Women's Caucus, to outlaw this practice. A federal budget amendment passed in 1996 and signed by President Bill Clinton in the 1997 appropriations bill outlaws the practice of female genital mutilation on anyone under eighteen and includes provisions for counseling immigrants about the law and the health dangers (Kent 1986). Unlike the proposed legislation, the amendment has no requirement for reporting the incidence of female genital mutilation. The result is only anecdotal evidence of the extent of this practice. Three states—New York, Minnesota, and North Dakota—have passed laws making the practice of female genital mutilation a felony unless it is medically necessary. Most U.S. legal experts also interpret child abuse laws broadly enough to cover female genital mutilation.

Female genital mutilation is viewed as a serious problem that is common among immigrant communities, including Somali enclaves in Los Angeles, Texas, Minnesota, Tennessee, Virginia, and New York (Kent 1986). Immigrant women who were circumcised as children have joined to fight the tradition among compatriots in this country. Among them is a Somali filmmaker who has toured the country with her film "Fire Eyes," which shows African children being circumcised. Another is Mimi Ramsey, an Ethiopian nurse who visits African businesses and communities in the United States proselytizing against female genital mutilation (Burstyn 1995). She has now formed a nonprofit organization called FORWARD United States to try to eliminate the practice through education (Kent 1986).

Social workers, usually unaware that such a practice exists, should learn the personal and community dynamics of accepting circumcision in order to identify and deal with this practice. Among the majority of girls and women, the psychological effects are often subtle and buried in layers of denial and acceptance of social norms. Circumcised immigrant women living in societies where the procedure is not performed may have serious problems in developing their sexual identity, and mental health professionals may be called in to deal with these issues (Toubia 1994:714). The victims need direct help for the public health consequences of this practice. Toubia concluded that one concern is how to deliver the most appropriate psychological support to girls and women who have already been victimized. In addition, guidelines and training materials must be developed to inform providers about how to manage the health needs of circumcised women and appropriate ways to counsel patients when they request circumcision or reinfibulation (*New England Journal of Medicine* September 15, 1997).

This issue also has implications for the larger human services community, although very few preventive measures, such as education and community outreach, have been implemented. As a result, social workers must educate the larger health and mental health community about the psychological and emotional consequences of female genital mutilation. Social workers should also be aware of those persons in the immigrant communities who are attempting to address this problem. Many other groups with which social workers could become affiliated are trying to persuade American lawmakers to address female genital mutilation as a serious health and human rights issue (Burstyn 1995).

ADAPTATION AND COPING

Waters (1996) raised the question of whether for nonwhite immigrants, the processes of immigration and assimilation are the same as for earlier white immigrants or whether nonwhite immigrants and their children face very different choices and constraints because they are defined racially by other Americans. She studied the development of an ethnic identity among the second generation of black Caribbean immigrants whose parents had distanced themselves from American blacks by stressing their national origins and ethnic identities.

She found that although they varied in their identities, perceptions, and opinions, these second-generation youngsters could be sorted into three general types: (1) those identifying as Americans, (2) those identifying as ethnic Americans with some distancing from black Americans, and (3) those identifying as immigrants and ignoring American racial and ethnic categories. The factors determining the type of identity were their parents' class backgrounds, their parents' social networks, the type of school the children attended, and the family structure. These factors reflected the degree to which the children could be shielded from antisocial values.

The ethnic-identified youngsters were mostly from middle-class backgrounds, and the poorest identified themselves as American or immigrant. The ethnic-identified youngsters shared their parents' perception of their differences from American blacks. These shared stereotypes describe African Americans "as lazy, disorganized, obsessed with racial slights and barriers, with a disorganized and *laissez-faire* attitude toward family life and child raising" (Waters 1996:173). These youngsters tend to do well academically and see opportunities and rewards despite the racism and discrimination. Waters attributed their dilemma to white and black Americans' perception of them as blacks because their ethnic differences were not readily noticeable.

The second group, American-identified youngsters, did not stress either their immigrant or their ethnic identities. They also disagreed with their parents' views of black Americans. Instead, they embraced their peers' culture, which brought them into direct conflict with their parents when they disdained academic achievement. In their identification with their peers, they also accepted the larger society's negative stereotypes of themselves.

The third group, the immigrant-identified youngsters, did not feel the pressures of choosing between, identifying with, or distancing themselves from African Americans. They had strong national-origin identities and were indifferent to American distinctions between ethnics and black Americans. These youngsters were able to retain their identity because their accents, clothing style, and behavior clearly identified them as immigrants. They did well in school because of the different educational system, and in inner-city schools. they tended to be the better students. Waters concluded by asking how long the ethnic-identified second generation would continue to identify with their ethnic backgrounds, given the racism and discrimination in the larger society and the fact that their "lack of clues that would telegraph their ethnic status to others" (1996:196).

In Waters's review of the theoretical approaches to assimilation for recent immigrants and their children, she described the multiple and contradictory paths that second-generation children follow. She also discussed the fact that the situation faced by immigrant blacks in the 1990s differs in many of the assumptions of the straight-line model of assimilation. First, if blacks assimilate, they become American blacks, and black immigrants believe that being an immigrant black has a higher status. Second, the economic opportunity structure is very different now as the unskilled jobs in manufacturing that provided mobility no longer exist. A further complication is that for the second generation, part of becoming an American black is becoming aware of racism and its subtle nuances. Some second-generation children achieve socioeconomic success and retain strong ethnic attachments and identities, whereas others assimilate the American subcultures with limited socioeconomic mobility. Those who achieve socioeconomic success might be the first group to acculturate less than the European second and third generations.

Tensions Between Black Immigrants and African Americans

In his 1930s study of the Negro immigrant, Reid (1939) concluded that Negro immigrants enter the United States in the dual role of Negro and immigrant. As they move into Negro population centers in large numbers, they threaten the existing order of Negro adjustments and set the foundation for intraracial conflict. Negro immigrants have a low visibility because the external characteristics of both native and foreign Negroes are the same. Because they look alike, they are not inherently estranged; rather, it is their different customs that keep them isolated. Reid saw the initial clashes between native and foreign born as related to status. Because the immigrants are fewer in number, they are forced to subordinate their wishes and desires to those of the majority group. But for economic and utilitarian purposes, they soon seek status, recognition, position, and prestige in the existing political and moral order. Reid regarded this struggle as the root of the conflicts between native and foreign-born Negroes.

A tense relationship exists between Ethiopians and African Americans, for example. Ethiopians are drawn to Washington, D.C., because of its highly developed black community; its black political, economic, and social structure; and its black artistic and cultural circles. It is less daunting than other cities as a place for Africans to settle. However, if Ethiopians establish businesses in black communities, they are seen as foreigners, regardless of their U.S. citizenship. Another area of tension is their religious differences. Although many Ethiopians are Christian and join the established black and white churches, they also have their own churches. Hostility from the African American community, which sees them as making money and taking opportunities away from African Americans, is surprising to the Ethiopians. This hostility in turn forces them to hire their own countrymen or relatives, which only aggravates the situation. They see themselves as Ethiopians first and not as Africans or African Americans, and as newcomers they do not want to be placed in the position of the African American—at the bottom rung of the ladder. This separation is seen as an extension of the cultural and physical isolation that Ethiopians experienced in Africa; thus the Ethiopians also tend to keep their distance from other African immigrants. As a result, they are seen as behaving in a haughty and racist manner and trying to avoid associating with other Africans, when in reality it is their differing language and customs that separate them.

African immigrants also face prejudice from African Americans, who fear being displaced from their housing by immigrants moving into inner-city neighborhoods in search of moderately priced housing. Some African Americans link unemployment to immigration, and cultural, political, and attitudinal differences between African Americans and African immigrants may exacerbate the tension, further dividing the African American and African communities and possibly contributing to the exploitation of both groups.

MAINTAINING CONNECTIONS WITH THE COUNTRY OF ORIGIN

Technology and the ready accessibility of communication around the world mean that immigrants—if their families have telephones or access to this technology—are able to stay in touch easily with their country of origin. Most African and Caribbean countries have embassies in the United States that provide contact with the larger immigrant community. For example, in the Washington, D.C., area, the Caribbean nations celebrate their national independence days at a series of events, including church services, dinners, parties, and programs, at which the countries' ambassadors, along with members of the Caribbean diplomatic community, are represented. The same practices can be assumed about the African embassies, although refugees or those out of favor with an existing government may avoid these occasions.

Although travel to the country of origin might not be possible during the time that an immigrant is establishing permanent residence and then citizenship, visits by relatives are possible, particularly from the Caribbean. Once citizenship is secured, these visits may take place regularly to maintain family ties, establish businesses, or provide care to extended family members.

Local newspapers for African or Caribbean communities report on news about the home country and issues affecting the local community. These newspapers also reflect the concerns or interests of the immigrant group, in advertisements from travel agencies, shipping companies, immigration lawyers, real estate companies, and insurance companies. These publications provide ongoing contact with the island communities and a listing of services provided by other immigrant groups in the United States.

THE IMMIGRANT POPULATION'S STRENGTHS AND NEEDS

In accordance with 1965 Immigration Act, the shift from a quota system to one based on labor needs has helped revitalize many inner-city areas, with the large numbers of professional immigrants making their presence felt in every sphere. At the lower socioeconomic end, the immigrants' labor has been used to meet the demand for various skilled and unskilled jobs, and their determination and hard work have often meant better opportunities for their children.

Immigrants to the United States are expected to succeed on their own and to require few if any services from the federal, state, or local government. As a result, no coordinated service programs exist to meet the special needs of immigrants to the United States. The exception has been the services to refugee groups that this country has offered at various points in its history. The federal government's Office of Refugee Resettlement, which was established after the Vietnam War to help resettle refugees from Vietnam and surrounding countries, provided funds to states and mutual aid associations to assist these groups in their resettlement. Similar support was given to Cuban refugees, Haitians, Soviet Russian Jews, and other groups. This support is the exception, however, and as a result, the services provided to immigrants in this country are haphazard and unplanned. Immigrants nonetheless have multiple needs that should be addressed, but there is an ongoing reluctance to do so. The passage of a welfare reform law in 1996 denying food stamp benefits to legal immigrants is an example of this reluctance. An example of a more positive response to this need was the establishment of the Haitian Community Health Information and Referral Center in 1983 by a Haitian immigrant. The agency, located in Brooklyn, is available to the 500,000 Haitians living in New York and provides a variety of social and health service referrals to low-income, Creole-speaking and other Caribbean families. As a result of welfare reform changes, this agency has taken the initiative to explain these changes to immigrants and to monitor their impact on the Haitian community (HCSSW Update, Spring 1998).

FAMILY DYNAMICS

In her 1988 study, Jenkins reported that according to the Haitian associations, in addition to families' problems of adjustment and communication or language barriers, the different roles of men and women (or husbands and wives) in the United States create an equally pervasive stress. Haitian women are more likely to be working outside the home in the United States, and because Haitian men

traditionally believe that they "possess" their wives, they find it diff
them work. Furthermore, traditional forms of control over wives an
are not acceptable in the United States, and in parent-child conflict
feel powerless when their children act more independently than the,
their home country. This independence is heightened because children often
serve as interpreters for their parents. For the Ethiopians, such stresses on the
family are its breakup, the unacceptability of "hands-on" punishment of children and wives, loneliness, adjustment and mental health, and living expenses
and health care costs.

West Indian Families

The family structure in the Caribbean differs from island to island, but except
for Jamaica, most have a similar family structure. (Consequently, when one
reads about the Jamaican family, one cannot assume that the information applies to all West Indian families. See, for example, Janet Brice-Baker 1997 on Jamaican families.) Gopaul-McNicol (1993) used Cohen's typology to describe
the West Indian family:

> First, the Christian family based on formal marriage and a patriarchal order.
> This structure carries much status and is seen among the middle and upper
> classes. The man's primary responsibility in these families is economic and he
> is expected to support his wife and children. Failure to do this is seen as
> grounds for divorce.
>
> Second, "the faithful concubinage" (called "living" in Trinidad). It has no
> legal status, is based on a patriarchal order, is culturally accepted, has at least
> three years' duration and may include children and they are seen as a family.
> The man performs all of the functions of a legal spouse and lives with the
> woman as if he was married to her.
>
> Third, is the companionate family where the individuals are living togeth-
> er primarily for pleasure and convenience usually for periods of less than
> three years.
>
> Fourth, is the disintegrated family, which consists of women and children
> only. In this type, the men may merely visit the women from time to time. In
> these latter three family structures women are less dominated by men.
> (Gopaul-McNichol 1993:20–21)

Some of the differences in the Jamaican family structure can be traced to the
following factors: Jamaica lies on the outer periphery of the West Indies and is

the least integrated with the other islands. It has the largest population in the West Indies, 2.4 million in 1990. It also has had the longest history of migration to the United States. Jamaicans tend to be more assertive, less tolerant of discrimination, and, because of the large numbers who have migrated, are able to maintain their cultural identification more easily than the other islanders can.

Because of the difficulties Jamaican men have had in securing employment, Jamaican women often must assume responsibility for the home and child care. Jamaican women's strength and independence are a notable difference compared with that of women from other islands. Jamaicans come to the United States looking for education and/or occupational advancement and retain an ethnic identity with their island or region. They have a sense of empowerment, since they have succeeded in casting off the burden of colonialism. Examples of black achievement are numerous, as many of their fellow Jamaicans have achieved prominence in their home island (Brice-Baker 1997; Gopaul-McNicol 1993).

Jamaican family relationships must be viewed within the context of their family and social class structure. Relationships between the European men who ruled the islands and the slaves created a colored middle class, a mixed-race population that had the benefit of education, moved into the professions, and became the new middle class. Upward mobility in Jamaica can also be achieved through education or marriage into the middle class. On the surface, sex roles are both traditional and stereotypical and vary little by class, race, or age. Girls are taught to be obedient and are discouraged from being assertive or sexually alluring. They are expected to date only boys known to their parents. Despite this emphasis on propriety, there are many unplanned, out-of-wedlock pregnancies and many extramarital affairs. A man's ability to have a mistress is a reflection of his status and wealth and his ability to feed and clothe another family. Although fidelity is seen as important and adultery is grounds for divorce, there is a double standard. A man can have extramarital affairs as long as they are discreet, but if they are discovered, they are not viewed as negatively as a woman's extramarital affair would be (Brice-Baker 1997).

The West Indian woman's primary responsibilities are rearing the children and taking care of her home and her husband in the same way that his mother did. The woman supports the husband's authority but holds power behind the scenes. In addition to this nuclear family is the extended family which encompasses those related by marriage and blood and can also include godparents, children who were adopted informally, and friends. All are expected to provide security for children and offer help in a crisis. Women rely on this structure for help with child rearing and household duties and also as a control against violence, as family members are expected to intervene in arguments and offer advice. Although in the United States, open communication is encouraged, in West Indian societies, gender, age, social and marital status, parenthood, educational level, and occupation determine who initiates conversation, speaks more readily, maintains eye contact, looks away, or changes the subject—all indications of who will dominate and who will submit. Women tend to avoid directness and confrontation but feel that their husbands are insensitive to their needs because of this lack of communication.

Feelings of love are usually expressed only toward infants. As the infant becomes a young child, affection is no longer openly expressed. Instead, love is affirmed through the parents' hard work to provide for the family and the mother's caring for the child's basic needs.

Respect is a core value, and disrespect for parents is an assault on the parent-child relationship. Respect for authority is learned in the home and reinforced in school and the community. The hierarchy of respect for parents is clearly defined, and parents do not try to have a friendship with their children. Children do not call adults by their first name and are expected to use titles when addressing them. It is considered impolite to contradict an adult, and children are expected to respect and obey their parents without exception. Younger siblings are expected to respect and obey their older siblings. Older siblings, in turn, are expected to help their parents take care of their younger siblings or grandparents. Respect is based on family hierarchy; it is not earned. Obligation also is an important spoken and unspoken concept in the family, and shame and reprimands are used to reinforce adherence to familial obligations.

In addition, males and females are socialized differently, with the most important child being the oldest son. Like the father, he commands more respect and receives better treatment. He is expected to be a lifelong role model to his siblings, and if he abdicates this role, the next son will take over. Boys are encouraged to enter a respectable profession, and girls are taught to handle domestic responsibilities so that they can be good wives and mothers. The eldest daughter is the "parental" child and shoulders more domestic responsibilities in the absence of the parents. Mother-child relationships tend to be strong, and the children's relationship with their father may be warm and affectionate. In an economically deprived family, the father may have to seek employment away from home, and so his role may be only an economic one. Adult children tend to stay home until they are married, and if they do, they are expected to contribute one-third to one-half their earnings for room and board. In the early years, fathers are not a source of emotional gratification or punishment, but as the child grows older, the father is the one to administer punishment at the

mother's instigation. Parents speak harshly to their children. Corporal punishment is quite common and includes spanking, slapping, or beating. The child
may be disciplined for taking too long; breaking items, even accidentally; or
being disobedient. This is an acceptable form of discipline and is not seen as
child abuse in West Indian culture (Brice-Baker 1997; Gopaul-McNicol 1993).

Haitian Families

The Christian family described by Gopaul-McNicol (1993) is typical of middle-
and upper-class Haitian families. In the lower socioeconomic classes, the pattern is the same as that described for the other West Indian islands. One family
pattern, called *placage* in Haiti, would be described in the United States as a
common law marriage. Another similar pattern is a man's cohabitation with
several partners and their children.

Haitian fathers are expected to be the financial provider and child discipli-
narian. Women are responsible for child rearing, and men act as the problem
solvers in unusual circumstances. Parent-child roles in Haitian families are also
clearly delineated, with limited tolerance of children's self-expression. Children
learn to absorb and not question; conformity and obedience are expected. Family business is expected to remain in the family. The extended family is valued
and, if available, is a source of support. Elderly grandparents take care of the
children while the parents work, and they expect to be treated with respect.
Adult children are expected to take care of their parents, and if they cannot do
so, the elderly grandparents are sent back home.

Like other West Indians, Haitians believe in corporal punishment, which
sometimes brings them into conflict with the larger society. Language adds another dimension to the issues faced by Haitian families in the United States. Few
Haitians speak French; most speak Haitian Creole. Fluency in French is associated with higher social status and formal knowledge, so Haitians who speak
only Haitian Creole are viewed as lower class (Bibb and Casimir 1997). Many
similar patterns exist in Haitian and West Indian families. The distinctions described by Charles in his discussion of the three sets of conditions prevailing in
the environment of Haitian children also apply to other West Indian families.
The first condition is that of households with children born in the United States
but living with their Haitian-born parents. These children are exposed to their
parents' values but at the same time are being acculturated into the American
value system.

In another family condition, children born in Haiti or other transitional islands are brought to the United States to rejoin their parents who are currently

living in the United States. The children acculturate more quickly than their parents do, which is alarming to the parents because they want their children to preserve their Haitian cultural identity.

In the third condition, the household contains both children born in the United States and those born in the island of origin. Often these siblings are reunited for the first time, and conflicts result from the different approaches used by parents toward the American-born and foreign-born children.

African Families

Ross-Sheriff stated that although immigrants from Africa "may share some similarities, they cannot be lumped together because of the many obvious distinctions—culture, language, religion, traditions and so on. There are also wide differences and disparities among conationals from single countries in Africa" (1995:135).

The first wave of immigrants from sub-Saharan Africa included highly trained and skilled workers such as technicians, engineers, physicians, and nurses. In the last decade, the number of African immigrants entering the United States rose dramatically. The 1990 U.S. Census reported more than 250,000 black Africans residing in the United States legally, primarily in the large cities. Nigerians accounted for 91,000, or 36 percent, of the Africans in the United States in 1990. We thus use Nigerian families here as an example of the African family, because of both their large numbers and the work of Nwadiora (1996) and Tikali-Williams (1997) on them and West African children. We should emphasize again, however, that each African group has its own cultural characteristics.

Nigeria, located on the West Coast of Africa, is the richest and most populous country in Africa, with a population of more than 100 million. Although the country has several modern cities, most of the population resides in rural villages. Nigeria was formed in 1914 when British colonialists combined three main tribal groups: the Hausa-Fulani, Igbo, and Yoruba. Since the nation's independence from Great Britain in 1960, it has experienced ethnic problems, a civil war, several military governments, and a succession of military coups.

The Hausa-Fulani live in the north of Nigeria and are one of the oldest Islamic civilizations in the world. Ninety-eight percent of the group is Muslim, and 42 percent of the families practice polygamy. In these families, children are named according to the dictates of Islam, and strict gender segregation is maintained in the home. "Women and children are cloistered in an emotionally enmeshed setting" (Tukali-Williams 1997:277). Age and rank regulate the social environment, and cultural expectations and knowledge remain constant over time. Boys and men have much social power and engage in highly symbolic communication with females while remaining a physical distance away from their dependent families. Girls marry when they are very young.

One percent of the Igbo, who live in the southeast, are Muslim, and the rate of polygamy is 30 percent. Forty-two percent of the Yoruba, who live in the southwest; are Muslim, and the rate of polygamy is also 30 percent. Although polygamy is a symbol of high status for men in the three tribal groups, figures indicate that most Yoruba marriages, and especially Igbo marriages, are monogamous. This change in marriage patterns is due to modernization and the influence of Christianity.

When Nigerian families arrive in the United States, they face an abrupt change from the social status of and affiliation with a majority group to that of a minority group. Because this stratification is based solely on skin color, the immigrant's social status is immaterial. This in turn leads to a resentment of racism and discrimination and is a major factor in the decision of 90 percent of the families who decide to return to Nigeria.

The family is the cornerstone of African cultures and is an extended family that includes one's blood relatives from several generations. Very strong ties are maintained with families and the home country, and only 10 percent of African immigrants, according to data from Apraku (1991) and Kamya (1997), had not returned home for a visit following immigration. Children are perceived as carriers of the future, the disseminators of cultural values, and economic insurance for their aged parents. The African elders are deeply respected and honored and are seen as repositories of wisdom who will soon join their revered ancestors. Homage is paid to ancestors, whom the Nigerians believe are still spiritually alive and influencing their daily affairs.

Festivities, rituals, and celebrations, which take place within the extended family and community structure, mark life cycle events such as birth, initiation to womanhood or manhood, marriage, and death. Marriage is an alliance between two extended families. Among the Igbo, the process leading to marriage may last for several months or even years. In addition to a middleman who investigates the respective families, a soothsayer or diviner determines the auspiciousness of the marriage. If the results are positive, a dowry is provided as a token of appreciation for the approval of the bridegroom's family to marry the bride. The husband and wife are expected to maintain moral virtues and their responsibilities to each other and not bring shame to their families, who are eternally tied through their marriage. They must remember that the eyes of their families, both living and dead, are constantly watching them, regardless of where they may reside.

The typical Nigerian family is patriarchal, with the man being the provider and the woman the nurturer. Both roles are important to the success of the family, but in the United States it is unusual for women to stay at home and raise children because they are usually involved in education, business, or employment. Because the male propagates the lineage of the family name and identification, the oldest male is given the title of the third parent.

The naming of the Nigerian child is an important ceremony which is celebrated three to ten days after the child's birth. Parents choose the name, which reflects the events surrounding the birth of the child, in conjunction with elders, who are considered to have the closest connections to ancestors. The naming ceremony may also be used to enforce social harmony and order by prescribing for the parents a program of actions or behaviors with respect to child rearing. Children derive their individual identity, familial and lineage positioning, and inheritance based on this program.

For the first three years of a child's life, Nigerian mothers have sole rights to a child, but because of economic pressures, surrogate caretakers may have to be used, which may be a source of great stress. The child must learn proper forms of address, including the correct use of titles, kinship, age and status terms, appropriate greetings, and the observance of rank, status, and power differences. Older siblings are held responsible for mishaps or infractions committed by their younger siblings, since children under six are not considered responsible for their behavior. Unlike Americans, Nigerians use only verbal skills to reinforce the social obligatory behaviors of their culture.

Nigerian culture is described as a "high-context culture" with less reliance on verbal communications than on understanding through shared experience, history, and implicit messages relayed through rituals and ceremonies. Nigerians tend to be more attuned to nonverbal cues and messages. Parents construct learning environments for their children that foster the acquisition of skills and virtues valued in their community. There is less maternal excitement or stimulation during infancy but more praise, structure, and support as the child grows older. Children are discouraged from talking to or seeking too much attention from adults, but older siblings are expected to provide as much attention as their younger siblings need.

Puberty is a major developmental milestone occurring between twelve and fourteen years of age, with various rites observed in Nigeria to mark it. Parents or godparents, in lieu of diviners and spiritualists, perform these rites, and parents hold social events to mark the occasion. Parents may change the youngster's wardrobe or provide jewelry as an indication of their change in status.

Boys reaching puberty also must assume additional social responsibilities, which may interfere with their peer-group activities. Teens are often sent to vacation in Nigeria, where they are exposed to traditional expectations and desires. The expectation is that the child will do well in school, but if not, the teen is commonly returned to Nigeria if other parental interventions fail. Girls are sheltered by their parents.

WOMEN

Bryce-Laporte (1981) characterized the 1965 Immigration Act as being marked by three features: (1) the elimination of the national-origin system; (2) the peak of the massive entry of immigrants into the United States, with Asia replacing Europe as the major source of immigration; and (3) the distinctive female majority that distinguished this new immigration. This pattern of female immigration has remained constant, and in 1995 the sex ratio was 86 males for every 100 females. One exception was between 1988 and 1992 when more men were admitted than women owing to the Immigration Reform and Control Act (IRCA). In 1991, during the peak year for IRCA legalization adjustments, the sex ratio reached 198 males for every 100 females (1995 Statistical Yearbook of the INS).

This movement of women, particularly Caribbean women, was enabled by a 1965 law that included a work provision permitting individuals to enter the United States to take jobs, such as domestic work, that could not be filled from the resident labor force. Employers had to show evidence that they had tried unsuccessfully to find a suitable worker in the United States (Kessner and Caroli 1982).

Earning a living has been as important to Caribbean women as it is to men. According to Gordon, these women have had to support themselves for the following reasons: "The westernized system of guaranteed male support for women and children has never been institutionalized among a large segment of Caribbean peoples," and "the economic marginality of some men negates any expectation of traditional male support" (1981:19). As a result, Caribbean women, unlike other immigrant women who are dependents of men, have migrated without male sponsorship.

With the 1965 Immigration Law opening the door to semiskilled and unskilled labor from the West Indies, the Caribbean women were able to fill the need for domestic workers in the United States. Because most of these jobs required that they live in their employers' homes, they moved without their children, who were left in the Caribbean with relatives such as maternal grandmothers or other persons in the extended kinship network. Another group that migrated was nurses, who were recruited to relieve shortages in hospitals in the New York area.

The provisions of this law determined the immigration pattern: adults who migrated alone with the expectation that they would later be joined by their family, those who immigrated as complete family units, single persons with no dependents, and those who left their family behind with no expectation of their joining them. Those who leave family behind with no expectation of being reunited with them usually come for a short period of time to supplement the family income and are generally professionals, such as nurses. Single women in various occupational categories have the best opportunity for self-improvement through occupational upgrading or education, since they have no other family obligations.

Adults who migrate by themselves with the expectation of being joined by their family have the hardest time because they must reorganize their lives and reconstitute their families. Many years may elapse before this process is completed. Although immigration law favors younger children, mothers who must work usually want the older children, who can care for themselves, to come first. These women also must demonstrate that they can support their children. The result is brief visits with children, and when they join her she is unable to exercise her parental authority because she is not accepted as an authority figure. In addition, because she must continue to work, she is also often absent from the home and cannot provide the support and guidance needed by her newly reconstituted family (Gordon 1981). When Jenkins (1988) asked women newcomers if they faced problems distinct from those of men, they mentioned two—the care of their children and how that care tied women to their homes, and the changed roles and relationships between men and women.

PROBLEMS FREQUENTLY ENCOUNTERED

Immigrant families have a variety of human services needs, including housing, employment and training, health and mental health issues, education, legal services, family support including day care, and services for young people, the elderly, and women. That is, they present the same problems for social services as do any other group of Americans, but their response to and use of these services are largely determined by the nature of the service. For example, immigrant families often come in conflict with the legal and social service system around the issue of child abuse because of their different attitudes toward discipline and corporal punishment.

Role of the Social Worker

Although much has been written about social work services for America's increasingly diverse populations, the term *diverse* is only a catchall phrase for a variety of groups. A text edited by Fisher, *Cultural and Ethnic Diversity: A Guide for Genetics Professionals* (1996), talks only about native-born blacks and does not address any other black groups. Canino and Spurlock's *Culturally Diverse Children and Adolescents: Assessment, Diagnosis and Treatment* (1994:45) makes the point that "clinicians should also be alert to cultural differences as well as similarities among those identified as Black or African-American." While those immigrants from the Caribbean islands and West and East Africa may bear some similarities to American-born blacks, for many the differences are much greater. "Identified as African Americans, they hold various beliefs about death and illness, some of which lead some to choose their traditional practitioners (e.g., Yoruba and voodoo priests) to alleviate their symptoms" of medical or psychological problems (p. 45). Clinicians should therefore determine how clients identify themselves rather than assume that an English-speaking person with dark skin and kinky hair is African American. The client may be proud to be Trinidadian and may identify himself or herself as black but not American (Canino and Spurlock 1994). Canino and Spurlock's book also provides clinical guidelines for social workers, psychologists, psychiatrists, and other community mental health workers who work with economically disadvantaged children and adolescents from culturally diverse backgrounds, but a true study of the social worker's role as it relates to the issue of black immigrants and their needs remains to be written for the social work professional.

AVAILABLE SERVICES, POLICIES, AND PROGRAMS

In 1980, a group of Ethiopians organized the Ethiopian Community Center (ECC) in Washington, D.C. They were criticized by some in the community for making it comfortable for people to stay here rather than return to their home country. But the founders saw it as a way to help Ethiopians adjust to life here. The ECC, which survives on government grants and private donations from Ethiopian businesses, sees one of its important tasks as the promotion and enhancement of a positive image of the Ethiopian community in the United States.

Jenkins wrote in 1988 that these ethnic associations are not a new phenomenon in the United States but that they reemerged with the rise in immigration of new groups with distinct cultural patterns. She then distinguished between what an ethnic association is and what it does. An ethnic association is an organization formed by individuals who consciously define themselves as members of an ethnic group, with the goal of fulfilling needs common to persons of that group and positioning itself as part of the ethnic community. The key elements are the basis of a self-defined ethnic group, the voluntary nature of the association, and the goal of mutual benefit. What is new is that these associations are being formed in a country that already has large institutionalized social welfare programs and professional social work bureaucracies. This led Jenkins to ask several questions: Are the benefits of the welfare state available to immigrants, refugees, and temporary workers? How can newcomers negotiate the system to obtain needed services? Can the ethnic associations, in their role as mutual support groups, become a conduit for the delivery of social services to immigrants and refugees? What links exist, or can be forged, between ethnic associations and the formal volunteer and public social service system? Using these questions, Jenkins studied New York City.

Three Haitian groups were identified for the study. The oldest was started in 1967 for Haitians in New York, to help Haitians find jobs, adapt to the city, gain access to social services, and bring family members to the United States. This association functions as an ethnic agency, and about 15 percent of its clients are newcomers who differ from earlier immigrants in that many are illiterate and have had no formal education. In 1975 another Haitian group was incorporated whose concerns are the social, cultural, and service needs of new Haitian immigrants and the immigration and adjustment problems of poor Haitians. This membership association also serves nonmembers. At least a third of those served arrived in the 1980s, and their educational levels were lower, more were undocumented, and more were from rural areas. A third Haitian association was organized in 1979 to provide a place where Haitians could come and feel at home and where new Haitian arrivals could be helped to get working permits and adjust to American society. Seventy-five percent of its clientele are newcomers. All three associations have paid employees and are funded by public money, subcontracts from volunteer associations, foundations, and/or fundraisers. Each of the three associations is in a different borough, with structural and operational differences, but all basically function as ethnic agencies to meet distinct needs. French Creole, the language of the people they serve, further distinguishes them from other English-speaking immigrants. They focus on immigration issues such as legal and civil rights, are actively involved in service delivery, and have an important community role because they can stretch their activities beyond their local situations. For example, in 1985 the first National Conference of Haitian Community Centers was held in New York as the first step in forming a national network of groups concerned with the problems of Haitians. Representatives of approximately fifty organizations met to discuss issues of common concern, such as housing, employment, language, and immigration counseling (Jenkins 1988).

Another association included in the Jenkins study was the Jamaican association established in 1938 to work for Jamaica's independence from Great Britain, which was achieved in 1962. Since then, the association's goal has been Jamaican economic independence from the United States. The association also provides services to Jamaicans and other West Indians in New York City. It is a membership organization with about two thousand members, 98 percent of whom are Jamaicans, and it also includes people from other Caribbean islands as well as North Americans. The association represents the earlier immigrant group but is not heavily involved with newcomers. Newcomers are seen as more aggressive and militant, as expecting too much, and as wanting to see more things happen, in contrast to the older immigrant group that saw themselves as more balanced. The association is primarily a volunteer organization and raises funds to support activities such as a Caribbean education group, immigration and legal advice, cultural activities, employment referral, student advisement, and informal referrals for jobs and housing (Jenkins 1988).

The two African associations examined in the Jenkins study were established to serve the Ethiopian population. Before the 1980 Refugee Act, Ethiopian immigrants were young, urban, educated, and single. But beginning in the 1980s, families and immigrants from rural areas and refugee camps began arriving in the United States. As a result, the associations were developed to serve the needs of refugees from Ethiopia. The first association was established in 1979 by an Ethiopian in New York to assist refugees in camps and newcomers with orientation, English classes, housing, counseling, and other needs. The second association was set up as a mutual assistance association in 1981, principally to identify Ethiopians' common needs and to help in the areas of immigration, civil rights, and welfare. The association has approximately one hundred dues-paying members and obtains funds through fund-raising, donations, and public support for refugees.

Jenkins's study also looked at newcomers' need for and knowledge and use of personal social services and the associations' role as provider and facilitator. The problems that the associations agreed had an adverse effect on family life were adjustment and communication or language barriers. The associations responded in different ways to meet the needs of their ethnic group. For example, the Haitian associations maintained a list of persons who would shelter women if they were abused, provided counseling, or referred them to a coalition of Haitian women. The Jamaican association, however, did not see the abuse of women as a problem at that time but viewed women working outside the home as paving the way for the men. The Ethiopian association reported no special problems with domestic abuse but felt that child care tied women to the home and inadequate education limited their employability.

How has the larger society, beyond these ethnic associations, responded to the needs of the immigrant population? The larger society usually responds, if at all, when the family comes in contact with a social service agency for any reason. These contacts may include child abuse and neglect cases, spousal abuse, difficulties in school, and the juvenile or criminal justice system, but seldom are contacts for services to a population in need. Exceptions occur when social workers or other helping professionals have an affinity or identification with a certain group. An early example of this was the work done by two West Indian social workers whose concern about the difficulties of a newly arrived immigrant student inspired them to secure funding to provide group counseling to a group of students with school problems. Because of the emphasis on education in West Indian families, the workers knew they could help the families if their approach centered on educational issues. Their purpose was to assist students with the cultural adjustment to life in America, facilitating their engagement with new family members, and getting reacquainted with a parent(s) who had not been a part of the child's life for many years (Sewell-Coker, Hamilton-Collins, and Fein 1985). In their group work in Canada, Glasgow and Grouse-Sheese (1995) supported these findings concerning the issues of rejection and abandonment among Caribbean adolescents. They pointed out that school and clinic personnel tried to make these students understand and appreciate the sacrifices that their parents made to bring them to Canada. But social workers have not always understood the need to appreciate how their parents' absence affected the children and how difficult the immigration process was for them. In addition, a "culture of silence" in which children are expected to be compliant makes it difficult for them to speak critically in the presence of their parents. Glasgow and Grouse-Sheese see the group work process as an opportunity for these young people to be heard by supportive adults and to understand their past experiences and current conflicts.

As the numbers of each immigrant group have increased, they have been able to develop their own resources. In New York City, with its large West Indian population, Medgar Evers College has opened a Caribbean Research Center, and the Caribbean Women's Health Association provides public education about health needs and, in particular, the prevention of AIDS. And every large city has religious and cultural organizations.

THE RELATIONSHIP BETWEEN IMMIGRANTS
AND THE WIDER SOCIETY

Black immigrants are entering a country with a distinct history of discrimination against people of African ancestry. Furthermore, both the white community and the African American community despise them. In her study of Jamaican immigrants (1987), Foner wrote that the most jarring change for Jamaicans was that being black took on a new and more painful meaning. Being black in a racially divided America became more of a stigma than it had been in Jamaica. Although black skin was not valued in Jamaica, it was not a barrier to upward mobility or to social acceptance "at the top." Because of their black skin, their distinctive problems and unique proclivities as Jamaicans are generally overlooked in the United States, and whites dismiss their demands and protests as being merely those of blacks as a whole (Foner 1987).

This shift from majority to minority status has heightened Jamaicans' consciousness of their ethnic identity, which some use as a way to distinguish themselves from black Americans. Many immigrants believe that setting themselves apart from black Americans has tangible benefits, and many feel they receive better treatment from whites than do black Americans. To summarize Foner's findings, Jamaicans felt they were different from and superior to African Americans because they had not experienced the same wholesale prejudice and discrimination and saw themselves as more ambitious, more hardworking, and more productive (e.g., they saved so they could buy a home) and, with more dignity and self-assurance, as less hostile to whites. The large number of Jamaicans in New York City has had an important effect on ethnic relations within the black population as well as on race relations between blacks and whites. More and more Jamaicans now live and work with native black Americans, and an increasingly large, ethnically diverse black population is confronting whites with an ever-growing percentage of foreign-born individuals (Foner 1987).

These attitudes of separation have created tensions between the West Indian and native black Americans. One problem is the group's different norms, values, and attitudes. West Indians emphasize discipline, drive, and dedication, and as a result, West Indians appear to do remarkably well. Gladwell discussed other factors in his article "Black Like Them" (1996), in which he reported on Kasinitz's work in the Red Hook section of Manhattan where he interviewed employers and discovered a pattern of what the employers called *positive discrimination*. Employers had devised an elaborate mechanism for distinguishing those they felt were "bad" blacks and those they saw as "good" blacks. Good meant that you were from outside the neighborhood and, if you were an immigrant, were willing to work hard. Another study (1996) by Harvard sociologist

Mary C. Waters found a similar pattern. In both studies, West Indians were regarded as superior blacks, praised for their hard work and emphasis on education. In the 1980s, Sowell pointed out that the West Indian advantage was the historical legacy of the Caribbean slave culture. Gladwell also noted that because of the recognition of the West Indians' achievement, one could say that racism was not aimed at all black people. But as the researchers found in their studies of hiring patterns, employers were drawn to the unfamiliar because they deemed unacceptable what was familiar to them—that is, the blacks who lived in their neighborhood. Gladwell stated that moreover, the success of West Indians was not proof that racism did not exist but, instead, was a way of giving another twist to racist attitudes. Thus employers' attitude was, I do not despise you for the color of your skin, because there are some black people whom I like; instead, I despise you for who you are. Gladwell labeled this *multicultural racism*, in which one ethnic group could be played off against another because of the color of their skin. But we will not really know where this discrimination originated until the second generation, when the children of West Indians become part of the African American mainstream and no longer are distinctive. Gladwell also explored the guilt of West Indians who have made a point of differentiating themselves from other African Americans, thereby making it easier for whites to join in their criticism. He concluded by noting that what has happened to the Jamaicans in Toronto, where they are looked down on, is further proof that what has happened in the United States is not the end of racism but an accident of history and geography. In the United States, because there is always someone else to despise, even in the "new" racism—as in the "old"— somebody must always be at the bottom.

Case Studies and Other Resources

In their discussion of families of African origin (1995), Black and Debelle note that therapists working with people of African descent in the United States must be aware of both cultural similarities and differences, raising questions and drawing distinctions so that the important differences can be discussed, understood, and celebrated. In his book *Communicating for Cultural Competence* (1998), Leigh uses an ethnographic model when interviewing clients so that the clients themselves become the social worker's cultural guides to learn about this other cultural world.

These techniques for entering the client's worldview are valuable for social workers serving a variety of clients. A knowledge base for working with these diverse families is currently being built, and social workers can consult books such as Leigh's on using ethnographic interviews or Canino and Spurlock's *Cul-*

turally Diverse Children and Adolescents (1994). In addition, other authors have developed various assessment techniques. Gopaul-McNicol recommends the use of a West Indian Comprehensive Assessment Battery (WICAB) instrument that "is aimed at assisting the clinical in assessing the client's various support systems, the social, emotional, and psychological functioning of the client and the cultural transitional conflicts being experienced by the client" (1993:18–19). Gloria Johnson-Powell (1997) has created the "culturologic" interview as a way of performing a cultural assessment when working with children and parents from different cultures.

In addition, many novels have been written about immigrants in the United States. The experiences of an earlier generation of Caribbean women are recounted in Paule Marshall's *Brown Girl, Brownstones* (1959), and Rosa Guy's *Ruby* (1976) talks about the experiences of the Caribbean immigrant child. Books about African immigrants include Mark Mathabane's *Kaffir Boy* and *Kaffir Boy in America* (1986 and 1989) and Kassindja and Bashir's *Do They Hear When You Cry* (1998).

There also is a large body of case material about the unique challenges faced by this new immigrant population. The following two brief case examples illustrate some of these issues:

> Chidi is the oldest son and is married with three teenagers. He recently returned to America after attending his father's funeral at home, where his elders cautioned him about living in the United States and neglecting his primary responsibilities at home. The village elders urged him to "come back home to fix things up and continue the work your father left behind." Chidi's conflict between his loyalty and desire to respect his family's wishes and traditional values and the need to live independently with his nuclear family in the United States precipitated depression that brought him, and eventually the whole family to treatment. Chidi became a workaholic, avoiding intimacy with unpredictable bursts of anger. A balance was brought about in the family through an agreement for Chidi to visit home every two years in order to "take care of things," and the family's need to remain in the United States but visit their home every 5 years. The family was also exposed to several other Nigerians in the area for cultural support.   (Nwadiora 1996:137)

In this case, the social worker skillfully recognized the Nigerian man's competing responsibilities and worked with the family to develop a reasonable compromise and, at the same time, arranged for additional supportive resources in their own immigrant community.

Aimee, age 8, was referred to the clinic because of nightmares, worries and concerns about her mother's safety. Her family had migrated recently from a rural area in the West Indies, where they had lived within a supportive extended family network. Aimee's father had remained in the West Indies. Her mother came to the United States in search of greater job opportunities and better education for her children.

Back in the West Indies, Aimee had enjoyed a large area to play in and had spent most of her free time outside. In contrast, she now lived in a crowded one-bedroom apartment and had to share her bed with her siblings. The apartment was in one of the worst crime-infested areas of the city; a crack raid had recently occurred in the next apartment. Aimee frequently heard shots at night and was often exposed to gang violence. Two older children in her school had been found dead in the previous 2 years. and she herself had been assaulted once. Aimee and her mother had become increasingly fearful, and Aimee was not allowed to go outdoors in the afternoons and on weekends.

Inadequate heat and electricity characterized the building in which the family lived. Because they had lived all their lives in a tropical climate, they were particularly sensitive to the cold weather.

Aimee met the diagnostic criteria for a separation anxiety disorder and was becoming school phobic. She also displayed symptoms of posttraumatic stress disorder. Hers was certainly a high-risk environment, and the number of stressful events she had experienced had overwhelmed her adaptive capacities.

Aimee's clinician was aware of the impact of these events on the family. He initiated the sessions by assessing the coping styles of the family in the past. He soon understood that Aimee's separation anxiety was precipitated by the dangerous neighborhood, the lack of the previously protective father, and the recent traumatic incidents. Aware of the added inability of this migrant family to access appropriate public resources, he consulted with a colleague from a social service agency. They orchestrated their efforts with those of a housing agency to locate an apartment in a more stable, safer community closer to a West Indian church. In a follow-up contact a year later, Aimee was free of symptoms and was adjusting well to her new school.

(Canino and Spurlock 1994:19–20)

In this case, once the social worker was able to arrange a move, Aimee's symptoms disappeared. A compilation of case illustrations like these, of the issues and dilemmas faced by immigrant families, is needed as a guide to the human service personnel who work with these new immigrant groups.

REFERENCES

The African Newsline. (1998). (April): 1–24.

Ahearn, F. L. Jr. (1995). Displaced people. In *Encyclopedia of Social Work.* 19th ed., vol. 1. Washington, DC: National Association of Social Workers Press.

Apraku, K. K. (1991). *African Emigrés in the United States: A Missing Link in Africa's Social and Economic Development.* New York: Praeger.

Bastien, M. (1995). Haitian Americans. In *Encyclopedia of Social Work.* 19th ed., vol. 2. Washington, DC: National Association of Social Workers Press.

Bibb, A., and Casimir, G. J. (1997). Haitian families. In M. McGoldrick, J. Giordano, and J. K. Pearce (eds.), *Ethnicity and Family Therapy.* 2d ed. New York: Guilford Press.

Black, J. S., and Debelle, G. D. (1995). Female genital mutilation in Britain. *British Medical Journal* 310: 1590–1592.

Brice-Baker, J. (1997). Jamaican families. In M. McGoldrick, J. Giordano, and J. K. Pearce (eds.), *Ethnicity and Family Therapy.* 2d ed. New York: Guilford Press.

Bryce-Laporte, R. S. (1972). Black immigrants: The experience of invisibility and inequality. *Journal of Black Studies* 3 (1): 29–56.

Bryce-Laporte, R. S. (1981). The new immigration: The female majority. In D. M. Mortimer and R. S. Bryce-Laporte (eds.), *Female Immigration to the United States: Caribbean, Latin American and African Experiences.* Washington, DC: Research Institute on Immigration and Ethnic Studies.

Burstyn, L. (1995). Female circumcision comes to America. *Atlantic Monthly* 276 (October): 28, 30, 32–35.

Canino, I. A., and Spurlock, J. (1994). *Culturally Diverse Children and Adolescents—Assessment, Diagnosis, and Treatment.* New York: Guilford Press.

Caribbean Daylight. (1998). (April 13).

Center for Immigration Studies. (1997). Immigration-related statistics—1997. *Backgrounder,* no. 3-97.

Cruse, H. (1967). *The Crisis of the Negro Intellectual—A Historical Analysis of the Failure of Black Leadership.* New York: Morrow.

Dinnerstein, L., and Reimers, D. (1975). *Ethnic Americans: A History of Immigration and Assimilation.* New York: Harper & Row.

Ethiopian Yellow Pages. (1997/98). 4th ed. Alexandria, VA.

Fisher, N. L. (ed.). (1996). *Cultural and Ethnic Diversity-A Guide for Genetics Professionals.* Baltimore: Johns Hopkins University Press.

Foner, N. (1987). Introduction: New immigrants and changing patterns in New York City. In N. Foner (ed.), *New Immigrants in New York.* New York: Columbia University Press.

Gladwell, M. (1996). Black like them: Why are West Indian immigrants perceived to be different from other African-Americans? *The New Yorker* (April 29 and May 6): 74–81.

Gladwell, M. (1998). Lost in the middle. *Washington Post Magazine* (May 17): 11–13, 27.

Glasgow, G., and Grouse-Sheese, J. (1995). Themes of rejection and abandonment in group work with Caribbean adolescents. *Social Work with Groups* 17 (4): 3–27.

Glazer, D. (1997). *We Are All Multiculturalists Now.* Cambridge, MA: Harvard University Press.

Gopaul-McNicol, S. (1993). *Working with West Indian Families.* New York: Guilford Press.

Gordon, M. (1981). Caribbean migration: A perspective on women. In D. M. Mortimer and R. S. Bryce-Laporte (eds.), *Female Immigration to the United States: Caribbean, Latin American and African Experiences.* Washington, DC: Research Institute on Immigration and Ethnic Studies.

Guy, R. (1976). *Ruby.* New York: Viking Press.

Haitian Community Health Information and Referral. (1998). *HCSSW Update* (Spring): 5.

Harrison, D. F., Thyer, B. A., and Wodarski, J. S. (1996). *Cultural Diversity and Social Work Practice.* 2d ed. Springfield, IL: Thomas.

Heilemann, J. (1996). The power of pragmatism. (In Talk of the Town.) *The New Yorker* (April 29 / May 6): 46–48.

Jenkins S. (ed.). (1988). *Ethnic Associations and the Welfare State—Services to Immigrants in Five Countries.* New York: Columbia University Press.

Johnson-Powell, G. (1997). The culturologic interview: Cultural, social, and linguistic issues in the assessment and treatment of children. In G. Johnson-Powell and J. Yamamoto (eds.), *Transcultural Child Development—Psychological Assessment and Treatment.* New York: Wiley.

Jones, N., Jacobs, N. R., and Siegel, M. A. (1995). *Information Plus—Compact Minorities—America's Rich Culture.* Wylie, TX: Information Plus.

Kabena, T. (1998). Town meeting unifies Nigerians. *African Sun Times* (September 7–13): 3, 10.

Kamya, H. A. (1997). African immigrants in the United States: The challenge for research and practice. *Social Work* 42 (2): 154–165.

Kasinitz, P. (1992). *Caribbean New York Black Immigrants and the Politics of Race.* Ithaca, NY: Cornell University Press.

Kassindja, F., and Bashir, L. M. (1998). *Do They Hear When You Cry.* New York: Delacorte Press.

Kent, C. (1986). Dangerous, deadly, scarring: AMA efforts advance ban on female circumcision: Culturally sensitive public education urged. *American Medical News* 39 (October 28): 3.

Kessner, T., and Caroli, B. B. (1982). *Today's Immigrants, Their Stories.* New York: Oxford University Press.

Lander, A., Foster, C. D., and Jacobs, N. R. (1994). *Information Plus—Minorities—A Changing Role in America.* Wylie, TX: Information Plus.

Leigh, J. W. (1998). *Communicating for Cultural Competence.* Needham Heights, MA: Allyn & Bacon.

Luxner, L. (1998). Ambassador interview—Ambassador of Grenada Denis Antoine—Tiny country with big agenda. *Embassy Flash* (February): 4, 11.

Marshall, P. (1959). *Brown Girl, Brownstones.* New York: Avon Press.

Mathabane, M. (1986). *Kaffir Boy.* New York: Macmillan.

Mathabane, M. (1989). *Kaffir Boy in America.* New York: Scribner.

Matthews, L. (1997). On the labeling of immigrants: Illegal aliens? *Caribbean Journal* (May 31): 5.

Millman, J. (1997). *The Other Americans—How Immigrants Renew Our Country, Our Economy and Our Values.* New York: Viking Press.

Nwadiora, E. (1996). Nigerian families. In M. McGoldrick, J. Giordano, and J. K. Pearce (eds.), *Ethnicity and Family Therapy.* 2d ed. New York: Guilford Press.

Ostine, R. (1998). Caribbean immigrants and the sociology of race and ethnicity: Limits of the assimilation perspective. *African American Research Perspective* 4 (1): 68–76.

Portes, A., and Stepick, A. (1993). *City on the Edge—The Transformation of Miami.* Berkeley and Los Angeles: University of California Press.

Reid, I. D. (1939). *The Negro Immigrant.* New York: Columbia University Press.

Reynolds, B. (1994). The move to outlaw female genital mutilation. *MS* 12 (3): 65.

Ross-Sheriff, F. (1995). African Americans: Immigrants. In *Encyclopedia of Social Work*, 19th ed., vol. 1. Washington, DC: National Association of Social Workers Press.

Sewell-Coker, B., Hamilton-Collins, J., and Fein, E. (1985). Social work practice with West Indian immigrants. *Social Casework: Journal of Contemporary Social Work* 66 (9): 563–568.

Toubia, N. (1994). Female circumcision as a public health issue. *New England Journal of Medicine* 331 (September 14): 712–716.

Tukali-Williams, J. (1997). West African children. In G. Johnson-Powell and J. Yamamoto (eds.), *Transcultural Child Development—Psychological Assessment and Treatment.* New York: Wiley.

Ugwu-Oju, D. (1995). *What Will My Mother Say—A Tribal African Girl Comes of Age in America.* Chicago: Bonus Books.

Ungar, S. J. (1995). *Fresh Blood: The New American Immigrants.* New York: Simon & Schuster.

U.S. Bureau of the Census. (1992). *Census of Population, 1990*: General Population Characteristics, United States. Washington, DC: U.S. Government Printing Office.

U.S. Immigration and Naturalization Service. (1995). *Statistical Yearbook of the Immigration and Naturalization Service.* Washington, DC: U.S. Government Printing Office.

Waters, M. C. (1996). Ethnic and racial identities of second-generation black immigrants in New York City. In A. Portes and R. G. Rumbaut (eds.), *The New Second Generation.* New York: Russell Sage.

CHAPTER 5
SOCIAL WORK PRACTICE
WITH EUROPEAN IMMIGRANTS

Howard Jacob Karger and Joanne Levine

Much of America's "melting pot" is made up of European immigrants, of which the majority are classified as Caucasian or white. Although American society is typically divided along the lines of "whites" and people of color, clumping all of white society into a single category is almost as misleading as ignoring the important cultural differences among people of color. For example, in 1850, it was relatively easy to describe white Americans because they probably had an Anglo-Saxon background and were Protestant. After the Civil War, however, immigrants began coming from southern and central Europe who were not Protestant and not Anglo-Saxon and whose language and culture were different from those people who preceded them. As a result, it is difficult in the 1990s to describe a white American, since about 200 million people can trace some of their ancestry back to the following groups (in descending order based on size): English, German, Irish, French, Italian, Scottish, Polish, Dutch, Swedish, Norwegian, Russian, Czech, Slovakian, Hungarian, Welsh, Danish, and Portuguese. In addition, the background of many white Americans is Hispanic. Although most of these groups have generally assimilated into American life, many continue to maintain some of the characteristics that have contributed to the uniqueness of American society (Bernardo 1981). To better understand European immigration, therefore, we will first examine the history of European immigration to the United States.

A BRIEF HISTORY OF EUROPEAN IMMIGRATION

Between 1800 and 1860, six million, mostly impoverished, European immigrants entered the United States. As early as 1796, officials of New York City's poorhouse complained of the "enormous and growing expense . . . not so much from the increase of our own poor, as from the prodigious influx of indigent foreigners into this city" (Trattner 1974:52). By 1820, the annual report of New York's Society for the Prevention of Pauperism listed "emigrants to this city from foreign countries as the single largest source of pauperism" (p. 53).

Between 1820 and 1860, more than four million immigrants to the United States came from more than twenty different countries, most from England, Ireland, Germany, and Scandinavia. Ireland suffered a serious potato famine in the 1840s, and an unsuccessful revolt in Germany in 1848 brought many political refugees. In general, the English blended with the larger population; the Irish settled in the larger cities; and the Scandinavians lived in relatively small frontier communities (Cohen 1958). Much to the chagrin of many American Protestants, most of the Irish and German settlers were Catholic, unlike the earlier English immigrants.

From 1850 to 1880, immigration continued at a rate of approximately 2.5 million people a decade, and between 1880 and 1890, immigration reached a high of 5.25 million. Newer immigrants arriving after 1865 differed from the earlier immigrants in that they came primarily from Poland, Russia, Austria, Hungary, Turkey, Portugal, Italy, and the Balkans. Most of the immigrants who came between 1880 and 1900 were eastern Europeans, and the largest number were Jews fleeing the pogroms in czarist Russia. For example, in 1820 there were only 6,000 Jews in the United States, but by 1900 that number had risen to 4 million. Between 1900 and 1910, the number of immigrants reached an all-time high of 8.8 million (Cohen 1958).

The Difficult Conditions Faced by European Immigrants

Between 1890 and 1920, 22 million immigrants came to the United States, and at the same time, the American people became more urban. Seventy-five percent of the immigrants lived in the cities; and during the decade following 1920, 6 million people moved from farms to cities (Axinn and Levin 1975). By 1914, almost one-fifth of the American population were European immigrants who had arrived between 1880 and 1914. In fact, 40 percent of the population of the twelve largest cities were immigrants, and another 20 percent were second-generation Americans. By 1915, 60 percent of the U.S. labor force was foreign born (Jansson 1993).

Life in late-nineteenth-century America was hard. The dream of milk and honey that motivated many immigrants to leave their homeland became, for many, a nightmare. The streets of American cities were not paved with gold; instead, they were overcrowded, riddled with disease and crime, and economically destitute.

The immigrants of the early 1900s came from many European nations and had distinct cultures. For example, most of the Italian immigrants were peasants who were forced to leave their villages because of high rents, rising taxes, and competition from factories that made products similar to those made in small cottage industries. Husbands or unmarried men often migrated to America in the hope that they would make a fortune and then return to Italy. Many, however, ultimately decided to pay for steamship tickets for their families rather than return to their homeland. Despite remaining in America, many Italians continued to maintain close ties to their native land (Jansson 1993).

In contrast, Russian and Polish Jews usually migrated with their entire families. They were often artisans and small merchants who left eastern and central Europe because of economic competition from large factories, economic discrimination and persecution, and fear of the pogroms directed against Jews. Like Italians, immigrant Jews maintained close ties with their families remaining in the "old country" and often brought over large numbers of relatives. Unlike the Italians, however, most did not want (or could not) return to the country they had left. In general, their main allegiance was to family and community rather than to the nation or place of their birth.

Many European immigrants of the early 1900s were wooed by steamship companies that promised them prosperity in the new land. Although word of mouth from earlier immigrants belied some of the actual conditions in the United States, many decided that the harsh life in America would be better than what they had at home. Often robbed en route to seaports by bandits, most immigrants also had to survive the diseases endemic to low-cost steamship passage. After a difficult journey, many immigrants were shocked to find themselves stuck in dark and crowded tenement houses, which differed dramatically from the fresh air of their native villages (Jansson 1993).

A typical tenement apartment contained two or three rooms, with a large tub in the kitchen where people bathed. There were often no inside toilets or just one toilet shared by each floor. The tenements were usually built extremely close to one another, which restricted ventilation, and some tenement apartments contained no windows or indoor plumbing. Immigrants moved frequently to escape exploitative slumlords and eviction or to be nearer a better job market.

Conditions in the immigrant sections of large cities were deplorable. Food poisoning was common in the absence of refrigeration and public health controls; many medicines contained toxic substances or had no medicinal value; and rodent infestation was the norm. Hastily constructed wood tenements that housed hundreds of families were firetraps, in the absence of few or no housing codes. In some cases (e.g., the Chicago fire of 1871), whole sections of cities burned. Crime rates, including murder, were high, as street gangs from various ethnic groups fought one another to stake out their territories. Tuberculosis was widespread, and among some groups, infant mortality was as high as 50 percent. Medical care for the poor was nearly nonexistent; there was little or no public education, and insanity, suicide, and prostitution were common (Bremner 1956).

The industrial and economic prospects were equally bleak. Factory conditions were abominable: Workers were expected to work six (or even seven) days a week, and twelve-hour days were common. Indeed, it was not unusual for workers to be required to work eighteen-hour days, especially in the summer. Whatever labor regulations existed could be overridden by "voluntary agreements" between employers and employees. Factories were poorly lit and unsanitary, vulnerable to fire, and offered almost no job security. Immigrants received extremely low wages. According to Jansson, "Though $15 per week was needed for survival by families in Pittsburgh in 1909, two-thirds of immigrants earned $12.50, and half of them earned less than $10. Barely half the workers in American industry could survive on one paycheck" (1993:114). Moreover, homework (piecework done at home, usually assembly done by whole families in one- or two-room tenements) was common (Karger 1988). Women were often forced to work at night and then take care of their home and children by day (Karger and Stoesz 1998). No special protective legislation for women existed until the early 1900s, and child labor was legal. According to Richard Hofstadter (1955), industrial accidents claimed one out of ten to twelve workers, and employees had neither worker's compensation nor disability insurance. When these conditions are added to the fact that American workers experienced an economic depression every fifteen or twenty years, it is clear that the lot of immigrants and of most working-class Americans was extremely difficult (Montgomery 1979).

Moreover, graft and corruption became the rule as urban immigrants competed for scarce food, housing, and jobs, eking out a marginal existence in squalid city tenements. Eventually, political machines emerged that converted city governments into fiefdoms of patronage (Kaplan 1974; Riis 1890). In short, it was no accident that Charles Loring Brace (1872), a pioneer of child welfare, entitled his book *The Dangerous Classes of New York.*

Because of the Depression of the 1930s, the number of immigrants fell below the legal quota, with only 699,375 entering the United States for permanent residence between 1930 and 1939. Then, however, the sweep of fascism across Europe forced thousands of people to seek refuge from political and religious persecution, and many turned to America. Since most of the refugees seeking asylum in the United States were from those countries with the smallest quotas (e.g., Germany), the immigration problem became acute, and by 1939, 185,333 refugees had entered the United States on temporary visas (Cohen 1958). This number, however, represented only a tiny fraction of those who were being persecuted. Many of them, especially Jews, who could not enter the United States because of immigration quotas, died as a result of the Nazis' "final solution." Of those who escaped from Nazi Europe, some refugees—such as Albert Einstein, Karen Horney, Otto Rank, Herbert Marcuse, Erich Fromm, and those scholars who started Manhattan's New School for Social Research—left an indelible imprint on American society.

AMERICA'S AMBIVALENCE TOWARD IMMIGRATION

American society has historically vacillated between believing that immigrants could be successfully absorbed into American society without serious economic and cultural consequences and fearing immigrants. During periods of optimism, it was believed that immigrants could be socialized and molded into model American citizens. But during periods of pessimism, it was feared that immigrants would take the jobs of native Americans, that the ranks of immigrants were composed mainly of anarchists and socialists, and that the rapid birthrate of European immigrants would result in the destruction of American society and its values. The Progressive Era belief in the positive aspects of immigration reached a peak in the social settlement movement.

The Settlement House Movement

The settlement house movement, which began in the 1880s and emerged in most large and medium-size American cities during the next two decades, was a response to immigration and the prevailing urban conditions. Most of the settlement houses were built in immigrant neighborhoods by wealthy benefactors, college students, single women, teachers, doctors, and lawyers, who themselves moved into the slums as residents. Rather than simply engaging in friendly visiting and outdoor relief, the upper- and middle-class settlement leaders tried to bridge class differences and to develop a less patronizing form of charity and socialization. Rather than coordinating existing charities, they tried to help the people in the neighborhoods organize themselves. Because they actually lived in the same neighborhoods as the impoverished immigrants, settlement workers could also provide fresh and reliable knowledge about the social and economic conditions of American cities (Karger and Stoesz 1998).

The foremost settlement house in the United States, Hull House, was established by Jane Addams in 1889. She approached the project—and the Chicago ethnic community in which it was housed—with a sense of Christian Socialism derived from a "rather strenuous moral purgation" (Hofstadter 1955) rather than a sense of noblesse oblige. The cofounder of Hull House, Ellen Gates Starr, described the values of the settlement house worker:

> After we had been here long enough and people see that we don't catch diseases and that vicious people do not destroy us or our property . . . we have well founded reason to believe that there are at least half a dozen girls in the city who will be glad to come and stay a while and learn to know the people and understand them and their ways of life; to give out of their culture and leisure and overindulgence and to receive the culture that comes from self-denial and poverty and failure which these people have always known.
>
> (Quoted in Davis 1973:57)

By 1915, this altruism was shared by enough settlement workers that more than three hundred settlement houses had been established, and most of the larger American cities could boast at least one or more (Davis 1973).

Although they provided individual services to poor immigrants, the larger settlements were essentially reform oriented. These reforms were achieved not only by organizing the poor to press for change but also by using interest groups formed by elite citizens and creating national alliances. Settlement-pioneered reforms included the prevention of tuberculosis, the establishment of well-baby clinics, the implementation of housing codes, the construction of outdoor playgrounds, the enactment of child labor and industrial safety legislation, and the promotion of some of the first studies of urban blacks in America, such as W. E. B. Du Bois's *The Philadelphia Negro*. Indeed, many of the leaders of President Franklin D. Roosevelt's New Deal had worked in settlements. For example, alumnae of Hull House included Edith Abbott, drafter of the Social Security Act; her sister, Grace Abbott, and Julia Lathrop, who became directors of the U.S. Children's Bureau; and Frances Perkins, secretary of labor and the first woman to be appointed to a cabinet post (*Encyclopedia of Social Work* 1995).

American Hostility Toward Immigration

The relatively benign paternalism that marked the Progressive Era settlement work gave way in the 1920s. to more strident techniques of social control. The inherently xenophobic and nativistic tendencies of America surfaced as a response to World War I and the Bolshevik Revolution of 1917. Fearful of an internal revolution, American society became less tolerant of foreign ideas and cultures and consequently demanded an uncompromising allegiance to what was perceived as Americanism. For example, the "Americanization crusade" pressured European immigrants into speaking English and identifying any Bolsheviks in their midst. This "red scare" ultimately led to the imprisonment and deportation of hundreds of foreign immigrants. It also led to the Immigration Act of 1924, which sought not only to curtail immigration but also to give preference—within this diminished flow—to northern Europeans. This was done by setting a quota of 2 percent of those nationalities who were living in America in the 1890s. Not surprisingly, during that period there were relatively few eastern European Jews, Italians, and Asians living in the United States. Only Mexican immigrants escaped the quotas (Jansson 1993).

Settlement houses—in many ways a mirror of their times—responded to this challenge by trying to create "100 percent Americans" out of their immigrant neighbors. With some notable exceptions (e.g., Chicago's Hull House), the Americanization emphasis, though always present in settlement work, reached a new zenith from roughly 1919 to 1929. For instance, immigrant families brought customs with them such as arranged marriages and the strict discipline of children and adolescents. In addition, while the father had the ultimate authority in the family, it was often the mother who collected the paychecks of all family members and parceled out money to each, subtracting the cost of food and household goods. This form of family organization was anathema to the American nativists, who believed that the father should have fiscal control and the children should be free to marry (within reasonable parameters) whomever they chose. Customs such as buying food in large, crowded markets and from street peddlers was frowned upon as unsanitary. So too was the immigrants' diets, which consisted mainly of potatoes, bread, or pasta. Their medical practices, such as using midwives instead of physicians, were also deplored by the more conservative settlement workers and the American nativists. This same contempt was leveled at the immigrants' clothing and their inability (or refusal) to speak English to one another.

What the nativists and the conservative settlement workers perceived as distasteful was an important cultural adaptation to American society. For example, a diet heavy in starch allowed immigrants to survive on relatively few resources. Collapsing the incomes of all family members allowed immigrant families to survive in hard economic times. The pooling of resources also allowed these families to accumulate capital, which they could later use to start a small business or educate a child. As Jansson put it, "each family constituted a small welfare state" (1993:114). The use of arranged marriages also encouraged more stable marriages based on similarities rather than differences; it helped combine the resources of two families (often leading to joint business ventures); and it helped keep the individuals tightly connected to the existing family structure and community. In theory, arranged marriages would reduce the likelihood of divorce, something that most of the immigrant population clearly could not afford.

With some exceptions (e.g., the relatively progressive Immigration and Nationality Act Amendments of 1965), America's ambivalence toward immigrants continues today. Moreover, immigration remains one of the knottiest social and legal issues facing American society. In response, anti-immigration groups such as the Federation for American Immigration Reform (FAIR) broadcast exclusionary messages. For these groups, immigration is a time bomb in terms of its negative impact on the U.S. economy and its effects on the interests of American workers. This hostility is also rooted in the fear of losing an already vaguely defined American identity. According to FAIR,

> Overall, current levels of immigration are reducing the quality of life for the average American. Our limited resources are being exhausted, our jobs are being taken, our wages are being depressed, our schools are being overcrowded, our highways are being congested and our welfare system is being overrun. In addition, certain segments of the population such as youths, the urban poor, and those employed in specific labor sectors such as nurses and cab drivers are being forced out of the labor market.   (FAIR n.d.)

In 1992, Republican presidential candidate Pat Buchanan made immigration policy a major plank in his bid for the presidency, explaining: "[One] reason that we are beset with conflict is that since 1965 a flood tide of immigration has rolled in from the Third World, legal and illegal, as our institutions of assimilation—public schools, popular culture, churches—disintegrated" (quoted in Rosen 1996:11).

Critics and proponents of immigration base their claims on three studies. The first, by economist Donald Huddle of Rice University, claims that post-1969 immigrants have created an annual net deficit in the economy of $44 billion. A second study, by the Center for Immigration Studies, calculated that post-1969 immigrants create a net deficit of $29 billion annually. But the proponents of immigration point to a 1994 Urban Institute study by Michael Fix and Jeffery Passel that found that post-1969 immigrants create an annual net benefit to the economy of $29 billion (FAIR 1994). At best, it is unclear whether immigration by itself creates a net benefit or a net drain on the economy.

Anti-immigration critics argue that immigrants constitute a growing part of welfare recipients. According to FAIR,

> Adult immigrants received 10.8 percent of all Aid to Families with Dependent Children (AFDC) in 1993, up from 5.5 percent ten years earlier. The total cost to taxpayers to provide AFDC to immigrants in 1993 was $1.2 billion. . . . Moreover, between 1983 and 1993, the percentage of SSI recipients who were immigrants tripled from 3.9 percent to 11.5 percent. . . . The actual number of immigrants receiving SSI benefits more than quadrupled from 151,207 in 1983 to 683,178 in 1993. Elderly immigrants now constitute 28.2 percent of recipients of SSI for the elderly. . . . The number of immigrants receiving SSI payments for disability grew from 22,600 in 1983 to 266,730 in 1993 more than a ten-fold increase. . . . Approximately 1.4 million legal immigrants were receiving SSI or AFDC in 1993; 6 percent of the immigrant population are on public assistance, compared with 3.4 percent of all citizens.   (1995:1)

Partly as a result of these contentions, Congress included immigration reforms in the Personal Responsibility and Work Opportunity Act (PRWORA) of 1996. The most comprehensive welfare reform legislation passed since the New Deal of 1935, this nine-hundred-page bill contained profound implications for both legal and illegal immigrants (U.S. House of Representatives 1996). Specifically, the original PRWORA disentitled most legal immigrants (including many who have been living in the United States for years but have elected not to become citizens) from food stamps, Aid to Families with Dependent Children (AFDC), and Supplemental Security Income (SSI). (Illegal immigrants were never entitled to these benefits.) Immigrants still entitled to benefits were (1) those who have become citizens or who have worked in the United States and paid social security taxes for at least ten years and (2) veterans of the U.S. Army who are noncitizens. In addition, the bill gave the states the option of denying Medicaid benefits to immigrants. In Texas alone, the PRWORA was expected to disqualify 187,000 legal immigrants from receiving food stamps, 22,000 from AFDC benefits, and 53,000 from SSI (Reinert 1996). As a result of changes in immigration policy, 1995 saw the steepest sustained drop in immigration since World War II. The current legal immigration is approximately 700,000 a year, in a U.S. population of over 260 million.

The United States accepts only a fixed number of refugees each year, a number determined by the president in consultation with Congress. For example, in 1997, 78,000 refugees were permitted to enter the United States The total number of "refugee slots" is divided among different regions of the world, and in 1997, the regions and numbers of slots were as follows:

- Africa—7,000
- East Asia—10,000
- Eastern Europe and the former Soviet Union—48,000
- Latin America and the Caribbean—4,000
- The Near East (southwestern Asia and the Middle East)—4,000
- Unallocated reserve—5,000 (this may be allocated to refugees fleeing unforeseen trouble arising during the year). The State Department decides from which countries within these regions the United States will accept refugees. For example, in 1997, the only African nationalities permitted were Somalians, Sudanese, Burundians, and Liberians.

Current Trends in European Immigration

Legal immigration to the United States has undergone several changes in the last ten years. From 1985 to 1988, the total flow of immigration into the United States remained relatively constant and then rose sharply from 1988 to 1991. The sharp rise after 1988 was due to the impact of the Immigration Reform and Control Act of 1986 (IRCA), which granted legal status to undocumented immigrants who had been in the United States continuously since 1982 or had worked in agriculture. In 1995, the total number of immigrants admitted to the United States was 720,461, less than half the 1,827,167 admitted in 1991.

Since 1965, the major source of immigration to the United States has shifted from Europe to Asia and Latin America, reversing the trend of nearly two centuries (see figures 5.1 and 5.2). According to the Immigration and Naturalization Service (INS), Europe accounted for 50 percent of all U.S. immigration during the decade between 1955 and 1964, followed by North America at 35 percent and Asia at 8 percent. In 1995, Asian immigration peaked at 37 percent, followed by North America at 32 percent and Europe at 17.8 percent. The total number of immigrants from Europe more than doubled, from 63,043 in 1985 to 160,916 in 1994. This change was due largely to the Immigration Act of 1990, which revised the numerical limits and preferential categories used to regulate immigration. Specifically, the act increased the level of employment-based immigration and allotted a higher proportion of visas to highly skilled immigrants, a preference resulting in a rise in the number of immigrants from most European countries

(U.S. Department of Justice n.d.). Table 5.1 breaks down European immigration on a nation-by-nation basis, though only those European nations with significant numbers of immigrants are included.

Most immigrants (66.6 percent) to the United States choose to settle in just seven states: 23.1 percent in California, 17.8 percent in New York, 8.6 percent in Florida, 6.9 percent in Texas, 5.5 percent in New Jersey, and 4.7 percent in Illinois. European immigrants tend to follow a similar migration pattern, although they are more likely to congregate in the larger urban areas of the Midwest (e.g., Chicago) and the Northeast (e.g., New York) (U.S. Department of Justice 1996).In 1995, roughly 61,000 immigrants came from eastern and central Europe and 19,000 from western Europe. Although 48,000 European immigrants remain unaccounted for (presumably from a large number of small European nations), the three-to-one ratio between eastern/central and western Europe immigrants is expected to continue.

The differences between eastern/central and western European immigrants

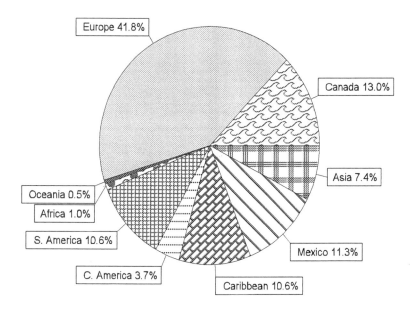

FIGURE 5.1 Immigrants by Place of Origin, 1964
Source: U.S. Department of Justice, Immigration and Nationalization Service, Washington, D.C. 1966

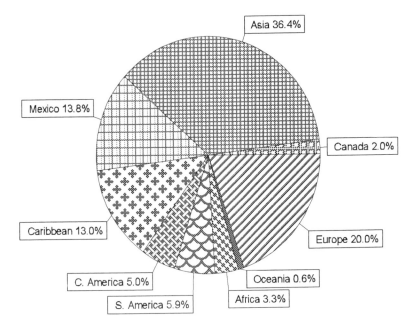

FIGURE 5.2 Immigrants by Place of Origin, 1994
Source: U.S. Department of Justice, Immigration and Nationalization Service, Washington, D.C. 1996

are noticeable. For example, of the 6,237 German immigrants to the United States in 1995, two-thirds were immediate relatives of a U.S. citizen. Of those migrating from the United Kingdom, almost half were immediate relatives of a U.S. citizen, with most of the remainder using employment-based preferences (i.e., needed skills in the United States). Presumably, these two groups of western European immigrants are either rejoining an immediate family member or occupying a job. But of the 17,432 Ukrainians migrating to the United States in 1995, almost 15,000 came seeking refugee or political asylum. Of the 14,560 Russians migrating to the United States in 1995, more than 8,000 entered as refugees or political asylees (U.S. Department of Justice 1996). Without a job or an immediate family member to look after them, many eastern and central European immigrants have a harder time adjusting to American society than do the majority of west European immigrants. Accordingly, the remainder of this chapter will focus on eastern and central European immigrants because (1) they make up the numerical majority of European immigrants to the United States and (2)

TABLE 5.1
European Immigration, 1993–1995

Country	1995	% 1995[a]	1994	% 1994[a]	1993	% 1993[a]	% Change, 1994–1995
Europe	128,185	17.8	160,096	20.0	158,254	17.5	-20.3
Ukraine	17,432	2.4	21,010	2.6	18,316	2.0	-17.0
Russia	14,560	2.0	15,249	1.9	12,097	1.3	-4.5
Poland	13,824	1.9	28,048	3.5	27,846	3.1	-50.7
UK	12,427	1.7	16,326	2.0	18,783	2.1	-23.9
Yugoslavia				0.4			
(former)	8,307	1.2	3,405		2,809	0.3	144.0
Germany	6,237	0.9	6,992	0.9	7,312	0.8	-10.8
USSR (unknown republics)	6,784	0.9	6,954	0.9	7,369	0.8	-2.4

Percentage of the immigrant population that entered the United States in that year.
Source: Adapted from U.S. Department of Justice, Immigration and Naturalization Service, *Immigration to the United States in Fiscal Year 1995* (Washington, DC: U.S. Government Printing Office, 1996), http://www.ins.usdoj.gov/graphics/aboutins/statistics/annual/fy95/132.htm.

they represent a serious challenge to social workers because they have more difficulty adjusting to American society as a result of their cultural, familial, and social differences.

THE CONTEXT OF EASTERN AND CENTRAL EUROPEAN IMMIGRATION

The effect of the global marketplace on the eastern European nations' economies is difficult to measure. First, we have only sketchy economic data for many of these countries. Second, their economies vary widely in their level of industrialization, the age of their industries, their physical infrastructure, and their per capita incomes. For example, the 1991 per capita GNP of eastern European nations ranged from a low of $1,390 in Romania to a high of $3,830 in Estonia. Moreover, these countries' average annual growth rates in 1991 ranged from 0 percent in Romania to 1.7 percent in Bulgaria. The GDP of these countries was similar, ranging from a low of $27.6 billion in Romania to a high of $78 billion in Poland (World Bank 1993). (The GDP of the Russian Federation was not recorded in that year.) Even though the economic data for these countries are incomplete, it is clear from the evidence that most eastern European economies were either stagnant or in decline throughout the 1980s and early 1990s. The continuing stagnation in the eastern and central European economies suggests that the wave of immigration will continue for the foreseeable future.

The character of the eastern and central European population—and to some extent the struggles they endure in the United States—is related to the economic and social system that dominated the eastern bloc nations for almost fifty years. The social system that marked the former Soviet Union and much of eastern Europe blended state paternalism with a blatant disregard for the needs of the population. Feher and Arato (1989) described the ways in which heavily subsidized food and rents; full employment; relatively high wages (compared with the average wage of the workers); initially generous social security benefits (representing a high percentage of the average wage); and free or inexpensive health care, education, and cultural services reflected a kind of social welfare contract between the Communist Party and the people. This contract was marred only by its inefficiency and by the hidden privileges extended to the Communist Party elite (Deacon 1992).

Most socialist societies had enshrined the right to work in their constitutions, and a job was made available to most of those people who wanted one. In fact, the state's paternalism was expressed most fully in activities connected with the workplace. Holiday homes, sanatoria, paid vacations, and holidays in state-owned resorts were reserved for workers with good records who were employed in established firms. In much of eastern and central Europe, social welfare benefits consisted mainly of state-provided work.

In contrast to the state's apparent generosity, no unemployment benefits were extended to those blacklisted by the Communist Party or to those who lost their jobs for other political reasons. Little was provided for people who simply refused to work. Although this system supplied jobs for almost everyone, real unemployment was hidden, since few worksites produced much work. As the saying goes, the state pretends to pay workers, and the workers pretend to work. Despite the outward generosity, wages were so low in many countries (e.g., Hungary) that workers had to hold second or even third jobs just to survive (Deacon 1992). Nonetheless, despite the paradoxes and hypocrisies, this system provided economic security and the basic necessities of life for the majority of the eastern and central European population.

This superficially egalitarian system coexisted with the hidden privileges of the many *apparatachiks* who had access to hidden incomes, foreign bank accounts, and superior welfare and health services. In fact, the problem of undeserved privileges became a sore spot for much of the population and helped lead to the overthrow of the Communist parties in eastern and central Europe.

Those contradictions found in labor policy also applied to health care. Although health care in eastern and central Europe was generally inferior to that in the West, it was available (many countries had a system of worksite-based medical provision) and was free. And even though the numbers of doctors and hospital beds were greater than in comparable Western nations, medical care in eastern Europe was generally inefficient, undercapitalized, and often lacking in basic equipment (Deacon 1992).

Extensive services and benefits to working mothers were offered in much of eastern Europe. The three-year child grant (family allowance) in Hungary and the former German Democratic Republic was complemented by a widespread system of day care and kindergartens. Women, on the other hand, were expected to be employed and also to maintain the home. Furthermore, because contraception was difficult to obtain, abortion often became the most readily available form of family planning (Deacon 1992).

Housing, like employment, was seen in many eastern European countries as a right. Because rents were subsidized, housing was generally inexpensive and represented only a small portion of family income. However, bad planning, inefficiencies, and corruption in the construction sector helped cause severe housing shortages in many eastern and central European countries, and twenty-year-long waiting lists for apartments were not uncommon. As a result of these shortages, multigenerational and even postdivorce communalism in housing was both common and enforced in many socialist countries. More often than not, preferred housing stock was allocated to Communist Party officials.

Social security protection against old age and sickness was well developed in many eastern and central European nations, with benefit levels representing a high proportion of wages. But because the benefits were not indexed to the cost of living (unlike U.S. social security), beneficiaries often had to rely on the largesse of the state to compensate for the erosion in benefits caused by inflation. Although social security benefits contained work-related components (benefits were based on work record rather than necessity), people could retire at a relatively early age. For those outside the accepted categories of recipients (the young, the disabled, single parents, etc.), benefits were inadequate (Deacon 1992).

The contradictions that marked the eastern European welfare system are obvious. The system's supposed egalitarianism and compassion coexisted uneasily with high levels of corruption and an underdeveloped and inefficient economy. It was precisely this economic inefficiency that hampered the provision of more generous social welfare benefits and higher-quality health care. Moreover, the supposed egalitarianism of the socialist society was tempered by a corrupt system that rewarded the better-off with dachas, subsidized apartments and villas, an alternative and higher-quality health care system, and hidden incomes. In the end, the elusive balance between economic efficiency and distributive justice was never reached in eastern Europe (Deacon 1992).

The profound social and economic changes resulting from eastern and central Europe's rapid immersion into a market economy will in all likelihood lead to increased migratory pressures. For example, instead of hiding unemployment in state make-work jobs, it is now a major social problem in eastern and central Europe. Other changes are equally dramatic. High levels of inflation are eroding already low standards of living. The removal of state subsidies has dramatically forced up the costs of rent and food. Many inefficient and underfunded medical establishments have been unable to operate under cost-accountability frameworks, and some have been forced to shut down. A number of educational institutions, notably the academies of science, have found themselves in difficult economic straits. Child care and the right to free abortion are also being threatened. Overall, the costs of shifting to a market economy have resulted in a decline of 30 percent or more in living standards and an unemployment rate of between 10 percent and 20 percent in many eastern and central European countries (Deacon 1992).

Although the social and economic landscapes of eastern and central Europe are rapidly changing, most current reforms include the following components: (1) a shift in the provision of social welfare services from bureaucratic/political to market relations; (2) an increase in local control over social provisions; (3) the end of privileged access to social provisions (including health care) previously based on Communist Party affiliation; (4) the substitution of Western-style social insurance programs for state security systems; (5) the transfer of the health and recreational facilities of state-owned industries to community and private hands; (6) the greater privatization of health and social care; (7) governmental encouragement for building private residential homes; (8) the removal of state subsidies for food, housing, and, increasingly, health care; (9) appeals for philanthropy and private initiatives to replace former state-sponsored services; (10) the development (often hasty) of unemployment benefits; and (11) the enactment of measures to curb the impact of inflation on wages. Because eastern European nations are not homogeneous, the scope and comprehensiveness of these reforms differ widely from country to country. Nevertheless, these reforms have made life difficult for millions of eastern and central Europeans and have thus spurred the desire for economic migration.

POLICY IMPLICATIONS

Instead of the current ad hoc approach to immigration policy, legislators, policymakers, and policy analysts must develop a proactive stance that assumes a less dependable marketplace and a more activist government. It would useful for American policymakers to look to other countries that have struggled with a large-scale immigration of eastern and central Europeans. One such country is Israel, which in the late 1980s and early 1990s was forced (with little preparation) to cope with a massive influx of Russian immigrants that exceeded 400,000 in a total population of just over 4 million.

Under Israeli immigration policy, each immigrant family is entitled to an "absorption basket" containing time-limited (two years) subsidized housing; low-interest housing loans; a time-limited tax-exemption status on certain items such as furniture, appliances, and automobiles; job training; and subsidized language courses. When combined with services and other rights, this "basket" is intended to facilitate the economic and social absorption of new immigrants (Doron and Kramer 1991).

American immigration policy also should provide a "basket of immigration services" similar to that provided by Israel, to include temporary food assistance, job training and reeducation, health care, personal social services (including alcohol and substance abuse counseling), subsidized language courses, and policies that help immigrants buy and not simply rent housing. In addition, the government should provide financial planning to help eastern and central immigrants understand and conform to a market economy and financial retirement planning to introduce immigrants to IRAs, since many will not have paid in the forty quarters of social security required to receive benefits when they reach retirement age. Others will have paid in so little that their benefits will be insufficient when they retire.

Housing is one of the first problems faced by eastern and central European immigrants, especially since most choose to live in relatively expensive midwestern cities such as Chicago or the even more expensive coastal regions (California and the Northeast) where rent and housing prices are the highest in the nation. After rent payments, many immigrants are left with little or nothing for food and clothing. One component of the U.S. immigration policy should be a time-limited subsidization of housing.

A more difficult problem than simply finding jobs is the need to secure employment at a fair wage and at an appropriate level of employee skills. Many eastern and central European immigrants have a scientific, academic, or other professional education. But because training and professional degrees do not always translate from one culture to the other, many immigrants are forced to lower their occupational status from that of their former careers. U.S. immigration policy should therefore provide updated training, retraining, and/or brush-up training for newly arrived immigrants.

Other, more aggressive policies should also be tried, such as the creation of economic incubators, which are, in effect, research and development centers that allow immigrant scientists and professionals to continue the research they started in their homeland. In addition, these incubators might attract venture capital for new projects and lead to the creation of private immigrant businesses as research enterprises are transformed into concrete products. Volunteer efforts may also be useful to aid the socialization of eastern Europeans into mainstream American society. Many immigrant families can receive important assistance from veteran Americans, including housing assistance, employment, furniture, clothes, informal advice, and so forth.

SOCIAL WORK PRACTICE WITH EASTERN AND CENTRAL EUROPEAN IMMIGRANTS

Eastern and central Europeans regard the socialist state as responsible for the material well-bring and living conditions of its citizens. The Soviet Union, for example, provided free and comprehensive health care to all citizens of its republics. This responsibility, assumed by the state, was given considerable prominence in the legal code under which the service was provided, which opened with "Protection of the people's health is one of the most important tasks of the Soviet State" (Ryan 1978).

But the state's paternalist mandate coexisted with widespread corruption; private entrepreneurship was illegal; and all goods were owned by the state. To gain personal wealth and privilege through the control of goods and services, they were illegally diverted from the state in exchange for other illegally diverted goods and services. The only way to acquire scarce consumer goods was to steal them either from the source of production or the point of distribution (Rosner 1996).

The socialist state is clearly different from what eastern and central European immigrants encounter upon their arrival in the United States. Until recently (before the PRWORA), it was assumed that if immigrants could not immediately enter the American mainstream, they would be temporarily support-ed by a maze of public assistance programs that included AFDC (now the Tem-porary Assistance to Needy Families Program, or TANF), food stamps, Medic-aid, and so forth. While these public welfare programs may allow most immigrants to live at a subsistence level, they do not promote economic and so-cial integration into American society.

Despite the greater influx of immigrants from eastern and central Europe during the past decade, understanding of these new groups lags far behind (Buchwald, Klacsanzky, and Manson 1993). In addition to conflicts related to the differing role of government in United States compared to their country of origin, other ethnic factors affect their adaptation, such as traditions and lan-guage.

SOCIAL WORKERS AS CULTURE MEDIATORS

Awareness of the implications of ethnicity when assisting immigrant groups has been a major focus of social work intervention and includes understanding how each immigrant group perceives the adjustment experience and what problems they will face while adapting (Nah 1993). Likewise, the ethnic influ-ences that motivate clients often need to be interpreted to others to ensure ap-propriate treatment (Fandetti and Goldmeier 1988).

Obtaining the necessary mental and physical treatment is crucial to eastern and central European immigrants, as several studies report a significantly greater prevalence of psychiatric disorders among these refugee groups than among the general population (Brodsky 1988; Buchwald et al. 1993; Eitinger 1959; Hitch and Rack 1980; Krupinski et al. 1973; Mezey 1960). Although gath-ered from many countries, the findings of these investigations have been consis-tent, with explanations being the impact of premigration factors, including the severity of war experiences; the lack of community cohesion; fewer social con-tacts; loss of contact with family members; and the absence of guaranteed work and social benefits (Brodsky 1988; Buchwald et al. 1993; Eitinger 1959; Hitch and Rack 1980; Krupinski et al. 1973; Mezey 1960).

These studies highlight the importance of ethnic factors in the experience and adjustment of eastern and central European immigrants. An important role for social workers, therefore, is that of culture mediator. A culture mediator focuses on those ethnic factors that impede the resolution of problems and the satisfaction of needs for maintaining or improving adaptive functioning. Social workers taking this role thus must remain vigilant in their efforts to see ethnicity as an emergent property rather than a static, unchanging phenomenon (Fandetti and Goldmeier 1988; Gelfand and Fandetti 1986).

This is not the first time that the role of social work in society has been conceptualized as that of a mediator. Social workers mediate the individual social engagement between group members and the systems that impinge on them and at the systems' boundaries. These interacting systems are recognized to have power and value differences, hence the need for a mediator (Lurie 1982; Parsons 1991). In this role, the social worker helps the client and social system reach out to each other in more realistic, rational, reciprocal ways through the collaborative skills of intercession, persuasion, and negotiation (Germain and Gitterman 1980).

The culture mediation process involves both an awareness of ethnic components and the use of a multilevel framework encompassing the complexity of an ethnic assessment. Ethnic factors may be addressed at the three levels of assessment and intervention in social work: the micro, mezzo, and macro. This framework (see table 5.2) identifies the areas of concern for ethnic intervention and planning (Fandetti and Goldmeier 1988).

CASE ILLUSTRATIONS

The following case vignettes involving eastern and central European immigrants illustrate how culturally sensitive multilevel assessments and interventions can occur at the micro, mezzo, and macro levels.

Case 1

The following case features multilevel ethnic assessment and intervention with issues centering on the impact of inadequate English skills and dislocation from the patient's native land.

Boris Z. is a sixty-year-old divorced Russian immigrant who has been living in the United States for five years. He emigrated to the United States because of the social and economic upheavals of the post-Soviet era. In the Soviet Union, he had worked as an architectural draftsman; a skilled trade that required specialized training. He has been unable to find comparable work in the United States and is working in a butcher shop in his neighborhood. Since arriving in this country, Boris has been living in an area of New York City that is heavily populated by other eastern and central Europeans. Because of this, Boris has been able to use his native language with customers and friends. His English is poor, and he is unable to read the language.

TABLE 5.2
Levels of Ethnic Assessment

Micro: The person

1. Assess the person's cultural orientation: for example, languages spoken, religion professed, and generation of immigration of the primary client.
2. Evaluate the importance of intra ethnic group variations affecting the person's orientation.
3. Consider the person's class membership as a mediating factor.
4. Select ethnically compatible solutions to personal problems.

Mezzo: The family, client group, and treatment team

1. Assess the ethnically based dynamics of the family, client group, or team.
2. Assess the responsiveness of a group or team, whose members may themselves reflect different ethnic orientations.
3. Evaluate the importance of intraethnic group variations in families, groups, and treatment teams.
4. Consider class membership as a mediating factor.
5. Select ethnically compatible solutions at the family, group, or treatment team level.

Macro: The local and nonlocal community

1. Understand family boundaries with the larger community in intervention and planning.
2. Facilitate community responsiveness to ethnic cultural needs.
3. Be aware of local-state-national policies affecting the integration of the ethnic groups.

Source: D. Fandetti and J. Goldmeier, J. (1988). "Social Workers as Culture Mediators in Health Care Settings," *Health and Social Work* 13 (3) (1988): fig. 1, 173.

Boris, who has had diabetes for several years, suffered a stroke that required an emergency admission to a local hospital where many of the staff spoke Russian. Formerly robust, the stroke left him with moderate deficits in speech and ambulation, although the physicians felt that with intensive, inpatient physical rehabilitation, he could regain much of his previous level of functioning. Once he was medically stable, he was transferred to a physical rehabilitation hospital located out of his neighborhood. The managed care company had a contract with this facility and arranged for his transfer.

Soon after his admission, the physical rehabilitation team found Boris becoming agitated and irritable when asked to sign consent forms for procedures. The nurses and nurse's aides notes consistently indicated that he was often resistant to efforts to help him with personal care, consequently making him a safety risk on the unit. During one evening round, a nurse's aide found Boris slumped on the floor of the bathroom. Despite being repeatedly cautioned by the staff to ask for assistance when walking, Boris had attempted this alone. Although not injured by his fall, the nursing staff was forced to keep his bed rails up in order to prevent this from happening again. This measure only increased the tension between Boris and the staff, especially when he began to try to bribe the nurses and nurse's aides to lower the bed rails and let him walk alone when he wanted to.

Several members of the staff became extremely upset by his behavior and complained to the head nurse. They felt that Boris was humiliating them and interpreted his efforts to slip them cash as disrespectful of their status as paid, hospital staff. Despite several efforts to convince Boris that helping him was their job, he continued to approach some of them with offers of money. As time passed, the tension between Boris and the nurse's aides grew worse as he became more resistant to their efforts to help him. Consequently, Boris missed several physical rehabilitation classes because of his refusal to get dressed.

The physician and nursing staff agreed that Boris still had the physical potential to make progress but that his noncompliance needed to be addressed. His lack of participation was putting him at risk for being discharged before maximizing his rehabilitation potential in the hospital. Through regular chart reviews and updates from the physician, the managed care insurance company knew that Boris was not fully participating in his rehabilitation program. The managed care case manager informed the physician that given the high cost of inpatient care, it would be more cost effective for Boris to continue his therapy at home through a home care referral. The physician disagreed, feeling that Boris would make better progress if he remained in an intensive inpatient rehabilitation unit and argued for this with the case manager. As a result, Boris was approved for four more days, after which he would need to be discharged and given home care services unless he began to participate fully in his program.

A social worker was urgently requested to evaluate Boris. She went to his bedside and was immediately struck by his inability to communicate adequately in English. Initially suspicious of the social worker, Boris became less hostile when she brought in a Russian-speaking translator from the hospital's volunteer department. With the help of the translator, Boris was able to communicate more easily. He expressed his gratitude and relief that one had been provided, because communicating in his limited English, compounded by his poststroke speech deficits, had been very difficult for him.

Although embarrassed, he revealed to the social worker that he did not read English and felt overwhelmed when the hospital staff gave him forms to sign. A proud man, Boris had been too ashamed to admit this inability to the staff. In the Soviet Union, he informed the social worker, he held a professional position. Since being here, because of difficulties with this language and different licensing requirements, all he was able to do was work in a local butcher shop. He was afraid that his poststroke deficits would prevent him from returning to even this job.

Boris also voiced his resentment at being transferred to a hospital out of his community, because the distance discouraged friends from visiting. Although divorced and childless, he had a sister and niece in Russia who would take care of him if they were here. It was at times like this, he noted, that he missed his family and homeland. Unfortunately, he added, until he became a U.S. citizen and saved more money, it would be impossible to bring his family here.

Boris was upset about his conflicts with the staff but was confused about how he had contributed to them. He described being hospitalized in the Soviet Union where shortages of medical supplies were common and frequently, it was necessary to slip the staff some rubles in order to get what was needed. Boris said that all he was trying to do here was to also make sure his needs were met so that he might get well as soon as possible.

After meeting with Boris, the social worker talked with the physician and nursing staff. She explained the implications of Boris's culture for his hospital adjustment and the cultural differences that were contributing to conflicts between him and the staff.

The social worker began by discussing the impact of Boris's limited English-language skills on his ability to participate in and make health care decisions. To help in his participation, it was crucial for a Russian translator to be present when medical procedures and/or consent forms were being discussed. This interpretation reframed Boris's hostility when the English-language forms were presented as a cultural issue rather than a power struggle between Boris and the staff regarding his care. It also allowed for a solution to be worked out with the volunteer department to provide a Russian-speaking translator.

Boris's conflict with the nursing staff also was mediated, keeping in mind the cultural components. The social worker explained Boris's perception of the health care system according to his earlier experiences with Soviet health care. There, supplies were often lacking, and so it was not uncommon to bribe the staff in order to get them. The social worker encouraged the staff to understand that this behavior was Boris's attempt to take control of his situation in a way that was customary in his culture. Therefore, his intent had not been to demean the staff but to take an active role in his recovery.

Boris's noncompliance with physician's orders to was also explained in the context of cultural differences; that is, eastern Europeans are often taught not to ask for help and so may be unlikely to use appropriate services (Buchwald et al. 1993; Knab 1986; Krause 1978; Young et al. 1987). The social worker further suggested that Boris's noncompliance with safety precautions were actually additional efforts to take control. By being transferred to a facility away from the community hospital with staff who understood his language and customs, Boris was again uprooted, which only served to reinforce his feelings of being dislocated from his native land (Althausen 1996). Therefore, Boris sought control by engaging in behavior that he knew—regardless of the consequences.

As a result of this social work intervention, Boris was given access to a Russian-speaking translator when needed. This enabled him to fully participate in his health care plan, mitigated his feelings of social isolation, and increased his sense of control over his recovery. In addition, this effort to accommodate his needs sent Boris the message that he was not being penalized by the hospital because he spoke a different language and was not presently engaged in professional work. This, in turn, enabled him to feel more receptive to receiving assistance when needed. He was soon attending all his therapy sessions, and the physician was able to obtain approval for him to continue his stay.

During the discharge-planning process, the social worker asked the managed care case manager for a referral to a home health agency in Boris's community that had a high percentage of Russian-speaking staff. The social worker argued that if Boris were comfortable with staff who understood his language and customs, he would probably be more likely to adhere to his home care plan and thereby avoid being readmitted to the hospital.

The Culture Mediation Intervention

The social worker's multilevel ethnic assessment helped her explain the misunderstandings about cultural values between the patient and the staff. By reframing these conflicts as cultural differences between the patient and staff, the social worker was able to relieve much of the tension between them.

At the micro level, the social worker helped Boris maintain a sense of control, which was crucial in order for him to cope with the losses associated with his disability and hospitalization. She did this by bringing up his earlier experiences which affected his behavior in the current situation. The difficulty lay in relating his efforts to remain in control to the current cultural context. Giving Boris access to a translator was an important intervention to help him take control.

Boris also was struggling to cope with his inadequate English skills and the loss of occupational status in this country. His experience in the hospital only served to remind him of this loss, his lack of family support, and his sense of shame regarding his losses. Again, giving him access to a translator enhanced his adaptive social functioning and increased his sense of self- esteem.

At the mezzo level, the social worker intervened with the physical rehabilitation team and was able to help the staff members understand and be more tolerant of behaviors that deviated from their cultural norms (Fandetti and Goldmeier 1988). Educating the staff about the certain aspects of the Soviet health care system and their impact on the patient's behavior helped diminish the staff's anger toward Boris.

The social worker mediated cultural issues on the macro level by identifying culturally relevant resources in both the hospital and the community. She demonstrated the need for greater cultural awareness and responsiveness both during an admission and when planning for aftercare.

A central mission of social workers is to maximize the resources and choices of patients. This is becoming a greater challenge under managed care, in which such decisions are in the hands of the case manager who controls funding for inpatient and posthospital care. The role of the social worker as a culture mediator is thus even more important to ensure that the cultural and ethnic influences that shape patients' health care practices and beliefs are not ignored.

Case 2

The following case highlights the culture mediation process in helping a Jewish Holocaust survivor adapt to living in the United States. For this group, ethnicity interacts with the patient's specific experience, the degree of discrimination experienced, and the impact of war (McGoldrick and Giordano 1996). This vignette looks at these traumas as they affect two generations, the Holocaust survivors and their adult children, demonstrating the complexity of a multilevel ethnic assessment that often requires a multigenerational perspective.

Henia A. was a seventy-eight-year-old widowed Polish Orthodox Jewish Holocaust survivor who lived alone with informal, minimal assistance from her two middle-aged daughters living nearby. During a routine visit, her daughters found her on the floor of her apartment. She was taken by ambulance to the hospital for treatment of a broken hip.

Henia had an extremely difficult time adjusting to her loss of functioning and hospitalization. She became very anxious when approached by hospital staff who wore uniforms, cowered when announcements were made on the overhead speaker, and briefly became delusional, believing that the physicians were Nazis. Her daughters spent hours by her bedside and often were hostile to staff who came to inform them that visiting hours were over. Henia's daughters frequently complained to the head nurse about a variety of matters while denying the extent of their mother's disabilities. They were hesitant to accept reports from the medical and nursing staff about Henia's fluctuating periods of confusion, her significant memory deficits, and her difficulties walking. Because of the daughters' resistance to accepting information about Henia's level of functioning and care needs, they were perceived by many of the medical and nursing staff as not being concerned about their mother's welfare.

The social worker assigned to the case met with Henia's daughters to discuss the staff's concerns regarding their behavior on the unit and their attitudes toward their mother's disabilities. The daughters discussed their feelings about their mother who they believed, as a Holocaust survivor, had suffered enough. It was their primary responsibility, as her only family members, to stay at her bedside as much as possible. They felt especially strongly about this matter, as Henia was reexperiencing the traumas of the concentration camp, and it was very difficult for them to see her suffering now.

Henia's daughters tried to minimize the impact of their mother's physical and cognitive deficits, telling the social worker that if she had survived the Holocaust, she could survive anything. They did share the social worker's concern about how Henia would manage at home alone, and the daughters began to consider having her live with one of them after she left the hospital. They were committed to keeping Henia in the community, as she had often expressed a fear of being placed in an institution where she might be abused.

The daughters expressed great displeasure with the hospital, which they regarded as failing to meet the special needs of their mother. For example, they felt that in her case, the visiting hours should be extended and that the family should be allowed to participate in her personal care. They stressed that Henia was obviously having difficulty adapting to the hospital environment and that her loss of functioning was caused by her past traumas. Her daughters believed that she would be less anxious and make a better recovery if her family were available as much as possible.

The social worker offered to help them by asking the hospital administration to extend Henia's visiting hours and suggesting to the medical and nursing staff that they determine how the daughters might participate in Henia's daily care. The social worker also arranged a meeting with the daughters, the head nurse, and the attending physician to explain the culturally based misunder-standings.

During the meeting, the social worker told them that for many Holocaust survivors, hospitals were dangerous places because they were an admission of sickness and deterioration, which in the concentration camp signified certain death. For some, the return to helplessness wrought by illness and hospitaliza-tion elicited delusions of being back in the camp. The hospital uniforms, the overhead sound system, and the background noise of ambulance sirens served to reawaken further memories of the camp, thereby increasing their anxiety.

The social worker then encouraged the daughters to explain how their caring and commitment to Henia were expressed through their desire to spend as much time as possible at her bedside and help with her physical care. They real-ized this conflicted with some hospital rules, but as family, they believed their role in Henia's recovery was crucial. They also were trying to give her emotion-al support and encouragement to survive her current situation by minimizing reports by the staff about her disabilities. This again was done out of caring and respect for what she had survived and endured in the past.

As a result of this meeting, several changes acknowledging the culturally rel-evant needs of the patient and family were implemented. The visiting hours for the daughters were extended; the daughters were trained by the nurses to help Henia in certain aspects of her physical care; and the physicians did not wear lab coats when attending to her. Consequently, the anxiety of the patient and fami-ly was significantly decreased, and they began to comply with medical orders and make appropriate aftercare plans.

The Culture Mediation Interventions

This case history shows cultural mediation in two areas: (1) the role of the fam-ily in caring for elderly members and (2) the impact of war and persecution on a group's dynamics. In this case, the social worker was able to underscore the important role of the Jewish family in providing emotional support in times of crisis—essential when a family member had survived the Holocaust. This re-sulted in a change at the macro level, with the institution agreeing to expand visiting hours for this patient and her family. At the micro level, this provided positive reinforcement for the daughters who were expending a great deal of ef-fort to maintain the centrality of the family; a major dynamic in the Jewish fam-ily. The reinforcement also validated the efforts of Henia's daughters to fulfill their traditional role of adult children caring for their elderly parent; a role rooted in Jewish religious principles (Rosen and Weltman 1996). The rest of

Henia's family had been murdered in the Holocaust, and she had been widowed for many years. As was common for adult children of survivors, her daughters were being called on to do the work of an extended family (Danieli 1994a; Rosen and Weltman 1996).

The social worker assumed a leadership role in mediating cultural differences at the mezzo level, by arranging a meeting with the family and staff. The social worker took an active role in interpreting their behavior in a cultural context, thereby modeling this intervention for the daughters, who could then share their perspective with the medical team. Through these efforts, the staff could appreciate why survivors perceived hospitals as dangerous places (Danieli 1988). In response, the medical staff did not wear white lab coats when at Henia's bedside.

The challenge for immigration policy is to meet the needs of new immigrants without adversely affecting the social and economic interests of the indigenous population. In the case of the United States, immigration policy has not been rationally thought out. In fact, most of the debate on immigration has centered on how many people would be permitted to enter the United States and under which clauses and/or conditions. Once here, immigrants are expected either to take care of themselves or to be taken care of by family members.

U.S. immigration policy also is not geared toward absorbing large numbers of economic refugees, such as many eastern and central European immigrants who are professionals and/or skilled workers. It is also not equipped to maximize these immigrants' economic contribution to American society. Instead, American immigration policy assumes a passive government and an aggressive employment market. Hence, at least in theory, large numbers of immigrants need only be released into the American economy, and the marketplace will both absorb and socialize them. It is a theory that has led to a great deal of social and interpersonal turmoil.

Social workers can help immigrants in several ways. First, by advocating for progressive reform in immigration laws, social workers can ease the difficult transition and acculturation of European immigrants into American society. There is a clear precedent for this in the American settlement house movement of the late nineteenth and early twentieth centuries. Second, social workers can deliver and mediate services such as health care, housing, and mental health services. Specifically, apart from being advocates for immigrants, social workers can become "culture mediators." As the preceding case examples illustrate, many Americans have little understanding of immigrants' day-to-day problems. Consequently, many Americans (including many service providers) do not appreciate the cultural adaptations necessary for immigrants to survive in a modern market economy. They often also do not understand how these immigrants view the world. In short, because of their training and cultural sensitivity, social workers are the best-equipped professional group in America to help immigrants.

REFERENCES

Althausen, L. (1996). Russian families. In M. McGoldick, J. Giordano, and J. Pearce (eds.), *Ethnicity and Family Therapy.* New York: Guilford Press.
Axinn, J., and Levin, H. (1975). *Social Welfare.* New York: Dodd, Mead.
Bernardo, S. (1981). *The Ethnic Almanac.* Garden City, NY: Doubleday.
Brace, C. L. (1872). *The Dangerous Classes of New York.* New York: Wynkoop and Hallenbeck.
Bremner, R. (1956). *From the Depths: The Discovery of Poverty in the United States.* New York: New York University Press.
Brodsky, B. (1988). Mental health attitudes and practices of Soviet Jewish immigrants. *Health and Social Work* (Spring): 130–136.
Buchwald, D., Klacsanzky, G., and Manson, S. (1993). Psychiatric disorders among recently arrived eastern Europeans seen through a U.S. refugee counseling service. *International Journal of Social Psychiatry* 39 (3): 221–227.
Central Bureau of Statistics. (1991). *Statistical Abstract of Israel, 1991.* Central Bureau of Statistics, Jerusalem [in Hebrew].
Cohen, N. (1958). *Social Work in the American Tradition.* New York: Holt, Rinehart and Winston.
Danielli, Y. (1988). Confronting the unimaginable. In J. Wilson, Z. Harel, and B. Karara (eds.), *Human Adaptation to Extreme Stress.* New York: Plenum.
Danieli, Y. (1994a). As survivors age. *National Center for Post-Traumatic Stress Disorder Clinical Quarterly* (4): 7–13.
Danieli, Y. (1994b). As survivors age: Part II. *National Center for Post-Traumatic Stress Disorder Clinical Quarterly* (5): 4–9.
Davis, A. (1973). *American Heroine: The Life and Legend of Jane Addams.* New York: Oxford University Press.
Deacon, B. (ed.). (1992). *The New Eastern Europe.* London: Sage.
Doron, A., and Kramer, R. (1991). *The Welfare State in Israel.* Boulder, CO: Westview Press.
Eitinger, L. (1959). The incidence of mental disease among refugees in Norway. *Journal of Mental Science* (105): 326–338.
Encyclopedia of Social Work (1995). 19th ed. Washington, DC: National Association of Social Work Press.

Fandetti, J., and Goldmeier, J. (1988). Social workers as culture mediators in health care settings. *Health and Social Work* 13 (3): 171–179.

Federation of American Immigration Reform (FAIR). (n.d.). *The Immigration and Nationality Act Amendments of 1965 and Their Aftermath.* Online: http://www. fairus.org/history/inaa65.html.

Federation for American Immigration Reform (FAIR). (n.d.). *Questions About Legal Immigration.* Online: http://www.fairus.org/issues/legs.html.

Federation for American Immigration Reform (FAIR). (1994). *Research Finds That Immigration Costs Nearly $30 Billion a Year.* Online (October): http://www. fairus.org/issues/studs.html.

Federation for American Immigration Reform (FAIR). (1995). *Immigrants and Welfare Use: Findings from the General Accounting Office.* Online (February): http:// www.fairus.org/issues/gaowelf.html.

Feher, F., and Arato, A. (eds.). (1989). *Gorbachev: The Debate.* Cambridge: Polity.

Gelfand, D., and Fandetti, D. V. (1986). Ethnicity: Dilemmas in assessment. *Social Casework* (67): 542–550.

Germain, C., and Gitterman, A. (1980). *The Life Model of Social Work Practice.* New York: Columbia University Press.

Higham, J. (1972). *Strangers in the Land: Patterns of American Nativism.* New York: Atheneum.

Hitch, P. J., and Rack, P. H. (1980). Mental illness among Polish and Russian refugees in Bradford. *British Journal of Psychiatry* (137): 206–211.

Hofstadter, R. (1955). *The Age of Reform.* New York: Vintage Books.

Jansson, B. (1993). *The Reluctant Welfare State: A History of American Social Welfare Policies.* Pacific Grove, CA: Brooks/Cole.

Kaplan, J. (1974). *Lincoln Steffens.* New York: Simon & Schuster.

Karger, H. J. (1988). *Social Workers and Labor Unions.* New York: Greenwood Press.

Karger, H. J., and Stoesz, D. (1998). *American Social Welfare Policy: A Pluralist Approach.* 3d ed. New York: Longman.

Knab, S. (1986). Polish Americans' historical and cultural perspectives of influence in the use of mental health services. *Journal of Psychosocial Nursing* (26): 31–34.

Krause, C. (1978). *Grandmothers, Mothers and Daughters: An Oral History Study of Ethnicity, Mental Health and Continuity of Three Generations of Jewish, Italian and Slavic American Women.* New York: Institute on Pluralism and Group Identity.

Krupinski, J., et al. (1973). Psychiatric disorders in east European refugees now in Australia. *Social Science and Medicine* (7): 31–49.

Lurie, A. (1982). The social work advocacy role in discharge planning. *Social Work in Health Care* 8 (3): 75–85.

McGoldrick, M., and Giordano, J. (1996). Overview: Ethnicity and family therapy. In M. McGoldrick, J. Giordano, and J. Pearce (eds.), *Ethnicity and Family Therapy.* New York: Guilford Press.

Mezey, A. G. (1960). Psychiatric illness in Hungarian refugees. *Journal of Mental Science* (106): 628–637.

Montgomery, D. (1979). *Workers' Control in America.* Cambridge: Cambridge University Press.

Nah, K. H. (1993). Perceived problems and service delivery for Korean immigrants. *Social Work* 38 (3): 289–296.

National Association of Social Workers. (1984). *Encyclopedia of Social Work.* 18th ed. Silver Spring, MD: National Association of Social Workers Press.

Parsons, R. (1991). The mediator role in social work practice. *Social Work* 36 (6): 483–487.

Reinert, P. (1996). Federal welfare plan hits legal immigrants. *Houston Chronicle* (August 2): 1A, 16A.

Riis, J. (1890). *How the Other Half Lives.* New York: Scribner.

Rosen, E., and Weltman, S. (1996). Jewish families: An overview. In M. McGoldrick, J. Giordano, and J. Pearce (eds.), *Ethnicity and Family Therapy.* New York: Guilford Press.

Rosen, J. (1996). The war on immigrants. *The New Republic* (January 7): 8–12.

Rosner, L. (1996). *The sexy Russian mafia.* Online at http://www.acsp.uic.edu/IASOC/rosner.htm.

Ryan, M. (1978). *The Organization of Soviet Medical Care.* Oxford: Basil Blackwell and Mott.

Trattner, W. (1974). *From Poor Law to Welfare State.* New York: Free Press.

U.S. Department of Justice. (1996). *Immigration to the United States in Fiscal Year 1995.* Online (August): http://www.ins.usdoj.gov/public/stats/119.html.

U.S. Department of Justice, Immigration and Naturalization Service. (1996). *Immigration to the United States in Fiscal Year 1995.* Washington, DC: U.S. Government Printing Service.

U.S. House of Representatives, Conference Committee. (1996). HR 3734: Personal Responsibility and Work Opportunity Act (Immigration Provisions)—Conference Committee Version. Title IV–Restricting Welfare and Public Benefits for Aliens. Washington, DC: U.S. House of Representatives, Conference Committee.

World Bank (1993). *World Development Report 1993: Investing in Health.* New York: Oxford University Press.

Young, R. F., et al. (1987). Health status, health problems and practices among refugees from the Middle East, eastern Europe and Southeast Asia. *International Migration Review* (21): 761–783.

CHAPTER 6

REFUGEES IN THE 1990S: A U.S. PERSPECTIVE

Nazneen S. Mayadas and Uma A. Segal

There never was a golden age of "pure refugees" in the 1950s and 1960s that has now dissolved into widespread abuse. And when asylum seekers are dismissed as "merely economic migrants" we need to remind ourselves of the vicious circle in which poverty and hopelessness breed social disorder, social disorder breeds repression, and repression breeds persecution, violence, and the forced movements of people.
—Phillip Rudge, *Refugees* (1991:35)

Since its historical beginning, the United States has been a country of refuge for those fleeing from persecution. Based on the words etched on the Statue of Liberty, it has fulfilled its commitment to the dispossessed and downtrodden over the past two centuries and continues to do so today. The United States has been a key donor to the Office of United Nations High Commissioner for Refugees' (table 6.1), and until the 1990s, it accepted the largest number of the world's refugees. Recently, however, its policies of asylum have not always been applied equitably to asylees and refugees. Although the United States has admitted the most Southeast Asian refugees for third-country resettlement, its treatment of refugees from Central America, Mexico, and the Caribbean has not been as generous. Just as Hong Kong in the 1980s placed Vietnamese refugees in closed camps and forced them to repatriate, the U.S. Coast Guard in the 1990s prevented the Haitian boat people from landing on its shores (Redmond 1992). Those Haitians who did manage to land were sent back, unlike the east Europeans, who arrived as victims of the cold war in Europe during that period. Perhaps this reversal of policy and selectivity in welcome can be explained by the increasingly xenophobic reactions of the 'public and the propaganda of the moral majority decrying the dissolution of the country's cultural heritage, economic stability, and national sovereignty. The rapid spread of "unfamiliar" ethnic groups that bring with them differences in race, creed, culture, and physical traits is thought to threaten the country's cherished homogeneity. As Pat Buchanan declared in his political platform of 1992, the 1965 Immigration Act

TABLE 6.1
Donations to the Office of the UN Commissioner for Refugees

Donor	Amount, millions of U.S. $
United States	254.4
Japan	107.8
European Commission	90.6
Sweden	51.6
Denmark	41.6
Netherlands	40.5
Norway	35.8
United Kingdom	28.8
Germany	18.9
Switzerland	18.6
Canada	12.3
Finland	12.2
Australia	9.6
France	8.8
Italy	8.7
Belgium	4.4
Spain	3.2
Ireland	2.7
New Zealand	1.1
Private sector, NGOs, UN	11.2
Other govts.	6.3
Total 1998 income from contributions as of 12/2/99[a]	769.1

Late recordings may affect the final 1998 figure slightly.
Source: http://www.unhcr.ch/fdrs/donorinc298.htm.

opened the gates to people of color and led to the disintegration of the culture and institutions of the United States (Karger and Stoesz 1994).

According to the definition in the 1951 convention and the 1967 protocol for the mandate of the UN High Commissioner for Refugees, a refugee is "any person who, owing to a well founded fear of being persecuted for reasons of race, religion, nationality, or political opinion is outside the country of his/her nationality and is unable or, owing to such fear or for reasons other than personal convenience, is unwilling to avail himself/herself of the protection of that country" (UNHCR 1996). This definition is accepted by the U.S. Immigration and Naturalization Service, as stated in the amended Refugee Act of 1980 which governs the present policy admitting refugees into the United States (U.S. Department of Justice 1995). Hence, persons entering the United States from a second country of asylum have already been rigorously screened and are recognized as bona fide refugees. Examples are the Southeast Asians from the Vietnam area. A second group of persons seeking asylum in the United States are those people whose claim to being persecuted is ambiguous for several reasons, the foremost being that their country of nationality is not seen as inimical to the United States.

Bound by the UN's convention of 1951 and the protocol of 1967, the United States is obligated to provide asylum to these people until their claim to a refugee status is established. These asylees are often placed in prisonlike conditions awaiting the verdict on their political status. If their case cannot be proved, they may be deported, regardless of the fate awaiting them back home. Persons in this category include the Haitians and El Salvadorans.

When determining whether to grant refugee status to asylees, the United States must also decide the extent to which it will address human rights violations. In 1994, two well-publicized requests for asylum were made by women who feared female genital mutilation in their home countries of Nigeria (Reed 1994) and Togo (Constable 1996) if they were deported. On May 1, 1996, the U.S. Senate voted to make female genital mutilation a federal crime and to repeal a recently signed antiterrorism law prohibiting illegal immigrants from entering the United States by claiming political asylum (Branigin 1996). A third group of persons who fail to qualify as refugees are those referred to as *undocumented aliens* or *economic refugees*. These people flee their countries to escape economic oppression, famine, and drought. Since starvation is not listed as a "well founded fear of persecution," the United States has a political right to strengthen its border patrol in the South and along the Rio Grande to keep these groups out. Therefore, the issue is not one of legal justification but of human rights and social justice.

DEMOGRAPHICS AND RESETTLEMENT PATTERNS IN THE UNITED STATES

Most refugees do not wish to leave their homes, and most hope to return. Since this is often not possible, many remain in the country to which they initially fled and whose language and culture are often similar to their own (http://www.in-teraction.org.pub/connect/strating/html 1997). A smaller group is approved for resettlement elsewhere, and about one million refugees annually are offered re-settlement in third countries; of these, 10 to 15 percent come to the United States. Census data collected between 1990 and 1996 from the Immigration and Naturalization Service indicate that approximately 100,000 refugees are admit-ted to the United States each year, and since 1975, more than two million have been resettled here. The census data further show that the number of refugee admissions between 1993 and 1995 has fallen; however, the proportion of refugees to other immigrants has been gradually rising (table 6.2). The total number of refugees admitted in 1995 was 114,664; the largest number was from Europe (46,998), followed closely by those from Asia (43,314). The countries of origin most often represented were Vietnam, Ukraine, Cuba, Russia, the former Soviet Union (unknown representation since its dissolution), and the former Yugoslavia, with refugees constituting the major proportion of the total num-ber of admissions from those countries (table 6.2). In 1995, California, New York, and Florida, in descending order, were the states that refugees first chose as their permanent residence, and despite some secondary resettlement, most refugees remain in the states into which they are first admitted.

The U.S. Immigration and Naturalization Service reported that in 1995, male refugees outnumbered females by approximately 3,500, and of the total number of admissions, females outnumbered males by about 53,000. The median age of the refugee group (31) was three years older than that of the total immigrant pop-ulation for that year. The refugees were fairly evenly distributed by gender across age categories, although there were 3,000 more males than females in the 15- to 29-year age bracket and 1,300 more females in the 65+ age group. In 1995, ap-

TABLE 6.2

1994–1996 Refugee Admissions and Percentages of Total Number of Immigrants

Category of Admission	1996	%	1995	%	1994	%
Ameriasians	956	0.1	939	0.1	2,822	0.4
Parolees, Soviet and Indochinese	2,269	0.2	3,086	0.4	8,253	1.0
Refugees and asylees	128,565	14.0	114,664	15.9	121,434	15.1

Source: http://www.ins.usdoj.gov//ext/aboutins/statistics/annual/fy96/993.

proximately 10 percent (11,069) of the refugees admitted were children under the age of 16 and therefore ineligible to work. The largest category of the 79,926 refugees between the ages of 16 and 64 were those who had no occupation outside the home (table 6.3). Of those who did have an occupation, the largest group was operators and laborers. Interestingly, this distribution was consistent with that of the total population admitted in 1995. Table 6.4 reveals a relatively proportionate distribution of occupations among the total immigrant and refugee populations. In 1995, clearly the refugees appear to have brought the same level of skills to the United States as did the other immigrants admitted in that year.

After a year in the United States, refugees have the option of changing their status to that of immigrant. The majority of those who entered the United States in 1994, numbering 106,827, chose this option and in 1995 changed their refugee status to that of permanent resident. (INS 1996: http:/www.usdoj. gov/ins/public/stats/118.html). But the number of refugees who became immigrants declined by 7.5 percent between 1994 and 1995 when compared with previous years, reflecting the recent decrease in the number of refugees admitted to the United States (INS 1996: http://www.usdoj.gov/ins/public/stats/115.html). Note that the ceilings set for refugees and immigrants in the United States are separate, so when refugees and asylees change their status to that of immigrant after the mandatory one-year stay, they remain exempt from the numerical cap preset for immigrants from their particular region of origin.

CUSTOM, TRADITIONS, AND VALUES

In the United States, refugees represent a cross section of the world's refugee population, bringing with them cultural diversity from almost all continents of the globe. Even though this enriches the range of cultures, it also presents value conflicts that either tolerate or condemn traditions and customs, depending on how they are regarded in the Western cultures. A recent news item (CBS *60 Minutes*, April 20, 1997) exemplified this cultural gap: The parents of an Iraqi family with their consent and in keeping with their traditions gave their two daughters, ages twelve and thirteen, in marriage to two adults of their community. The young men were charged with rape and the parents with child abuse. This is certainly an extreme, although not an isolated, case of cultural miscommunication. The result was that the INS denied asylum to refugees from the Jaffa area of Iraq. Issues such as these require understanding and sensitive handling of the situation, not penalization, as meted out in this case (Buckman, Lipson, and Meleis 1992).

TABLE 6.3
Admission Patterns of Immigrants and Refugees to the United States

Region/Country of Birth

	Number
All countries	*114,664*
Africa	7,527
Asia	3,314
Europe	6,998
North America	16,265
Caribbean	14,888
Central America	1,335
Other North America	42
Oceania	63
South America	497

State of Intended Stay

	Total	Refugees
All states	*720,461*	*114,664*
California	116,482	26,104
New York	128,406	19,721
Florida	62,023	14,527
Illinois	33,898	5,069
Washington	15,862	4,793
Texas	49,963	4,272
Massachusetts	20,523	3,639
Minnesota	8,111	3,635
Pennsylvania	15,065	3,125
Michigan	14,135	2,979
Georgia	12,381	2,672
Maryland	15,055	2,244
New Jersey	39,729	2,058
Virginia	16,319	2,054
Wisconsin	4,919	2,052
Ohio	8,585	1,791
Missouri	3,990	1,303
Colorado	7,713	1,296
Tennessee	3,392	1,152
Connecticut	9,240	956
North Carolina	5,617	863
Oregon	4,923	766
Iowa	2,260	733

Region/Country of Birth

Arizona	7,700	628
Nebraska	1,831	574
Kansas	2,434	473
District of Columbia	3,047	445
Kentucky	1,857	43
Indiana	3,590	424
Oklahoma	2,792	418
Utah	2,831	414
Nevada	4,306	411
Louisiana	3,000	376
Rhode Island	2,609	287
Hawaii	7,537	240
New Mexico	2,758	179
South Carolina	2,165	154
Puerto Rico	7,160	84
Alabama	1,900	67
Guam	2,419	13
Other and unknown	1,934	1,252
Country of birth	*Total*	*No. of refugees*
Vietnam	41,752	28,595
Ukraine	17,432	14,937
Cuba	17,937	12,355
Russia	14,560	8,176
Soviet Union (unknown republics)	6,784	5,060
Yugoslavia	8,307	4,744
Haiti	14,021	2,502
Ethiopia	6,952	2,006
Iran	9,201	1,245
China	35,463	803
India	34,748	323
El Salvador	11,744	283
Poland	13,824	245
Peru	8,066	241
Pakistan	9,774	197
Guatemala	6,213	158
Colombia	10,838	102
Philippines	50,984	80

TABLE 6.3 Continued
Admission Patterns of Immigrants and Refugees to the United States

Country of birth	Total	No. of refugees
Germany	6,237	61
Hong Kong	7,249	48
Mexico	89,932	37
Nigeria	6,818	26
Dominican Republic	38,512	22
Ecuador	6,397	11
United Kingdom	12,326	9
Korea	16,047	5
Canada	12,932	5
Jamaica	16,398	4
Guyana	7,362	3
Taiwan	9,377	2

Source: United States Trade Service, *Statistical Overview* (Washington, DC: U.S. Government Printing Office, 19), table 4.

Most refugees from the developing world have a traditional group orientation with a hierarchical familial power structure and clear role definitions (Segal 1994). Authority is gender based, with males maintaining instrumental and females maintaining nurturant roles. This neatly stacked pattern of behavior is upset on arrival in the United States and sometimes even earlier while awaiting resettlement in second-asylum camps. Since women are more likely to find jobs as domestics, they become the breadwinners exposed to the outside world. In school, children move toward the process of "Americanization," and the men are left at home in a state of bewilderment (Hirayama 1982). The family equilibrium is shattered and mental health problems replace order. Unlike immigrants, refugees leave their countries under duress and extreme trauma and with no preparation for their departure. They do bring psychological stress from unfinished business, material and emotional losses, loss of their home and country, and the knowledge that their country no longer wants them (Mayadas and Lasan 1984). Coupled with this is their reception in the country of resettlement, such as xenophobia, a loss of status, unemployment or employment in a menial job, inadequate language skills, and dependence on governmental welfare for survival.

This triangle of negativism—a disjointed family structure, the forced up-

TABLE 6.4
Age, Gender, and Occupational Distribution of Immigrants and Refugees, 1995

Age and Gender	Occupation of Persons Aged 16-64 Years	
	Number	*No. of refugees*
Male	333,859	59,023
Female	336,582	55,638
Unknown	20	3
Total	720,461	114,664
Age		
< 15 years	157,325	22,959
15–29 years	237,385	32,766
30–44 years	185,838	24,737
45–64 years	105,863	23,737
65+ years	33,993	10,350
Unknown	57	13
Male		
< 15 years	79,494	11,890
15–29 years	109,270	17,929
30–44 years	84,524	12,757
45–64 years	46,028	11,978
65+ years	14,513	4,465
Unknown	30	4
Female		
< 15 years	77,824	11,069
15–29 years	128,110	14,837
30–44 years	101,310	12,081
45–64 years	59,832	11,758
65+ years	19,479	5,884
Unknown	27	9
% Distribution	*100*	*100*
Male	46.3	51.5
Female	53.7	48.5
Median age	*28*	*31*
Male	27	30
Female	29	32
	Occupation of People Aged 16 TO 64 Years	
	Total	*Refugees*
Architects	472	15
Engineers	8,990	335

TABLE 6.4 Continued
Age, Gender, and Occupational Distribution of Immigrants and Refugees, 1995

	Occupation of People Aged 16 TO 64 Years	
	Total	Refugees
Math/computer scientists	2,127	78
Natural scientists	2,371	77
Physicians	4,072	120
Nurses	8,118	120
Other health professionals	4,330	176
College/school teachers	10,871	372
Artists, writers, athletes	5,036	191
Technologists, technicians	6,639	713
Administrators	24,306	602
Sales	11,329	1,095
Administration support	18,177	1,189
Production, craft, repair	18,068	1,858
Operators, laborers	50,755	14,622
Agricultural workers	11,282	121
Service occupations	45,609	7,263
Other	5,188	721
Total	514,993	79,926
Professional and technical	58,214	2,434
No occupation	*239,704*	*35,301*
Homemakers	88,890	5,962
Unemployed, retired	78,093	19,658
Students and/or < 16 years	72,721	9,681
Occupation not reported	37,549	15,441

rooting with multiple losses, and a xenophobic reception—contributes to the marginality of the refugee status and the dehumanization of the person, becoming the all-absorbing refugee culture. Although many people succumb to it, some transcend it. For example, one survey showed that in Canada, only 4.5 percent of all Southeast Asian refugees were on social assistance, compared with 7 percent of all Canadians (Na Champassak 1995). This study also attributes this welfare differential to the refugees' tolerance of hardship, reliance on informal support networks, and, despite the odds, the drive toward self-sufficiency. Perhaps another factor contributing to self-sufficiency is the growing recognition in the United States of cultural pluralism and the subsequent movement away from the traditional demand of newcomers to assimilate to the country (Gordon 1961; Mayadas 1997).

ADAPTATION AND COPING IN THE MAINSTREAM UNITED STATES

Historically, refugees have preferred to resettle in ethnic enclaves that can provide social support and a semblance of the old world now lost to them (Nguyen 1994). Most refugees hope to resettle in an industrialized country where, theoretically, they can more easily make a new start than they could in the country they left behind. Western countries maintain clear immigration policies, laws, and selection guidelines that determine the entry criteria used to select refugees for resettlement. For example, in the United States, Southeast Asian refugees' can opt to become permanent residents after a year's residence, but except for certain minor welfare privileges, they face the same opposition as do other voluntary immigrants from the developing world (DeVita 1996).

The United States is both an asylum and a resettlement country. Although it was seen in the 1970s and early 1980s as almost exclusively a resettlement haven for Southeast Asian refugees, it has since served as a first-asylum country to refugees from Latin America, Africa, Asia, and the Middle East. Whereas other asylum countries may accept refugees temporarily, asylees entering the United States, if identified as bona fide refugees fleeing from persecution (Hofferman 1998), they are eligible for legal residence in the country and may eventually apply to become U.S. citizens. This makes the United States a highly desirable country of resettlement. In fiscal year 1996, however, the U.S. admission rate dropped by 18 percent, bringing down the ceiling from 110,000 to 90,000 on the refugee quota. This reduction in numbers may appear as an attempt to curtail the admission of new arrivals, but it is consistent with the overall reduction in numbers and the UN High Commissioner for Refugees' emphasis on repatriation as the preferred solution to the refugee problem (Tarnoff 1995). Repatriation suggests that the fear-inducing emergency in the refugees' homeland has subsided and that the country is now willing to grant amnesty to its exiled citizens. But the policy of repatriation does not take into account that although the refugees' home country may once again seem stable (Bertalanffy 1955), it is nonetheless very different from what it was when the refugees fled. Settling back into a niche may not be possible, since the niche itself may have disappeared. In other words, repatriation may be the best solution from the international community's perspective but not from the refugees. The ambivalence of the Vietnamese refugees repatriated from Hong Kong is an example of this double-edged sword.

The 1990s have brought the largest numbers of international refugees and immigrants to the United States who are themselves diversified, multiethnic groups. The waves of refugees from the developing world follow a pattern, in which the first waves are composed of professionals, followed by tradespeople and unskilled laborers and, finally, by rural populations (Williams and Westermeyer 1986). The rationale for this pattern is that the first groups, the country's intelligentsia, are political and ideological dissenters associated with the attempt to overthrow the government. As such, they fit the definition of the traditional refugee seeking asylum from persecution related to ideological issues. These groups adjust easily to U.S. culture. Subsequent waves of refugees flee their war-torn country during or after the revolution. It is these second and third waves that have the most trouble adjusting and are frequently viewed as a drain on the United States' resources.

MAINTAINING A CONNECTION WITH THE COUNTRY OF ORIGIN

Whereas immigrants can return periodically to their home country, refugees may not do so. Their status is that of exiles. Yet contact with the home country, although severed, continues through memorabilia, symbolism, and ruminations, such as (1) observance of rituals, religious practices, and festivals; (2) adherence to the native language and communication patterns; (3) practice of ethnic values through customs and behavioral and attitudinal codes; and (4) familial, fraternal, and other ethnic group and interpersonal relationships. Another way of maintaining contact is through a perceptual distortion of reality, in which the past is overglorified to compensate for the disillusionment of the present (Mayadas and Lasan 1984). Both refugees and immigrants maintain continuity with their past and ancient culture, even though they may never actually return to their homeland. Groups from a common geographic area of origin are bound by the ethnicity and socioeconomic status of their home country. Interactional patterns are determined by this similarity, or the lack of it, rather than the political/naturalization status under which they are admitted into the United States The association with their country of birth is not only kept alive, but it is also transmitted to their children. The establishment of ethnic enclaves, with ethnic shops, restaurants, and other small businesses all attest to this symbolic allegiance to the home country and the desire for continued contact with its culture.

THE REFUGEE POPULATION'S STRENGTHS AND NEEDS

Like all immigrants and new arrivals in the United States, refugees wish to join the mainstream of their adopted country. They come with renewed hope, not so much for their generation, as for the generations to follow and seldom, if ever, feel that the country owes them a living. On the contrary, their recent experiences with governments, border authorities, and asylum/refugee-processing centers have been so horrific that they prefer to maintain a low profile, make no demands, and may even forgo their legitimate rights for goods and services owing to their fear of being mistreated. Furthermore, since language poses an additional barrier, refugees seldom can communicate their needs to the community and mental health services, and they also avoid service providers because of their fear of all authority. Another reason for not coming forward may be cultural, especially in regard to Asian refugees, who carry the burdensome label of *model minority.* This stereotype is an insidious way of denying this group access to the rights and privileges—such as federal funding, job opportunities, quota-based academic programs, and target-of-opportunity positions—extended to other minority groups. Moreover, since these groups are presumed to have traits like "diligence, frugality and willingness to sacrifice," they are expected not only to compete equally but also to excel in the open market in order to obtain those rewards, which are, at best, equal to and more likely less than what the average member of the majority group receives. Consequently, this group is frequently victimized by the glass ceiling in all walks of life: professional, corporate, academic, labor, and political (Crystal 1989:405).

Several studies have examined mental health issues related to refugees (Cole, Rothblum, and Espin 1993; UNHCR 1995; Williams and Westermeyer 1986). The interest in this subject stems from the assumption that groups, traumatized by war, torture, and persecution, must bear the scars of the ordeal. The cumulative findings of these studies show that war trauma does affect social functioning, job employment, and adaptation to new conditions, in addition to the cultural adjustment and climatic adaptations that most immigrants encounter (Flaskerud and Anh 1988; Gonsalves 1990; Hauff and Vaglum 1993; Hirayama and Cetingok 1995; Lin, Tasuma, and Masuda 1979; Tran 1993; Verdonk 1979). But these studies have only scratched the surface. First, the studies concerned with mental health focus only on clinical populations. Second, because of cultural factors, lack of knowledge, and apprehension, even those refugees with mental health needs are reluctant to utilize services. Finally, because most of the refugee population uses its own resources to adjust to the changed circumstances, the first two kinds of studies may not be representative of the population as a whole.

Refugees are not victims but survivors of disaster. Some refugees originally held professional and skilled-labor jobs in their native countries (table 6.4) and thus have adapted to their changed circumstances more easily and moved more quickly toward self-sufficiency (Williams and Westermeyer 1986). Refugees form communities in which self-generated private entrepreneurship allows the growth of a refugee economy. For example, refugees who own and operate ethnic restaurants often hire members of their own group yet attract customers from both the majority and ethnic populations. Most refugees do not stay on welfare for long but move on to jobs and small businesses as soon as they are able (Na Champassak 1995). Their family structure and group-oriented culture contribute much to this sense of self-reliance. Large extended families live under the same roof and pool their incomes to become family-run cooperatives in which every member has a stake (Crystal 1989). Whereas the West thrives on individualism, the refugees are interdependent and strive toward self-sufficiency. Furthermore, refugees not only bring cultural diversity and talent to the country, but they also contribute to its economy. They are, in the long run, an asset, but they do need help initially from organizations such as the Refugee Resettlement Program and voluntary agencies.

The goal of the Refugee Resettlement Program is to enable refugees to become economically self-sufficient as soon as possible after locating in a state. Because the program concentrates mainly on material self-sufficiency, it does not resolve cultural or social problems but forces refugees to adopt a U.S. lifestyle (Muecke 1987). But enforcing conformity is not conducive to a satisfactory resettlement. Without structural assimilation, cultural assimilation will be only superficial (Gordon 1961). If the goal is to have "one nation, indivisible," then institutional structures need to merge; that is, intermarriages and integrated neighborhoods need to become the norm instead of the exception; and all religious, social, and civic institutions should be regarded as equal, not only those that perpetuate the traditions and values of western Europe and England.

FAMILY DYNAMICS

When people cross national boundaries and settle in different countries, they often find themselves in alien social and cultural environments whose norms of behavior and family role relationships are unfamiliar and challenge the traditional patterns of their family interaction.

Reviews of anthropological and cross-cultural literature indicate that unlike the individualistic orientations of the North American and northern European cultures that reward independence and equality, numerous societies in other parts of the world reinforce allocentrism and interdependence among nuclear family members, between the nuclear family and extended family, and between the family and the community. Often age, gender, and roles strictly define status, power, and the parameters of acceptable behavior and relationships. Traditional family structures provide stability, interpersonal intimacy, social support, and a relatively stress-free environment in which expectations of behavior and responsibility are clear (Segal 1991). But the experience of being a refugee can cause major disruptions in the continuity of family life and create tremendous pressures that destabilize established family relationships and affect role performance. In cases such as these, the refugee network can provide support.

Often refugee communities serve as surrogate families, providing both emotional and material support, yet these pseudofamily structures cannot totally substitute for the natural family (Lum 2000). Although not suffering some of the traumas and difficulties faced by their parents, the children of refugees frequently face immense acculturation stress as they grow up in impoverished households. Their parents, who should be their primary support, often lack the experience and material resources to help them negotiate poor educational systems, street crime, lack of employment, racism, and intolerance (Bean et al. 1994; Segal 1994). Furthermore, because the children usually become more fluent in English than their parents do and rapidly adopt the customs of the new country, their roles often reverse (Potocky 1996a). That is, children serve as the English-language negotiators and interpreters of cultural norms for their parents (Carlin 1990; Drachman 1992; Stepick and Dutton Stepick 1994), which frequently undermines the authority of and respect for the elders (Furuto and Murase 1992), an important value in many cultures. And even though all adolescents in the United States feel a certain amount of intergenerational tension, children of refugees often find themselves torn between the two vastly different worlds of their refugee parents and their American peers (Rumbaut and Rumbaut 1976; Segal 1991; Suro 1992), and so they tend to emulate the patterns of personal vulnerability and family disintegration that often characterize other minorities in the United States (Vega and Rumbaut 1991). For parents this is a dual loss. They endured being refugees and now must endure cultural disintegration through the younger generation, for whose betterment many left their native land in the first place.

Resettlement is a lengthy process. Not only must all refugees adjust to a foreign culture, they must also come to terms with the events that forced them from their homes. Hulewat (1996) suggested that the refugee experience always produces a family crisis that can have long-term effects, that this happens regardless of the country or continent of origin. The cultural dissonance felt by each family is also affected by the family's particular dynamics (Hulewat 1996), its history, and the collective experience of that refugee group. Difficulties posed by the inability to speak English and different cultural patterns are often exacerbated by the xenophobia of both the host country and the refugee, making social integration a major hurdle (Mayadas and Elliott 1992; Mayadas and Lasan 1984).

In the United States, even for those who eventually are successful, the struggle is usually long and arduous, and "its impact is felt for a lifetime" (Nguyen 1994:25). The scars left from the strife manifest themselves in various ways, through family upheavals, psychosomatic illnesses, and/or social unrest. Whatever the outcome, it is important to remember that the refugee experience in itself is terrible, and when coupled with the reception in the resettlement country, it surpasses the negative experiences of other immigrants and minority groups. This is a crucial point to bear in mind when designing services for the refugee population.

POLICIES, PROGRAMS, AND SERVICES

The U.S. government's official definition of resettlement that guides policy regarding refugees is Public Law 96-212, the Refugee Act of 1980, which focuses on economic self-sufficiency in the shortest time possible. Refugees are considered to be economically self-sufficient if they are not receiving welfare benefits (Potocky 1996b). But a number of studies have found that many refugees in the United States are barely surviving economically, and a significant number receive public assistance. In addition, many refugee families who are considered to be economically self-sufficient are, in fact, living well below the official poverty level (Bach 1988; Kibria 1989; Office of Refugee Resettlement 1991). Refugees spend a greater percentage of their income on housing and live in much more crowded conditions than do other groups (Potocky 1996b; Vu 1990).

Potocky (1996b) and Kuhlman (1991) believe that this measure—self-sufficiency in the shortest amount of time— is too restrictive to truly assess economic integration, which should instead be measured by the following features:

1. Adequate participation in the economy.
2. An income that allows an acceptable standard of living.
3. Access equal to that of the host population to those goods and services to which access is not determined solely by income level.
4. The impact of refugees on the host society is such that on balance, the position of the various socioeconomic categories within the indigenous

population with respect to criteria 1, 2, and 3 has not deteriorated (Kuhlman 1991:16).

In keeping with those available to the rest of the population, programs and services for refugees are divided into those offered by governmental and by nongovernmental organizations. Governmental programs for refugees, however, have the clear aim of providing the assistance necessary to allow refugees to achieve economic self-sufficiency in the shortest time possible following their arrival in the United States. In fiscal year 1996, the Department of Health and Human Services (HHS) allocated approximately $417 million for refugees through the following five different federal programs: cash and medical assistance, employment services, preventive health services, the volunteer-agency matching grant program, and the targeted-assistance grant program (Judiciary Homepage 1997).

Cash and Medical Assistance

Cash and medical assistance are available to needy refugees who are not eligible for other such programs (e.g., Aid to Families with Dependent Children, Supplemental Security Income, Medicaid) and who arrive in the United States without financial resources. This assistance is paid entirely from federal funds but is available only for the eight months following entry into the country.

Employment Services

HHS provides funding to state and private nonprofit agencies to deliver services, such as English-language classes and employment training, to help refugees become self-sufficient as rapidly as possible. Individuals receiving cash and medical assistance are required to be enrolled in these training programs and to accept offers of employment.

Preventive Health Services

In 1996, HHS allocated resources to the Public Health Service to screen refugees for health problems before they entered the United States. Additional allocations were made to state public health departments in the form of grants to assess and treat refugees for contagious diseases.

Volunteer-Agency Matching Grant Program

During the first four months of a refugee's arrival in the United States, several volunteer agencies assume responsibility for helping in the resettlement process, thereby permitting many refugees to become self-sufficient through private initiatives and without needing resort to public cash assistance. These agencies match federal funds from either private money or similar goods and services.

For example, the American Near East Refugee Aid (ANERA) has regular fund-raising drives for refugee relief, and the American Refugee Committee (ARC) offers self-sufficiency–focused job training. The Guatemala Partners supports education and leadership training programs; the Haitian Refugee Center offers legal help in political asylum cases; and the Pontifical Mission for Palestine (PMP) provides funding for relief rehabilitation and development (Miller and Miller 1996). By recognizing the cultural differences and various needs of refugee groups, several ethnically focused agencies were formed to meet the specific requirements of particular groups of refugees.

Targeted-Assistance Grants

The targeted-assistance grants direct additional resources to those communities in which there is either a high concentration of refugees or a heavy use of public aid by the refugee population that has resettled there. Special efforts are made for those refugees who are dependent on public assistance. Since 1995, the goal of refugee assistance programs has been to provide culturally and linguistically appropriate services. Service providers should respond rapidly, visibly, and flexibly, especially to sudden refugee needs. A new group of discretionary initiatives was begun through the preferred communities and unanticipated arrivals grant programs to provide timely funding to both public and private service providers, to enable them to respond promptly to unanticipated influxes of refugees (Judiciary Homepage 1997). At the state and local levels, several alternative programs have been created using the "Fish/Wilson" authority. In 1985, Congress passed the Fish/Wilson Amendment to the Refugee Act to encourage HHS and the Office of Refugee Resettlement (ORR) to experiment with new approaches to providing welfare and job services. These innovative alternative programs may be developed and administered by either public or private agencies with the aim of finding employment for refugees—a goal consistent with the government's policy of economic self-sufficiency as the sole criterion for satisfactory resettlement.

USE OF PROGRAMS AND SERVICES

An audit by the Office of the Inspector General in 1995 found that many of the refugees who received financial aid through the social service and targeted assistance grants awarded by the Administration for Children and Families' ORR had been in the United States for more than five years and that some did not need financial aid. For example, since current refugee programs do not require time eligibility for social services and targeted assistance, in Florida about 95 percent of these grants were distributed to refugees who had been in the United States for more than five years (Office of the Inspector General 1995). A more troubling finding by the ORR was that the longer refugees remain out of the labor force, the less likely are they to begin searching for a job or to find a job. Refugees are most likely to join the labor force during the first and second years and steadily less likely as time passes (Office of the Inspector General 1995).

Gersten (1996) stated that welfare dependency continues to be a serious problem, especially in the states with the highest AFDC payments. The results of ten years of pilot projects indicate that the private sector is more effective than the public sector in securing employment for refugees. An amendment to the Immigration and Nationality Act proposed by Congressman David Obey called for transferring all responsibility to private agencies, including funds to strengthen services already being provided. The amendment is based on the results of the ORR study, that if refugees are shut out of any state or federal programs of cash assistance during their first twelve months in this country, they will be forced to seek employment for survival and thus become self-sufficient through necessity. In this way, most refugees find employment, and only the few who are not employed are then eligible for a welfare program (Gersten 1996).

In 1992, the ORR reported that the Planned Secondary Resettlement Program gave unemployed refugees the opportunity to relocate from areas of high welfare dependency to communities that offer more favorable employment. Approximately 1,750 relocated refugees found jobs, and the government recovered its relocation costs within eight months (Sullivan 1992). Nevertheless, Gersten (1996) who was then director of the ORR, became more skeptical of the secondary resettlement program later in 1996 and suggested that refugees knew which states paid the highest welfare allowances (California, Oregon, Washington, Minnesota, Massachusetts, and Wisconsin) and so arranged to move there.

OTHER PROGRAMS AND SERVICES

Governmental and volunteer organizations are beginning to recognize the need to address not only refugees' economic needs but also their psychosocial needs and the issues concerning their expectations of acculturation. Accordingly, several programs and services have been developed, or accommodated, for refugees, with the recognition that economic self-sufficiency will not solve all their problems.

Over a six-year period beginning in 1987, the ORR provided $3 million through the Administration for Children and Families (ACF) to educate law enforcement and refugee communities about each other. And in partnership with the Department of Justice and the National Crime Prevention Council, the ORR has enabled police departments and Asian refugee communities to train multilingual community service officers to conduct workshops, assist in criminal investigations, and mediate and prevent conflicts between refugees and the larger community. By these means, the ORR's crime victimization plan has established outreach and educational programs. Crime prevention services include neighborhood crime watches; increased law enforcement presence; and the prevention of, and intervention into, domestic violence and violence against children (Glickman 1993). Despite these efforts, it is clear that the crime is only one of many problems that can beset refugees, which may be divided into the following three categories (Dine 1995:4B):

Individual—as people cope with traumatic situations they endured back home or suddenly face a plunge in status here.

Family—as those already rendered fragile try to cope with a new society or as traditional values meet modern ones.

Group—with suspicions and envy keeping countrymen apart, at a time when they could help one another adjust.

As a rule, immigrants come to the United States with more resources, both tangible and intangible, than do refugees who, therefore, encounter many more urgent problems. Most refugees tend to gravitate toward cities, where the largest number of agencies are located and rents are lower. Cities such as St. Louis are becoming aware of the needs of refugee adults and children, and some of the schools and a few health care providers now have programs to treat the emotional and psychological aspects of their adjustment (Dine 1995). But despite the growing number of programs to help refugees, most are hesitant to seek mental health services, because of their cultural conditioning regarding privacy, coupled with fears of reliving their trauma.

The literature and services tend to focus on the needs of adult refugees and their experience of violation and relocation. In most instances, the voices of children are not heard, nor does their experience of victimization receive much attention. Only when isolated incidences in schools bring their traumatization into the public eye (see Dine 1995) is professional attention directed their way. A book edited by Ahearn and Athey (1991), the outcome of the Conference on Refugee Children Traumatized by War and Violence held in Washington, D.C., in 1988, made apparent that refugee children, especially those who fled countries in the midst of war or other forms of violence, have several special physical, social, and mental health needs. War, violence, economic deprivation, religious persecution, famine, and difficulties associated with flight make children particularly vulnerable to a variety of traumas. Refugee children often experience the death of a parent or loved one, the loss of their home, and the destruction of their community. They suffer separation, torture, and starvation and rarely understand the cause.

Programs such as the Fresh Air Program in San Antonio, Texas, are designed to assist all refugee children, but especially at-risk youth, to acquire knowledge and skills necessary to cope with the U.S. culture. Its aims are to reduce stress, develop self-sufficiency, involve families, preserve culture, and educate and sensitize the community at large to the needs and contributions of a multicultural environment (Stevens 1990). The Massachusetts Department of Mental Health's Refugee Assistance Program stresses the importance of integrating trauma education, cross-cultural approaches traditional methods of healing, and interagency collaboration to support the child, the child's family, and the service provider through the recovery process (De Monchy 1991). Other programs are designed to modify traditional family therapy methods to help refugee families deal with torture and forced exile. The Center for Family Therapy and Hypnosis in Oakland, California, has worked with many refugees, including those from Latin America, who have survived torture. In addition to identifying what constitutes torture, the program stresses the family's role in helping refugee deal with their experiences (Ritterman and Simon 1990). Innovative programs that combine a variety of traditional methods tailored to the needs of refugee populations can also be effective. Kellogg and Volker (1993) presented a model of multifamily group therapy that combines group methods, family therapy, and art therapy, to provide crisis intervention services to recent refugee arrivals to the United States. This program provides a supportive environment in which refugees can express and process their experiences.

Although many of the refugees' experiences are similar, service providers must recognize that their histories and the events leading to their seeking refuge may differ substantially. In addition, the refugees in the United States are, themselves, multicultural. Essential to the delivery of services is cultural sensitivity that goes beyond recognizing the traumatization and victimization experienced by refugees to acknowledging the differences in their heritage, values, norms, and expectations. Georgeski (1987) explored the differences among refugees from eastern Europe, the Middle East, and Ethiopia and found considerable variations in their level of acclimatization to U.S. culture—much of which was a reflection of their own backgrounds and traditions. Refugee services thus need to be designed to address these cultural attitudes toward health and illness, language barriers, limited access to health care, lack of community support, and their previous experiences with suffering (Boehnlein 1987).

ROLE OF SOCIAL SERVICES

The overall experience of many refugees, including the trauma of relocation, isolation from family and friends, problems with acculturation, and the economic stresses associated with the inability to find and hold a job may increase depression, lower self-esteem, damage psychological well-being, hurt coping skills, and increase anger and frustration. The United States' policy for refugees, aimed toward "economic self-sufficiency in as short a time as possible," may well not be sufficient to truly resettle individuals and families. Policies regarding refugee resettlement may need to include the identification and allocation of fiscal resources to allow practitioners to engage in active outreach, continuing support programs, and intervention services that can be implemented specifically to help refugees deal with the social and emotional traumas of relocating and adjusting to an alien land, such as the problems of acculturation, intergenerational conflict, and posttraumatic stress.

Since so many social service policies and services are directed to acculturative concerns, relatively little attention has been given to the refugees' other, more common familial and socioemotional problems. Although a few researchers have addressed child abuse (Ima and Hohm 1991; Jang et al. 1991; Korbin 1991), domestic violence (McCloskey et al. 1995; Norton and Manson 1992), HIV/AIDS (Snider et al. 1983; Sullivan et al. 1987), gay and lesbian issues (Aldershvile et al. 1980; Espin 1996; Sullivan et al. 1987; Swenson et al. 1991), and the concerns of the elderly (Barresi and Stull 1993; Furuto and Murase 1992; Tran 1990, 1991; Yee 1992), these studies have been episodic and not global. Hence there is little empirical evidence to indicate whether these problems are specific to any one refugee group or are present across cultures. Nevertheless, it suggests that the refugee population is not immune to such problems. The minimal attention given to these only reinforces society's primary interest in "resettlement and self-sufficiency in the shortest time possible."

What, then, can humanitarian services do to help refugees integrate into a society to which they do not feel welcome? Working with refugees requires, first, a recognition of the triangulated problem involving the refugees, the community, and the current state of mental health services. A three-dimensional approach is therefore needed (Mayadas, Ramanathan, and Suarez 1999). So far attempts have been made to integrate refugees into the surrounding community using an educational approach (Glickman 1993). Although this is a major step forward, it still does not take into account the existing services which are designed mainly for the North American population. For example, the treatment of psychosocial disorders basically follows a medical model using drugs and talk therapy. Service providers maintain a professional distance and take pride in their objectivity in handling "cases" and not "people." But this treatment model is unfamiliar to many refugees, who can understand it at best as indifference and a lack of concern for their welfare. The service providers, interpreting their response according to a psychopathology model, are likely to see it as resistance (Ivanoff, Blythe, and Tripodi 1994; Rooney 1992) or some other form of system manipulation. In a three-dimensional interventive approach, however, the focus would be on the match among the three elements of refugee, community, and mental health services, and both assessment tools and intervention plans may have to be modified. For example, to the Vietnamese, there are basically three models of help: "familial," "philanthropic," and "medical"—there is no concept equivalent to therapeutic help. Accordingly, service providers may be labeled by the refugee as "relational," "benevolent," or "expert." Service providers will be more effective if they respond likewise. For instance, if the service provider is viewed as a respected elder or a family member and the refugee offers a gift in gratitude for the kindness rendered, the service provider should graciously acknowledge it and even reciprocate in some small way, rather than reject it with the antiseptic psychoanalytic incisiveness inherent in the psychotherapeutic modalities.

Furthermore, not only is the understanding of the refugees' frame of reference and culture necessary, but the extent of their acculturation to the United States must be determined before they are assessed. Once refugees have entered the resettlement country, adjusting to it is seen solely as their responsibility, without recognizing that the host country also must be willing to accommodate them. Thus the service providers' role extends beyond service to the refugee and must take into account interventions at the community and society levels. The providers must ask questions like What jobs are available? Do they match the refugee's qualifications? How do the wages, salaries, and so forth compare with those of similar jobs held by the majority culture and other ethnic groups? What are the policies regarding welfare and medical benefits, housing, family reunification, and immigration of family members? What economic opportu-

nities (e.g., bank loans for small businesses, cooperatives, and other self-sufficiency projects) should be considered and concurrent interventions required?
The role of social services and service providers working with refugees is complex, requiring the ability to view concurrently the issues from different perspectives and levels, while keeping the focus on the refugee as the beneficiary
(Elliott and Mayadas 1996).

One skill that is seldom discussed is that of language. Although interpreters
are definitely an asset, they also may distort the meaning of what the refugee is
trying to say (Mayadas and Lasan 1984). Thus knowledge of the refugees' culture includes not only an understanding of their customs and rituals but also
what it means to be a refugee and how they differ from other ethnic groups of
immigrants. Haines (1997) identified six factors essential to understanding the
refugee experience: demographics, socioeconomic condition, familial and cultural variables, the flight experience, and the impact of American society on the
refugees when they arrive in the United States. Working with this population
also requires awareness of the United States' ever changing policies and laws
and their repercussions on the current and future refugee status. Who is offi-
cially recognized as a refugee, an asylee, or an undocumented alien in the United States? What are their rights? Where and when does the federal jurisdiction
regarding refugees end and the state's authority take over?

The complexity of the refugee situation requires a model of social work practice
that has global applicability. Unless we take advantage of the refugees' potential
and the country can accommodate and sustain their progress, no amount of
economic aid and institutional development will be able to help those who have
fled their countries of origin to start anew in the United States

In addition, the call for an all-inclusive model of practice is inherent in the
complexity of refugee work. This model must allow for multilevel interventions. For example, when refugee populations flee their countries because of
war or political upheaval, they need protection in the asylum country. Conditions at this level are dependent on national policies and political allegiance and
need macro-level intervention competence. At the same time, refugees also require adequate infrastructure and local services, such as medical aid and advocacy. These basic survival needs are compounded by highly individualized trauma, which requires support and understanding on a personal level. Thus the
macro, mezzo, and micro levels of concern must be attended to simultaneously.

Refugee workers must understand that all the refugees have left is their cultural heritage, their traditions, and their skills of survival. These have been pre-
served at a high price and have helped them escape conditions to which many of

their relatives and friends succumbed. At this initial stage of reestablishing stability, reliance on outside resources is a necessity, but the refugee community
also needs to be involved in its own rehabilitation, to retain its identity, self-re-
spect, and capability to make decisions. The empowerment perspective in a social development context allows service providers to focus simultaneously on
the economics of refugee self-sufficiency and the psychology of self-esteem (Elliott and Mayadas 1996). Such a model enhances cooperation between the local
population and refugees, reduces xenophobia, improves communication, and
above all, provides resources for the refugees' economic self-sufficiency.

REFERENCES

Ahern, F. D. Jr., and Athey, J. L. (eds.). (1991). *Refugee Children: Theory, Research, and
Services*. Baltimore: John Hopkins University Press.
Aldershvile, J., Skinhoj, P., Frosner, G. G., Black, F., Deinhardt, E., Hardt, F., and
Nielsen, J. O. (1980). The expression pattern of hepatitis B e antigen and antibody
in different ethnic and clinical groups of hepatitis B surface antigen carriers.
Journal of Infectious Diseases 142 (1): 18–22.
Bach, R. L. (1988). State intervention in Southeast Asian refugee resettlement in the
United States. *Journal of Refugee Studies* 1: 38–56.
Barressi, C. M., and Stull, D. E. (eds.). (1993). *Ethnic Elderly and Long Time Care*.
New York: Springer.
Bean, R. D., Chapa, J., Berg, R., and Sowards, K. (1994). Educational and sociodemo-
graphic incorporation among Hispanic immigrants to the United States. In B.
Edmonston and J. S. Passel (eds.), *Immigration and Ethnicity: The Integration of
America's Newest Arrivals*. Washington, DC: Urban Institute.
Bertalanffy, L. (1955). General systems theory. *Main Currents in Modern Thought* 2:
77.
Boehnlein, J. K. (1987). A review of mental health services for refugees between 1975
and 1985 and a proposal for future services. *Hospital and Community Psychiatry*
38 (7): 764–768.
Branigin, W. (1996). Senate votes to make female genital mutilation a federal crime.
Washington Post (May 2): A7.
Buckman, C. L., Lipson, J. G., and Meleis, A. I. (1992). The cultural consultant in
mental health care: The case of an Arab adolescent. *American Journal of Orthopsychiatry* 62 (3): 359–370.
Carlin, J. E. (1990). Refugee and immigrant populations at special risk: Women,
children, and the elderly. In W. H. Holtzman and T. H. Bornemann (eds.), *Mental Health of Immigrants and Refugees*. Austin, TX: Hogg Foundation for Mental
Health.

Cole, E., Rothblum, E. D., and Espin, O. M. (1993). Refugee women and their mental health: Shattered societies, shattered lives. *Women and Therapy* 13 (1/2, 3), parts I and II (entire issue).

Constable, P. (1996). INS says mutilation claim may be basis for asylum. *Washington Post* (April 24): A3.

Crystal, D. (1989). Asian Americans and the myth of the model minority. *Social Casework* 70 (7): 405–413.

De Monchy, M. L. (1991). Recovery and rebuilding: The challenge for children and service providers. In F. D. Ahern Jr. and J. L. Athey (eds.), *Refugee Children: Theory, Research, and Services.* Baltimore: John Hopkins University Press.

DeVita, C. J. (1996). Immigrants' impact on U.S. society. *Migration World Magazine* 24 (3): 28–30.

Dine, P. (1995). An invisible population: The terrors and tensions live on. *St. Louis Post-Dispatch* (June 25): 1B, 4B–5B.

Drachman, D. (1992). A stage-of-immigration framework for service to immigrant populations. *Social Work* 37 (1): 68–72.

Elliott, D., and Mayadas, N. S. (1996). Social development and clinical practice in social work. *Journal of Applied Social Sciences* 21 (1): 61–68.

Espin, O. M. (1996). Immigrant and refugee lesbians. In E. D. Rothblum and L. A. Bond (eds.), *Preventing Heterosexism and Homophobia: Primary Prevention of Psychopathology.* Vol. 17. Thousand Oaks, CA: Sage.

Flaskerud, J., and Anh, N. T. (1988). Mental health of Vietnamese refugees. *Hospital and Community Psychiatry* 39 (4): 435–437.

Furuto, S. M., and Murase, K. (1992). Asian American in the future. In S. M. Furuto, R. Biswas, D. K. Chung, K. Murase, and F. Ross-Sheriff (eds.), *Social Work Practice with Asian Americans.* Newbury Park, CA: Sage.

Georgeski, J. D. (1987). Nature of differences in adjustment to and valuing of the American culture among refugees from Eastern Europe, the Middle East and African countries. Ph.D. diss., U.S. International University, CA.

Gersten, C. (1996). Refugee resettlement by private organizations. Testimony of Chris Gersten, former director of Office of Refugee Resettlement, Department of Health and Human Services, before the House Judiciary Committee on Immigration and Claims (August 1). Online: http://www.house.gove/judiciary/632.htm.

Glickman, L. (1993). Refugee resettlement assistance (October 6). Re: 1993.10.06. Online: http://www.os.dhhs.gov/news/press/pre1995pres/931006.txt.

Gonsalves, C. J. (1990). The psychological effects of political repression on Chilean exiles in the U.S. *American Journal of Orthopsychiatry* 60 (1): 143–53.

Gordon, M. M. (1961). Assimilation in America: Theory and reality. *Daedalus, Journal of the American Academy of Arts and Sciences* 90 (2): 263–285.

Haines, D. W. (1997). Introduction to D. W. Haines (ed.), *Case Studies in Diversity: Refugees in America in the 1990s.* Westport, CT: Praeger.

Hauff, E., and Vaglum, P. (1993). The integration of Vietnamese refugees into the Norwegian labor market: The impact of war trauma. *International Migration Review* 27 (2): 388–405.

Hirayama, K. K. (1982). Evaluating the effects of the employment of Vietnamese refugee wives on their family role and mental health. *California Sociologist* 5 (1): 96–110.

Hirayama, H., and Cetingok, M. (1995). Amerasian refugees: Social characteristics, services needs, and mental health. *Journal of Sociology and Social Welfare* 22 (4): 69–84.

Hofferman, J. (1998). *Caring for the Political Refugee.* New York: Garland.

Hulewat, P. (1996). Resettlement: A cultural and psychological crisis. *Social Work* 42 (2): 129–135.

http://www.interaction.org.pub/connect/strating/html. (1997). Starting over: Refugee resettlement in the United States: 1–4.

Ima, K., and Hohm, C. F. (1991). Child maltreatment among Asian and Pacific Islander refugees and immigrants: The San Diego case. *Journal of Interpersonal Violence* 6 (3): 267–285.

Ivanoff, A., Blythe, B. J., and Tripodi, T. (1994). *Involuntary Clients in Social Work Practice.* New York: Aldine De Gruyter.

Jang, D., Lee, D., and Morello-Frosch, R. (1991). Domestic violence in the immigrant and refugee community: Responding to the needs of immigrant women. *Response to the Victimization of Women and Children* 13 (4): 2–7.

Judiciary Homepage. (1997). http://www.house.gov/judiciary/631.htm.

Karger, H. J., and Stoesz, D. (1994). *American Social Welfare Policy: A Pluralist Approach.* White Plains, NY: Longman.

Kellogg, A., and Volker, C. A. (1993). Family art therapy with political refugees. In D. Linesch (ed.), *Art Therapy with Families in Crisis: Overcoming Resistance Through Nonverbal Expression.* New York: Brunner/Mazel.

Kibria, N. (1989) Patterns of Vietnamese refugee women's wagework in the U.S. *Ethnic Groups* 7: 297–323.

Korbin, J. (1991). Child maltreatment and the study of child refugees. In F. D. Ahern Jr. and J. L. Athey (eds.), *Refugee Children: Theory, Research, and Services.* Baltimore: John Hopkins University Press.

Kuhlman, T. (1991). The economic integration of refugees in developing countries: A research model. *Journal of Refugee Studies* 4: 1–20.

Lin, K., Tasuma, L., and Masuda, M. (1979). Adaptation problems of Vietnamese refugees: Health and mental status. *Archives of General Psychiatry* 36 (9): 955–961.

Lum, D. (2000). *Social Work Practice and People of Color: A Process-Stage Approach.* 4th ed. New York: Brooks/Cole.

Mayadas, N. S., and Elliott, D. (1992). Integration and xenophobia: An inherent conflict in international migration. In A. S. Ryan (ed.), *Social Work with Immigrants and Refugees.* New York: Haworth Press.

Mayadas, N. S., and Lasan, D. B. (1984). Integrating refugees into alien cultures. In C. Guzzetta (ed.), *Education for Social Work Practice: Selected International Models*. New York: Council on Social Work Education.

Mayadas, N. S., Ramanathan, C. S., and Suarez, Z. (1999). Mental health, social contexts, refugees, and immigrants: A cultural interface. *Journal of Inter-Group Relations* xxv(4): 3–14.

McCloskey, L. A., Southwick, K., Fernandez-Esquer, M. E., and Locke, C. (1995). The psychological effects of political and domestic violence on Central American and Mexican immigrant mothers and children. *Journal of Community Psychology* 23 (2): 95–116.

Miller, E. W., and Miller, R. M. (1996). *United States Immigration: A Reference Handbook*. Santa Barbara, CA: ABC-CLIO.

Muecke, M. A. (1987). Resettled refugees reconstruction of identity: Lao in Seattle. *Urban Anthropology* 16 (3– 4): 273–289.

Na Champassak, N. (1995). Strategy for survival. *Refugees*. UN High Commissioner for Refugees, Geneva 100: 16–19.

Nguyen, N. (1994). Life's biggest lemon. *Refugees*. UN High Commissioner for Refugees, Geneva (94: 25).

Nguyen, W. H. (1994). Psychological well-being of the former Vietnamese political prisoner in the United States. Ph.D. diss., University of Texas at Arlington.

Norton, I. M., and Manson, S. M. (1992). An association between domestic violence and depression among Southeast Asian refugee women. *Journal of Nervous and Mental Disease* 180 (1): 729–730.

Office of Inspector General. (1995). *Refugee Assistance Programs Should be Limited to Newly-Arrived and Needy Refugees*. U.S. Department of Health and Human Services, report no. 1-04-93-00062. Online: http://www.sbaonline.sba.gov/ignet/internal/hhs/acf/hhs6469.html.

Office of Refugee Resettlement. (1991). *Refugee Resettlement Program: Annual Report to Congress FY 1990*. Washington, DC: U.S. Government Printing Office.

Potocky, M. (1996a). Refugee children: How are they faring economically as adults? *Social Work* 41 (4): 364–373.

Potocky, M. (1996b). Toward a new definition of refugee economic integration. *International Social Welfare* 39: 245–256.

Redmond, R. (1992). Slamming doors. *Refugees*. UN High Commissioner for Refugees, Geneva 88: 21–25.

Reed, C. (1994). Female genital mutilation fear cited in U.S. deportation case. *The Guardian* (March 21), section 1: 13.

Ritterman, M. K., and Simon, R. (1990). Understanding and treating Latin American torture survivors. In M. P. Mirkin (ed.), *The Social and Political Contexts of Family Therapy*. Boston: Allyn & Bacon.

Rooney, R. H. (1992). *Strategies for Work with Involuntary Clients*. New York: Columbia University Press.

Rudge, P. (1991). A new ethnic for Europe. *Refugees.* UN High Commissioner for Refugees, Geneva 83: 35.

Rumbaut, R. D., and Rumbaut, R. G. (1976). The family in exile: Cuban expatriates in the United States. *American Journal of Psychiatry* 133: 395–399.

Segal, U. A. (1991). Cultural variables in Asian Indian families. *Families in Society* 72 (4): 233–242.

Segal, U. A. (1994). Delinquency, substance abuse and gang behavior as indicators of family difficulties among Southeast Asian refugees. Paper presented at the 10th International Congress of Child Abuse and Neglect 1994, Kuala Lumpur, Malaysia.

Snider, W. D., Simpson, D. M., Nielsen, S., Gold, J. W., Metroka, C. E., and Posner, J. B. (1983). Neurological complications of acquired immune deficiency syndrome: Analysis of 50 patients. *Annals of Neurology* 14 (4): 403–418.

Stepick, A., and Dutton Stepick, C. (1994). *Preliminary Haitian Needs Assessment: Report to the City of Miami.* Miami: Immigration and Ethnicity Institute, Florida International University.

Stevens, L. D. (1990). Refugee services in San Antonio: The Fresh Air Program. In W. H. Holtzman and T. H. Bornemann (eds.), *Mental Health of Immigrants and Refugees.* Austin, TX: Hogg Foundation for Mental Health.

Sullivan, R., Linneman, C. C. Jr., Clark, C. S., and Walzer, P. D. (1987). Seroepidemiologic study of giardiasis patients and high-risk groups in a midwestern city in the United States. *American Journal of Public Health* 77 (8): 960–963.

Suro, R. (1992). Generational chasm leads to cultural turmoil for Mexicans in the U.S. *New York Times* (January 20): A14.

Swenson, P. D., Reiss, J. T., and Krueger, L. E. (1991). Determination of HBsAg subtypes in different high risk populations using monoclonal antibodies. *Journal of Virological Methods* 33 (1–2): 27–28.

Tarnoff, P. (1995). FY 1996 refugee admissions program. U.S. Department of State Dispatch 6 (34) (August 31): 643–644.

Tran, T. V. (1990). Language acculturation among older Vietnamese refugee adults. *Gerontologist* 30 (1): 94–99.

Tran, T. V. (1991). Family living arrangements and social adjustment among three ethnic groups of elderly Indochinese refugees. *Journal of Aging and Human Development* 32 (2): 91–102.

Tran, T. V. (1993). Psychological traumas and depression in a sample of Vietnamese people in the United States. *Health and Social Work* 18 (3): 184–194.

UN High Commissioner for Refugees (UNHCR). (1995). *The State of the World's Refugees in Search of Solutions.* New York: Oxford University Press.

UN High Commissioner for Refugees (UNHCR). (1996). *Community Services Manual.* Rev. ed. Geneva, UNHCR.

U.S. Department of Justice. (1995). *Statistical Yearbook of the Immigration and Naturalization Service:* M-367.

U.S. Immigration and Naturalization Service (INS). (1996). *Immigration to the United States in Fiscal Year 1995*: Highlights. Online: http://www.usdoj.gov/ins/public/stats/115.html.

U.S. Immigration and Naturalization Service (INS). (1996). *Immigration to the United States in Fiscal Year 1995*: Immigration Not Subject to Numerical Cap. Online: http://www.usdoj.gov/ins/public/stats/118.html.

Vega, W. A., and Rumbaut, R. G. (1991). Ethnic minorities and mental health. *Annual Review of Sociology* 17: 351–383.

Verdonk, A. (1979). Migration and mental illness. *International Journal of Social Psychiatry* 25 (4): 295–305.

Vu, T. Q. (1990). Refugee welfare dependency: The trauma of resettlement. In W. H. Holtzman and T. H. Bornemann (eds.), *Mental Health of Immigrants and Refugees*. Austin, TX: Hogg Foundation for Mental Health.

Williams, C. L., and Westermeyer, J. (eds.). (1986). *Refugee Mental Health in Resettlement Countries*. Washington, DC: Hemisphere Publishing.

Yee, B. W. (1992). Elders in Southeast Asian refugee families. Generations 16 (3): 24–27.

CONCLUSION

Pallassana R. Balgopal

The United States, a nation of immigrants, has evolved into a rich tapestry of intricately woven cultures, ethnicities, languages, religions, customs, and values. As chapter 1 showed, the three dimensions of Anglo conformity, melting pot, and assimilation have influenced immigrants' adaptation to their new homeland. Becoming an American means thinking, speaking, and behaving like an American—and often having to give up one's original lifestyle, customs, culture, language, and the like.. All immigrants are expected to assimilate into the mainstream society, and the sooner they do, the more quickly they will be accepted.

Throughout the nineteenth and early twentieth centuries, most of the immigrants coming to the United States were from European countries, but today most of them are from Latin America and Asia. At the present time, therefore, the United States is more ethnically and culturally diverse than at any other time in its history. And with the projected continuation of this immigration pattern, U.S. society should become even more diverse. The needs of the various ethnic groups differ as well, as should the social worker's role in working with them.

The chapters in this book discuss demographic data, the history of immigration, and the characteristics of various cultures, their methods of coping and adaptation, and their social welfare needs. Each chapter describes a specific geographical region, but there also are substantial differences among the groups in this region. For example, there are noteworthy differences between East Asians and South Asians. Similarly, Mexican Americans differ from other Latinos. Moreover, because of the close proximity of and the historical flow of farm workers between Mexico and the United States, undocumented Mexican immigrants present special problems. Immigrants of African descent coming from Africa are different from those coming from the Caribbean. Likewise, the language spoken by African-descent immigrants leads to different adaptation problems. For example, Haitians who speak French have different issues from those whose primary language is Spanish, such as immigrants from Cuba and the Dominican Republic. European immigrants from the former Soviet Union and Yugoslavia find themselves having to live in mixed social and ethnic neighborhoods, which often leads to conflict and adaptation issues. That is, these European immigrants are viewed as belonging to the dominant (white) group and thus as having access to certain privileges and power in American society that racial minorities do not. And it is true that because of their color, these white immigrants are able to blend more easily into the mainstream, but because of the language barrier, they too may have difficulties in obtaining employment, being accepted at educational institutions, and so on.

In addition to the problems encountered by immigrants, refugees have their own, unique issues, such as leaving their native countries under life-threatening circumstances and, upon coming to the United States, having to settle initially in regimented and regulated refugee camps. Unlike most immigrants, who settle in large metropolitan areas along with other immigrants, refugees must live in camps often located in areas where there is little ethnic and cultural diversity. Furthermore, these communities often resent the refugees' "invasion" of their territories. Wausau, Wisconsin, for instance, which for decades had been a peaceful community, suddenly was in the news in early 1990s when a serious racial clash erupted between the local residents and the new Hmong and Laotian refugee families who had been placed there. The handful of refugees who came to Wausau in the late 1970s had dramatically increased to more than 4,200 by the mid-1980s, and the community feared that they might become the majority population. At first when the refugees arrived, the community regarded them as novel and "neat," but soon this optimistic view changed, especially when school district's property tax skyrocketed (Beck 1994).

The preceding chapters of this book described in detail the role of social work in regard to specific immigrant groups. This conclusion briefly summarizes those dimensions that have implications for the social work practice perspective.

THE HISTORY OF IMMIGRATION TO THE UNITED STATES

When and why did immigrants start coming to the United States, and where did they first settle? What is the current pattern of immigration? What do these immigrants contribute to the United States? What kind of work did they do in their native country? How were these immigrants received by American society in the past, and how are they received now? How have these immigrants both assimilated into American society and retained their cultural heritage and customs? Social workers must have a basic knowledge of their clients' immigration experience, and they also should recognize the positive contributions to the United States made by the different immigrant groups.

A Theoretical Framework

With its dual focus on the person and the environment based on an ecological perspective, social work has a theoretical framework suitable for developing culturally sensitive interventions. But the profession must look beyond its ideological acceptance of cultural pluralism or multiculturalism. Although this acceptance has been regarded as fundamental to the profession's mission of developing services and policies for immigrant groups, in reality an assimilationistic philosophy still prevails. Assimilation is a process in which minority groups and their members are expected to give up their ways of life in favor of those of the dominant group. Often this process is a prerequisite to acceptance as part of the society.

Assimilation should not be the primary goal of social work practice, however, as it is antithetical to its professional values and ideologies. It is an approach based on power, the power of the dominant group. New immigrants, especially those who belong to ethnic minorities of color, are expected to assimilate behaviorally without being given opportunities to assimilate structurally. According to Chan (1991:xiv), "assimilation does not depend solely on the predilections of the newcomers. It can occur only when members of the host society give immigrants a chance to become equal partners in the world they share and mutually shape."

CONFLICTS REGARDING RELOCATION AND SETTLEMENT

Leaving one's country and familiar environment and entering a new arena with a different language, customs and lifestyle, and expectations is, not surprisingly, a very stressful event for immigrants, no matter where they come from, Europe, the Far East, or Central America.. According to Hulewat (1996), for immigrants to be able to resettle successfully, three cultural concepts need to be addressed. The first concept is the resettlement stage, which has five progressive phases: the preimmigration or preparatory phase, the actual migration, the arrival in the receiving country; decompensation or the recognition of losing one's past; and the transgenerational phase in which unresolved conflicts from the immigration experience are passed on to succeeding generations. The second concept is the immigrants' cultural styles and psychological dynamics, such as child-rearing practices and self-esteem. The third concept is the family's individual dynamics, including how its resources and strengths influence its members' abilities to tolerate cultural dissonance and adapt to their new country.

Direct service needs range from relieving the transitional stresses of moving to a strange environment to resolving emotional and interpersonal issues. In addition to these problems of the initial phase, immigrants encounter other conflicts in the later phases of their settlement in this country.

THE PARENT-CHILD RELATIONSHIP

One of the principal areas of conflict in immigrant families is that between parent and child. These generational differences become even more pronounced when children question and rebel against their parents' cultural expectations of behavior such as dating. In many traditional ethnic groups—such as South Asians—dating is simply not tolerated. But because this is an accepted American norm, youngsters in immigrant families want to date, and so it becomes a source of conflict. Interethnic dating creates additional family tensions. For instance, in Korean American families, which usually are Christian, parents insist that their children go out only with Christian youths. But when a youngster who is very active in church activities starts dating another person who is also a devout Christian but is not Korean, the parents object.

Immigrant parents want their children to do well in studies and succeed in life. They want them to achieve the "American dream" even if that means their acting like Americans. But the parents' toleration of such behavior is limited to that outside the home. That is, the children can be "American" outside, but when they come home, they have to behave as their parents want them to. These double expectations create tension between the parents and children, with the result that the youngsters do poorly in school or get involved in antisocial activities such as abusing alcohol or drugs or joining gangs.

Child-rearing practices, including disciplining, are culture specific and are often very different from those followed in this country. According to Nah (1993:294), "school age children [of Korean immigrants] are often left alone at home without parental guidance, feeding themselves and going to sleep by themselves while their parents work until late at night." When such "questionable" practices become visible to external constituencies such as schools or neighbors, they are brought to the attention of child welfare agencies, and of course, the parents are made to feel confused, humiliated, and ashamed.

To explore the identity conflicts encountered by Indian American youths, Pettys and Balgopal (1998) conducted an in-depth ethnographic study that revealed that immigration and acculturation produce a number of identity problems. The authors suggest that accordingly, social work interventions need to help families openly express their differences, concerns, and expectations. Family members need to be assisted in adapting to or "Americanizing" important aspects of their native culture without losing their essential meaning and intent.

DOMESTIC VIOLENCE

In immigrant communities, domestic violence is a growing problem whose roots often lie in the cultural beliefs and ideological framework that immigrants bring with them from their countries of origin. The victims/survivors' submission to violence is facilitated by their acceptance of several interlocking layers of bondage that block their will to resist the abuse or their opportunities to escape.

In many traditional cultures, people are taught not to think as individuals but to develop a collective identity. Thus ideal womanhood is demonstrated by a wife's dependence on and deference to the opinions and decisions of her husband and other authority figures (Das Dasgupta and Warrier 1995). A woman's commitment to her affinal and natal families include observing strict codes of privacy and public silence to protect the families from public shame, including the shame of marital discord, brutality, dysfunctionality, divorce—and even the need for external help. For many immigrants, this code of privacy discourages victims from divulging details about their trauma to "outsiders" such as community members, work colleagues, physicians, mental health professionals, police, or social workers. The far-reaching consequences of a woman's "betrayal" of the people she loves are often too overwhelming for her to break the code of silence.

Their recent immigrant status further victimizes some women who are already vulnerable to abuse. Many immigrant groups, such as South Asian men who are U.S. citizens or permanent residents, 'import' wives from their native countries. According to the Marriage Fraud Act of 1986, an imported wife has conditional residency for two years, after which a joint petition for permanent residency must be filed to avoid her deportation. The refusal to petition for permanent residency and the threat of imminent deportation without access to her children become powerful weapons for control and manipulation.

Transplanted into an alien environment, immigrant wives are especially physically and emotionally dependent and helpless. Their helplessness opens them to domestic battery, and their dependence makes it easier for their husbands to prevent their access to people and resources that could rescue them. These women are unfamiliar with American institutions and immigration laws and ignorant of their rights in this country. For instance, most new immigrant women would not know about the Violence Against Women Act of 1994, which allows abused women to petition for a waiver of the joint petition and to seek residency status on their own. The Personal Responsibility and Work Opportunity Reconciliation Act of 1996 makes sponsors responsible for the medical needs and expenses of dependent wives, thereby perpetuating neglect in violent homes. A dependent is not eligible for public assistance before five years of residency, unless she has paid taxes as a member of the labor force. Without a way to support herself and her children on her own, a dependent wife has no choice but to remain with her abuser. Likewise, the Work for Welfare program is often not accessible to dependent wives, since many do not have the opportunity or financial support to acquire the required work skill.

Immigrant families, especially those of color, often face racist hate crimes and discrimination that force them to remain socially isolated in their ethnic community. As a consequence, if an abused immigrant wife of color reported her husband—especially if he were a respected member of the community— the community would turn against her. The prospect of relocating, losing the shield of community protection, and becoming an easy target for racial hostility during employment or accepting services or resources is often terrifying for an immigrant woman.

DILEMMAS OF THE ELDERLY

Because of the decline in their health as well as in their economic status, elderly immigrants need both informal (social and kinship) and formal (human and health services) support. For elderly immigrants and their families, one of the biggest problems is whether to adopt a collectivist perspective, which implies dependence on and nurturance from family and kinship networks, or the dominant individualist perspective of their new environment, which implies minimal dependence on others. For example, placing a family member in a nursing home is not an easy decision for any family, but for an immigrant family, this option simply does not exist. Even if an immigrant family did decide on such a option, they would have tremendous difficulty carrying it out.

As another example, although Asian Americans' coping and adaptation to growing old is greatly influenced by their cultural norms, Asian American eld-erly face several other problems, such as conflict with the younger generation who may not accord them the traditional respect and place them in nursing homes; financial insecurity; and difficulty in obtaining basic services. In addi-tion, Asian American elderly frequently grieve for the loss of their tradition and family values, for they know they probably will not have an opportunity to re-turn to their native countries.

ALCOHOLISM AND SUBSTANCE ABUSE

The influence of ethnicity and culture on the use and abuse of alcohol and drugs has been recognized and also identified as a strong determent of a soci-ety's chemical usage patterns (McNeece and Dinitto 1998). Determining such patterns in immigrant groups is complicated by additional factors such as the history of the ethnic group's immigration to the United States, including their struggles, hardships, the circumstances under which they came, the duration of their stay here, their resettlement and its impact on them and their family, their housing, their employment, their children's' education, the availability of for-mal and informal support services, and their interaction with fellow immi-grants. Also important is how the different immigrant groups "use" alcohol and drugs in their native countries, including when this is seen as abusive behavior, and the ethnic communities' patterns in the United States of the acceptance, tolerance, and rejection of alcohol and drug abusers.

Hispanic immigrants, for example, differ with respect to their country of origin, current living environment, socioeconomic status, and so forth. Despite these differences, their common language, religion, and traditions have resulted in certain recurring patterns among these groups. It has been reported, for in-stance, that heavy drinking and alcohol-related problems among Hispanic American men in general seem to be more common than for the population as a whole. Furthermore, Hispanics often do not see chemical dependency as an illness or problem but, rather, as a moral weakness and so rely on divine inter-vention instead of seeking professional help (McNeece and Dinitto 1998).

Current research findings suggest that alcohol and substance abuse by African Americans is linked to three factors: (1) economic deprivation, (2) racism, and (3) stress. In addition, the use of illicit drugs is much higher among African Americans nationally, compared with other ethnic groups. The easy availability of alcohol and other drugs in impoverished African American neighborhoods is another risk factor (Fisher and Harrison 1997).

INTERGROUP CONFLICTS

The history of immigrants to the United States is a repeated pattern of tension and conflict between the native born and new arrivals. The pecking order of where each ethnic group belongs has been clear and explicit. In his 1992 book *Divided We Fall*, Perlmutter describes the history of ethnic, religious, and racial prejudice experienced by immigrant groups coming to this country. Added to their deplorable working conditions was the threat of replacement or dismissal by other minorities, which led to ethnic and religious rivalries. "The result was a multiple pattern competition, exploitation, and succession in which prejudice and discrimination were integral parts, reflecting old and generating new inter-group animosities" (Perlmutter 1992:166).

Intergroup conflicts are inevitable because of variety of differences between and among individuals and their reference groups. The differences may be both implicit and explicit, such as physical and psychological characteristics, ethnic and religious differences, economic and social status and background, gender and sexual orientation, and personal and cultural values. Balgopal and Vassil (1983) refer to them as *allogeneic conflicts*. Their conceptualization is based on the genetic principles of allogeneic process, according to which individuals that belong to the same species and yet have sufficient genetic differences may inter-act antigenically. Examples are the conflict between Indians and Pakistanis that has lasted for centuries because of their differences in religious beliefs; the con-flict between African Americans and European Americans that is based on racial differences; and the conflict between educated and professional immi-grant groups and their fellow ethnics who, because of their lack of education, are marginally employed. With the continued expansion of diversity among American ethnic groups, allogeneic conflicts are bound to become more com-mon and to include the new immigrant groups.

In recent years, the intergroup conflict between African Americans and Ko-rean Americans has erupted at different locations and times. In addition to the obvious racial and cultural differences between these two groups, the conflict has been exacerbated by the African Americans' resentment of the Korean Americans' taking over the small businesses in their neighborhoods. As a result, during the 1992 riots in Los Angeles, nearly 2,300 Korean-owned stores were burned and/or looted by African American and Hispanic rioters, an example of the fate of a middleman minority group in a society that is highly stratified racially and ethnically (Min 1995).

As chapter 2 pointed out, labeling Asian Americans as a model minority has contributed to the tension between them and other minorities, especially

African Americans and Hispanics. Affirmative action policies are another factor adding to intergroup conflict, although chapter 1 noted that these policies were not originally formulated with immigrants in mind (Beck 1996). At times, the dominant European Americans have used minority individuals to fight affirmative action policies; for example, in California, the supporters of Proposition 209 recruited an African American ally, Ward Connerly of the University of California's board of regents, as one of their main spokespersons (Lipsitz 1998). Regarding the success of Proposition 209, Lipsitz observed,

> Young people of color interested in higher education in California face a stark new reality. Already victimized by diminished state spending on recreation centers, libraries, counseling services, health, and schools, they now face a program targeted expressly against those among them who have the most ambition, who have studied the hardest, and who have stayed away from drugs and gangs.   (1998:228)

EMERGING CHALLENGES

The passage of the anti-immigrant Proposition 187, the anti-affirmative action Proposition 209, and the Personal Responsibility and Work Opportunity Reconciliation Act of 1996 were wake-up calls to which we social workers should pay heed. We must respond aggressively to regressive policies. We must not abandon our mission to work with the vulnerable, disadvantaged, and oppressed, which include many new immigrants and refugees. We must advocate for public policies and programs that accept and respect cultural diversity. As Podilla stated,

> Social workers need to take a national political stance on social welfare legislation that threatens to adversely affect children and other vulnerable immigrant, populations . . . [they need to] become involved in the legislative process—organize for community-based services and form coalitions to respond to the immediate impact of the current welfare reform legislation.
> (1997:604)

To avoid stereotyping and generalizing about new immigrant groups, social workers must find answers to the following: (1) Who are the new immigrants and refugees coming to the United States? (2) How are they adapting to this society's sociocultural environment? (3) What are these groups' main coping and adaptation problems? (4) How are they received by the host society, its citizens, and its institutions? (5) How do the new immigrant groups relate to their fellow ethnics who are native-born Americans? (6) How do different ethnic immigrant groups interact with one another? (7) How do national, state, and local policies affect these new arrivals? (8) What is the response of ethnic-specific sociocultural and religious institutions in assisting these immigrants? (9) What is these groups' pattern of help seeking and utilization of social welfare services? (10) What new policies and programs are needed to improve the quality of life of these new Americans? These are just a few examples from a long list of questions and issues that social workers must consider.

Gans (1997) compared both the researchers and the research on earlier European immigrants and today's newcomers and found two differences influencing both the findings and the respective positions of the researchers. According to him, the earlier researchers who studied European immigrants were outsiders who obtained most of their data from the second generation of immigrants. Not surprisingly, these second-generation immigrants' visible public acculturation—rather than their private ethnic retention—made the researchers believe that they were homogeneous and holistic groups who were easily assimilating into American society. Indeed, these European immigrants came to the United States at a time of rapid economic growth that encouraged them to move out of their ethnic enclaves, which in turn facilitated their acculturation. Now, however, according to Gans, contemporary researchers studying the new immigrants are obtaining their data directly from the first generation. Many of these new immigrant groups are nonwhite but middle class and often highly educated and professionally trained. In addition, the researchers themselves frequently belong to the groups they are studying and thus have an insider's perspective. The factors influencing today's researchers have changed, therefore, and they see very little acculturation by first-generation immigrants and even less assimilation.

Gans's conclusions regarding the interplay between acculturation and ethnic retention is relevant to social work researchers— whether outsiders or insiders in background and values—studying the second and subsequent generations of immigrants. In addition, social workers must be sensitive to those immigrants and refugees who, because of their economic status and lack of mastery of the English language, have yet to produce social science researchers. That is, the profession must welcome even outsider researchers studying these groups' coping and adaptation processes.

The role of the social worker is to learn how to assess immigrants' situations, advocate for their rights and needs, determine which community resources they need, help them adapt to their new country without leaving behind their cultural customs and traditions, and monitor their progress. Not only should the immigrants learn English; the social workers also must either speak the language of their clients or have access to bilingual and bicultural paraprofessionals. Because of such language barriers, social workers also must advocate on behalf of their immigrant and refugee clients for access to service providers located in the mainstream society. Using their knowledge, expertise, and skills, social workers need to organize peer-support and self-help groups to help the new arrivals assume their various new roles. At the neighborhood level, they should organize interethnic groups so as to develop a sense of community and reduce intergroup tensions and conflicts.

For social work to live up to its mission and commitment to work with the immigrant and refugee groups is a challenge, but it is a challenge it can and must accept. The profession has all the skills needed to win this challenge. Social workers must be prepared to work on both micro and macro levels with multicultural clients, through either ethnic-specific or multiservice agencies. Working with the client in his or her own environment is preferable. Community-based social service agencies often can respond most effectively to immigrant groups' needs. Their work must include intergroup activities and avoid getting trapped in the myths and stereotypes of the model minority, who often are the "hidden poor," thus neglecting to provide needed services to certain ethnic groups. In sum, social workers should keep an open mind and learn from their clients and be willing to try culture-specific interventions to respond to the needs and priorities of new as well as settled immigrants.

REFERENCES

Balgopal, P. R., and Vassil, T. V. (1983). *Groups in Social Work: An Ecological Perspective*. New York: Macmillan.

Beck, R. (1994). The ordeal of immigration in Wausau. *Atlantic Monthly* 273 (4) (April): 84–90.

Beck, R. (1996). *The Case Against Immigration: The Moral, Economic, Social and Environmental Reasons for Reducing U.S. Immigration Back to Traditional Levels*. New York: Norton.

Chan, S. (1991). *Asian Americans: An Interpretive History*. Boston: Twayne.

Das Dasgupta, S., and Warrier, S. (1995). *In Visible Terms: Domestic Violence in the Asian Indian Context*. Bloomfield, NJ: Manavi.

Fisher, G. L., and Harrison, T. C. (1997). *Substance Abuse Information for School Counselors, Social Workers, Therapists and Counselors*. Boston: Allyn & Bacon.

Gans, H. J. (1997). Toward a reconciliation of "assimilation" and "pluralism": The interplay of acculturation and retention. *International Migration Review* 31: 875–892.

Hulewat, P. (1996). Resettlement: A cultural and psychological crisis. *Social Work* 41 (2): 129–135.

Lipsitz, G. (1998). *The Progressive Investment in Whiteness*. Philadelphia: Temple University Press.

McNeece, C. A., and Dinitto, D. M. (1998). *Chemical Dependency*. Boston: Allyn & Bacon.

Min, P. G. (1995). *Asian Americans: Contemporary Trends and Issues*. Thousand Oaks, CA: Sage.

Nah, K. H. (1993). Perceived problems and service delivery for Korean immigrants. *Social Work* 38 (3): 289–296.

Perlmutter, P. (1992). *Divided We Fall: A History of Ethnic, Religious and Racial Prejudice*. Ames: Iowa State University Press.

Pettys, G. L., and Balgopal, P. R. (1998). Multigenerational conflicts and new immigrants: An Indo-American experience. *Families in Society* 79 (4): 410–423.

Podilla, Y. C. (1997). Immigrant policy: Issues for social work practice. *Social Work* 42 (6): 595–606.

LIST OF CONTRIBUTORS

PALLASSANA R. BALGOPAL is a professor emeritus of social work at the University of Illinois at Urbana-Champaign. He received his Ph.D. from Tulane University. Before joining the Illinois faculty in 1978, he taught at the Universities of Michigan, Maryland, and Houston, and he has held visiting professor appointments at the University of Madras and Delhi in India and the National University of Singapore. Professor Balgopal has been the recipient of two senior fellowships from both the Fulbright Program and the American Institute of Indian Studies. He has published widely on social group work and issues related to new immigrants, including three coauthored books and numerous book chapters and articles. He also serves on the editorial boards of the *Journal of Sociology and Social Welfare, Employee Assistance Quarterly,* and *Management and Labour Studies.*

E. ARACELIS FRANCIS is the director of the minority fellowship program of the Council on Social Work Education and is an adjunct associate professor at the School of Social Work at Howard University, where she teaches in the macro sequence. Her areas of interest are in African and Caribbean immigration and multicultural issues. Francis has also taught at the schools of social work at Adelphi University in New York and the University of Maryland in Baltimore. She received her bachelor's degree in the social sciences from the Inter American University of Puerto Rico, her master's degree in social work from the University of Chicago, and her doctorate in social welfare from Columbia University.

HOWARD JACOB KARGER is a professor and the Ph.D. program director at the Graduate School of Social Work at the University of Houston. Dr. Karger is an internationally recognized scholar in the field of social welfare policy. He is the author of, with D. Stoesz, *American Social Welfare Policy;* with J. Levine, *The Internet and Technology for Human Services;* and with L. Costin and D. Stoesz, *The Politics of Child Abuse and Neglect in America.* A two-time senior Fulbright Fellow, Dr. Karger has published widely in national and international journals.

JOANNE LEVINE is an assistant professor in the Graduate School of Social Work of the University of Houston. Dr. Levine coauthored, with H. Karger, *The Internet and Technology for Human Services.* Before her appointment at the University of Houston, she spent many years working with economically and ethnically diverse populations in New York City's academic medical centers. Her areas of research include the effects of massive psychic trauma on current refugees and asylees and ethical issues arising from the use of electronic information technologies in the human services. She received master's degrees in both social work and public health from Columbia University and a doctorate in social welfare from the Graduate School of the City University of New York.

JOHN F. LONGRES is a professor of social work at the University of Washington in Seattle. He received his Ph.D. in social work and social psychology from the University of Michigan. He was a Fulbright lecturer at the Catholic University in Guyaquil, Ecuador, in 1982/83 and a visiting professor at the University of Puerto Rico from 1981 to 1998. Dr. Longres has published extensively in the areas of human behavior and the social environment, ethnic and race relations, Latino social service issues, and mental health. He has been very active in professional activities and has sat on the board of directors of several Latino community agencies. For the Council on Social Work Education, he served on the Commission on Accreditation and chaired the nominating committee, the Commission on Minority Concerns, and the Publications and Media Commission. He also was the editor in chief of the *Journal of Social Work Education* from 1994 to 1997.

NAZNEEN S. MAYADAS is a professor of social work at the University of Texas at Arlington. She has worked with refugees on a global level through the Office of the United Nations High Commissioner for Refugees. Her publications include three coedited international handbooks on social welfare, social work education, and social work theory and practice.

JAYASHREE NIMMAGADDA is an assistant professor at Tulane University's Graduate School of Social Work. Dr. Nimmagadda's teaching expertise is in practice, research, addictions, human behavior, and the social environment (mental health). Her primary research interests are in the development of culturally relevant theories and the indigenization of traditional Western treatment models in addiction treatment and prevention. She does qualitative research and is also interested in international social work education.

DAVIS G. PATTERSON is a doctoral candidate in sociology at the University of Washington in Seattle. His publications and research interests include couple relationships and immigration, both with an emphasis on lesbians and gay men. A researcher in the Department of Medical Education at the University of Washington's School of Medicine, he has also published in the area of minority medical education and is currently a coinvestigator of a federally funded program to improve minority recruitment and retention in medical careers. Mr. Patterson has lived, worked, and traveled in Central America and Mexico.

UMA A. SEGAL is an associate professor of social work and fellow in the Center for International Studies at the University of Missouri in St. Louis. She has been involved in the field of child welfare since 1975 and, since 1988, has focused on the impact of the immigrant and refugee experiences on families. Her current research is on family violence among Southeast Asian refugees and perceptions of child abuse in cross-cultural and cross-national contexts. In addition to her teaching, research, and service responsibilities, she serves as program evaluator for the International Institute of Metropolitan St. Louis, a resettlement agency for refugees and immigrants.

INDEX

Regardless of when first-generation immigrants entered the United States, immigrant status is implicit in all compound main entries like European Americans, except Native Americans.

Boldface page numbers refer to definitions. *Italic page numbers* followed by italic letters *f* or *t* refer, respectively, to a figure or table. Parenthetical numbers indicate frequency of mention per page. The letter *n* following page numbers refers to chapter notes (e.g., 26n.1 is note 1 on page 26).

blend of ethnic identities, 79–80; fears of, 6, 75, 79, 171, 173–174; health needs and, 101, 110; as Hispanics, 83, 84–85, 167; household characteristics, 50, *87t, 96t*; people of color and, 85, 160, 167; suicide and, 47–48; as WASPs, 2, 4, 8, 167. *See also* European immigrants
Wilson, D., 102, 103(2), 126
Wilson, F. D., 75(2)–76, 126
Wilson, President Woodrow, 11
Woods, Tiger, heritage, 128
work ethic, 50–51, 129, 139, 160–161

work permits, 4, 72, 73, 157
working conditions, 16, 170, 180–181

xenophobia, 198, 205, 207, 213, 221, 230

Yamashiro, G., 46, 64
Yee-Bradbury, C., 48, 63
Yugoslavian immigrants, *179t, 204t,* 230
Yugoslavian refugees, 201, *204t*

Zairian refugees, 132
Zamanian, K., 98, 99, 100, 126
Zane, N., 49, 55, 56, 63
Zangwill, I., dramatist, 11